**Cambridge School**
**Shakespeare**

D1632819

# JULIUS CAESAR

Edited by Rob Smith and Vicki Wienand
Series editors: Richard Andrews and Vicki Wienand
Founding editor: Rex Gibson

# CAMBRIDGE
## UNIVERSITY PRESS

University Printing House, Cambridge CB2 8BS, United Kingdom

One Liberty Plaza, 20th Floor, New York, NY 10006, USA

477 Williamstown Road, Port Melbourne, VIC 3207, Australia

314–321, 3rd Floor, Plot 3, Splendor Forum, Jasola District Centre, New Delhi – 110025, India

79 Anson Road, #06–04/06, Singapore 079906

Cambridge University Press is part of the University of Cambridge.

It furthers the University's mission by disseminating knowledge in the pursuit of education, learning and research at the highest international levels of excellence.

www.cambridge.org
Information on this title: www.cambridge.org/9781107615519

First published 1992
Second edition 2008
Third edition 2014

20  19  18  17  16  15  14  13

Printed in Italy by L.E.G.O. S.p.A.

*A catalogue record for this publication is available from the British Library*

ISBN 978-1-107-61551-9 Paperback

........................................................................................................................................

# Contents

# Introduction

This *Julius Caesar* is part of the **Cambridge School Shakespeare** series. Like every other play in the series, it has been specially prepared to help all students in schools and colleges.

The **Cambridge School Shakespeare** *Julius Caesar* aims to be different. It invites you to lift the words from the page and to bring the play to life in your classroom, hall or drama studio. Through enjoyable and focused activities, you will increase your understanding of the play. Actors have created their different interpretations of the play over the centuries. Similarly, you are invited to make up your own mind about *Julius Caesar*, rather than having someone else's interpretation handed down to you.

**Cambridge School Shakespeare** does not offer you a cut-down or simplified version of the play. This is Shakespeare's language, filled with imaginative possibilities. You will find on every left-hand page: a summary of the action, an explanation of unfamiliar words, and a choice of activities on Shakespeare's stagecraft, characters, themes and language.

Between each act, and in the pages at the end of the play, you will find notes, illustrations and activities. These will help to encourage reflection after every act and give you insights into the background and context of the play as a whole.

This edition will be of value to you whether you are studying for an examination, reading for pleasure or thinking of putting on the play to entertain others. You can work on the activities on your own or in groups. Many of the activities suggest a particular group size, but don't be afraid to make up larger or smaller groups to suit your own purposes. Please don't think you have to do every activity: choose those that will help you most.

Although you are invited to treat *Julius Caesar* as a play, you don't need special dramatic or theatrical skills to do the activities. By choosing your activities, and by exploring and experimenting, you can make your own interpretations of Shakespeare's language, characters and stories.

Whatever you do, remember that Shakespeare wrote his plays to be acted, watched and enjoyed.

**Rex Gibson**
Founding editor

This new edition contains more photographs, more diversity and more supporting material than previous editions, whilst remaining true to Rex's original vision. Specifically, it contains more activities and commentary on stagecraft and writing about Shakespeare, to reflect contemporary interest. The glossary has been enlarged, too. Finally, this edition aims to reflect the best teaching and learning possible, and to represent not only Shakespeare through the ages, but also the relevance and excitement of Shakespeare today.

**Richard Andrews and Vicki Wienand**
Series editors

This edition of *Julius Caesar* uses the text of the play established by Marvin Spevack in **The New Cambridge Shakespeare**.

Beware the Ides of March: Shakespeare's play dramatises the political machinations surrounding the assassination of Julius Caesar. The action is focused on three characters: Mark Antony (left), Julius Caesar (centre) and Marcus Brutus (right).

There has been a terrible civil war. Pompey and Caesar – both formidable figures of the Roman world – have fought each other for supreme power in Rome, and Caesar has won. Caesar makes a triumphant entry into Rome.

Marcus Brutus is Caesar's close friend and military comrade. His ancestors were famed for driving the tyrannical King Tarquin from the throne and helping to found the Roman Republic.

A group of conspirators, envious of Caesar's increasing power, grow restless in Rome. They are initially led by Cassius (far right).

Brutus (right) becomes convinced that Caesar is greedy for power and intends to turn Republican Rome into a monarchy. He decides that Caesar must die for his ambition to be king, and agrees to assist in the assassination attempt planned by the conspiring senators.

PEACE

FREEDOM

LIBERTY

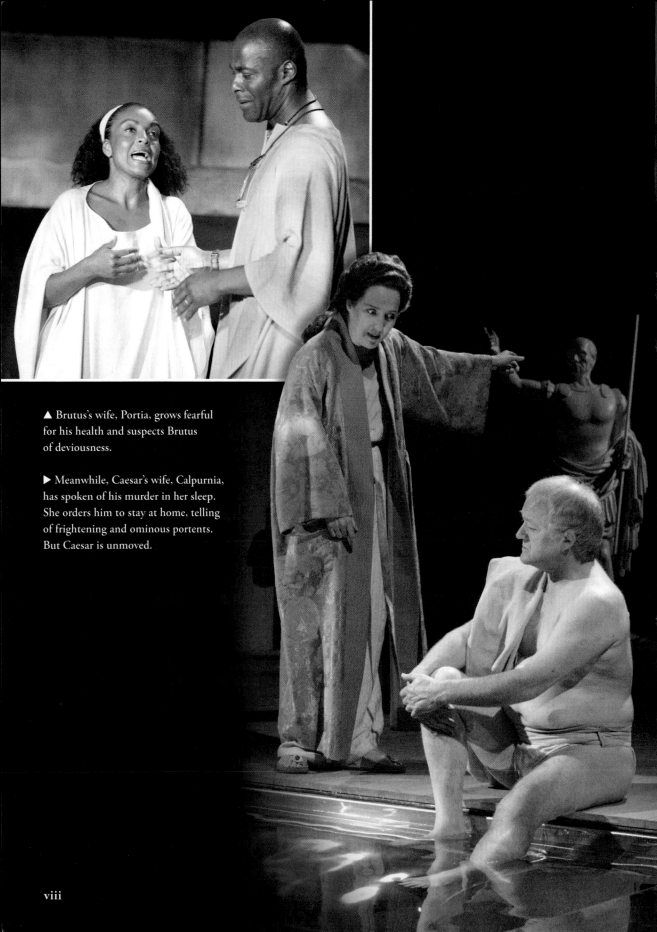

▲ Brutus's wife, Portia, grows fearful for his health and suspects Brutus of deviousness.

▶ Meanwhile, Caesar's wife, Calpurnia, has spoken of his murder in her sleep. She orders him to stay at home, telling of frightening and ominous portents. But Caesar is unmoved.

'*Et tu, Brute?*' Ignoring the Soothsayer's and his wife's premonitions, Caesar resolves to go to the Senate and is caught at the mercy of the conspirators. Having declared himself the world's only constant man, he is stabbed to death. His friend Brutus's betrayal shocks him profoundly.

'Friends, Romans, countrymen, lend me your ears.'
Following Caesar's death, his friend Mark Antony delivers
an eloquent and rousing speech over Caesar's corpse.
He deftly turns public opinion against the assassins.
The common people drive the conspirators from Rome.

Caesar's great-nephew, Octavius, arrives in Rome and forms
the Triumvirate with Antony and Lepidus. Antony and
Octavius (standing, centre) decide to go to war against
Brutus (seated right) and Cassius (seated left).

Brutus (left) berates Cassius for corruptly and dishonourably accepting bribes. He is also distressed by the news of his wife's death. Brutus and Cassius are reconciled but, as they prepare for war, Caesar's ghost appears to Brutus with a warning of defeat.

Events go badly for the conspirators during the battle. Both Cassius and Brutus (the latter pictured here with his slave Strato) choose to commit suicide rather than be captured.

The play ends with Antony's tribute to Brutus, who has remained 'the noblest Roman of them all', and hints at the friction between Mark Antony and Octavius that will characterise another of Shakespeare's plays, *Antony and Cleopatra*.

# Before the play begins

## The origins of the Roman Republic

When the **Roman Senate** granted Julius Caesar the title of dictator of Rome for life, it effectively signalled the end of the **Roman Republic** that had governed the city and its territories for more than four hundred years.

The Republic had been founded when the inhabitants of Rome drove out the tyrannical **Tarquin** kings and set up their own form of government, in which they could elect their own leaders rather than being ruled by hereditary kings.

## The Republican government

At first, control of the Republic was entirely in the hands of the **patricians**, Rome's aristocratic class. Only patricians could be elected members of the Senate, or parliament, and only patricians could be chosen as heads of state, or **consuls**. To prevent any one man obtaining too much power, there were always two consuls elected at any one time, who could rule for one year only. Consuls were primarily military commanders who would lead Rome's armies in war. In times of great emergency a dictator (supreme commander) was appointed in place of the consuls, but for a period of no more than six months.

In time the **plebeians**, the ordinary citizens of Rome, campaigned for and achieved the right to have their say in how they were to be ruled. They were allowed to elect two **tribunes** to represent them in government and protect their interests. Eventually the plebeians gained their own assembly, and the right to propose laws and to require one of the two consuls to be chosen from their own class. But despite these concessions, the patricians still retained overall control of government, while the plebeians – who were far greater in number than the patricians – remained poor, discontented and ready to riot.

## The size of the Roman world

As the centuries passed, the Roman Republic secured control of the rest of Italy, then Greece, Spain and North Africa, until it had conquered most of the countries surrounding the Mediterranean Sea.

But as Rome's wealth increased, so the quality of its ruling classes declined. The patrician class became more interested in luxurious living than in public service, and power gradually gravitated into the hands of a few men who could use their wealth and private armies to control the power of the Roman Senate and eliminate their political enemies.

Two such great rivals were Caesar and **Pompey**. Although for a while it suited the two men to form an uneasy political alliance, it was inevitable that they would eventually come to blows. In the bitter civil war that followed, Pompey was defeated and fled to Egypt, where he was murdered. In 48 BC, the Senate appointed Caesar as 'dictator' (i.e. made him head of government) and granted him many other powers and honours. There was even a statue of him placed in one of the Roman temples with the inscription 'To the Unconquerable God'. Caesar was now sole ruler of Rome and its territory. He was king in all but name.

Caesar was, however, surprisingly merciful to most of his defeated Roman opponents (including Brutus and Cassius) and gave a number of them responsible positions in his new regime. But the great unanswered question was how he would use his supreme power over the government of the Republic. Would he use it to reform and strengthen the old Republican system, which had so clearly failed to maintain control of Rome's vast territory? Or did he intend to establish a new monarchy with himself as the first king or emperor?

Some of the patricians were genuinely fearful that Caesar secretly intended to return Rome to monarchical rule. One such was Marcus Brutus, once a supporter of Pompey but now a close friend of Caesar. Brutus was a committed Republican and boasted a distinguished ancestor who had helped expel the Tarquin kings and establish the original Republic. Some patricians became so desperate that in 44 BC they conspired to assassinate Caesar before he could make himself king. One of the leaders of this conspiracy was Caius Cassius, another former supporter of Pompey in the recent civil war.

This is the point at which Shakespeare begins his story.

◆ Working in a small group, research each of the elements of the above summary that appear in bold font. Prepare a mini-presentation on the context of the play, including additional details and images to accompany the text. Share this with your class.

## Julius Caesar and the Elizabethans

The figure of Julius Caesar held a particular fascination for the Elizabethans. Some admired his military skill, strong leadership and generous treatment of former enemies. Others condemned him for his ruthlessness, for his weakening of the powers of the Senate and above all for his ambition.

Some Elizabethans may also have felt that the play reflected contemporary anxieties about what England might become following the death of the childless Elizabeth. They were divided in their attitude to the conspirators. If some felt Caesar's murder was justified to help preserve the Republic, others believed it to be a wicked act, or at the very least a major political misjudgement resulting in the very thing the conspirators were trying to prevent: the collapse of Rome's Republican governmental system. Brutus in particular enjoyed a double reputation. He was seen as an honest man of principle and a champion of liberty. Yet by joining the conspiracy he became also the man who treacherously murdered his friend and benefactor.

Whatever the Elizabethans may or may not have thought of Julius Caesar and the rights or wrongs of his assassination, less than fifty years after Shakespeare wrote his play the English people executed their king and set up their own Republican form of government under Oliver Cromwell.

▼ The Roman Republic *c.* 44 BC

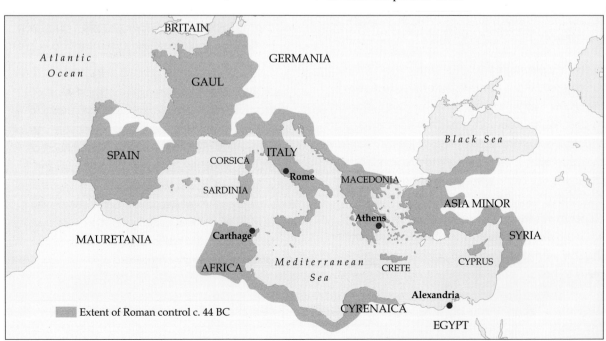

# Pompey and the Senate! Caesar and the people!

**(in groups A and B of four or five each)**

There has been a terrible civil war. Pompey and Caesar – heroes always named in one breath – have fought each other for supreme power in Rome, and Caesar has won.

All of you are Romans after the war. Group A still supports Pompey's views, believing in a more democratic type of government, through the elected assembly of the Senate. Group B supports Caesar, upholding the direct personal rule of a dictator.

- Use the opinions and details on the relevant scroll on the right to make a list of the benefits of senatorial (Group A) or one-person (Group B) rule as you see it. Include the views of both patricians and plebeians.
- After making their lists, Groups A and B should choose one person from their group who will speak at Caesar's celebratory 'triumph'. The other group members should help the nominated speaker to prepare a 60-second speech outlining the group's views to the assembled crowd.
- In your group, find and watch clips of political addresses. Suggest how the speaker might build into their own delivery any effective performance techniques that you identify. As the speaker practises the speech, the rest of the group should offer constructive feedback on what is good and what could be improved!
- Make placards, banners, badges and leaflets to distribute, or create other types of publicity material to be used at the triumph. Show clearly where your loyalties lie and either what you want to celebrate about Caesar's success or what you fear might happen under his rule.
- Then stage the triumph, allowing each group the chance to present their arguments. If you can, film it!
- Play the recording back and judge which group made the stronger case.

## A The Pompeyite point of view

*Pompey believed in the Senate. He fought for the Senate, he died for the Senate. One-person rule is dangerous – what's to stop Caesar becoming a tyrant now that the Senate has made him permanent head of government and granted him many special powers? Let's face it, he's even being worshipped like a god now that one of his statues has been erected in the temple. One ruler may serve us well, but what will happen when that person dies? Do we want to return to the days of the monarchy when power was handed on unopposed and we had no say in who ruled us? That's one of the reasons we killed the last king we had – four hundred years ago!*

## B The Caesarite point of view

*People in Rome are poor. Only the rich get votes in the Senate. Yes, the rich look after themselves. But with Caesar, you ask and you get. He listens and then he takes action – and he's richer than the Senate, because he's been off on his conquests again. Yes, it's true that he saw off Pompey, but look how decent he's been in forgiving the other rebels like Brutus and Cassius. They've now taken up positions of responsibility in his government, so we can trust him to put the good of the people first. Let him rule! Let him be a dictator! We need a strong man after the wars. But we'll never let him be king, of course.*

# Caesar's triumph

Study this photograph from a modern production of *Julius Caesar*.
How effective do you think it is in suggesting the kind of admiration
that Caesar was held in by some of his public? Why?

# List of characters

## Caesar and his supporters

JULIUS CAESAR
CALPURNIA  Caesar's wife
MARK ANTONY
OCTAVIUS CAESAR  } The ruling Triumvirate after Caesar's death
LEPIDUS

## The conspirators against Caesar

### Conspirators

BRUTUS        CASCA        CINNA        METELLUS CIMBER
CAIUS CASSIUS    DECIUS BRUTUS    TREBONIUS    CAIUS LIGARIUS

### Family and followers

PORTIA  Brutus's wife          VARRUS
LUCIUS  Brutus's boy servant   PINDARUS  Cassius's slave
CLAUDIO                        LUCILIUS
LABEO*                         TITINIUS
FLAVIUS*  } Personal followers  MESSALA    } Officers of Brutus
CLITUS    } of Brutus          YOUNG CATO } and Cassius
STRATO                         VOLUMNIUS
DARDANIUS                      STATILIUS*

## Other Romans

CICERO                        CINNA THE POET
PUBLIUS CIMBER                A CYNIC POET
POPILLIUS LENA  } Senators    1ST, 2ND, 3RD, 4TH PLEBEIANS
OTHER SENATORS*               CARPENTER
FLAVIUS    } Tribunes critical  COBBLER
MURELLUS   } of Caesar        MESSENGER
SOOTHSAYER   } Who try to
ARTEMIDORUS  } warn Caesar    1ST, 2ND, 3RD SOLDIERS
SERVANTS TO CAESAR, ANTONY
  AND OCTAVIUS                OTHER PLEBEIANS*

*non-speaking parts

Two Tribunes, Flavius and Murellus, ask some tradespeople why they are taking the day off. A Cobbler gives riddling replies.

## 1 Tribunes versus common people (in fours)

The opening of the play immediately establishes a sense of conflict. The Tribunes Flavius and Murellus (officials of the Roman government) are loyal to the defeated Pompey. They are angry that the common people celebrate Caesar's triumph in carnival mood. The Cobbler (which can also mean a person who plays with words) responds to the Tribunes' wrath with witty wordplay at their expense.

* Take the parts of Flavius, Murellus, the Cobbler and the Carpenter, and read lines 1–30 together. Experiment with different ways of bringing out the Tribunes' disapproval and the common people's celebration.

▼ Which line do you think is being spoken in the photograph below?

## Stagecraft

### Setting the scene

Shakespeare does not give any overt stage directions. The script has to be searched for references to the time of day, the location and the weather, for example, and then the director has to decide how to stage the play. They could choose to highlight in the staging a particular idea that runs throughout the play; to make the location specific, even familiar to their audience; or to go for a more neutral setting. Some directors choose to open this play with a powerful statement about the triumph of Caesar over Pompey.

* In groups, discuss your reactions to the staging shown in the picture above.
* Begin a Director's Journal to record your ideas about the staging of *Julius Caesar*, as if you were a director. Make a note in the journal outlining your discussion. Add any of your own ideas for staging afterwards.

---

**mechanical** manual workers, craftsmen

**rule** measuring ruler
**apparel** clothes

**in respect of** compared to
**cobbler** mender of shoes or one who mends clumsily
**directly** clearly, plainly

**soles** (a pun on 'souls')
**naughty** worthless
**be not out** don't be angry
**if you be out** if you (your shoes) are worn out
**mend** repair (shoes) or reform (souls)

# Julius Caesar

# Act 1 Scene 1
## Rome   A street

*Enter* FLAVIUS, MURELLUS, *and certain* COMMONERS *over the stage*

FLAVIUS     Hence! Home, you idle creatures, get you home!
Is this a holiday? What, know you not,
Being mechanical, you ought not walk
Upon a labouring day without the sign
Of your profession? Speak, what trade art thou?     5

CARPENTER   Why, sir, a carpenter.

MURELLUS   Where is thy leather apron and thy rule?
What dost thou with thy best apparel on?
You, sir, what trade are you?

COBBLER   Truly, sir, in respect of a fine workman, I am but, as you would    10
say, a cobbler.

MURELLUS But what trade art thou? Answer me directly.

COBBLER   A trade, sir, that I hope I may use with a safe conscience, which
is indeed, sir, a mender of bad soles.

FLAVIUS     What trade, thou knave? Thou naughty knave, what trade?    15

COBBLER   Nay, I beseech you, sir, be not out with me; yet if you be out, sir,
I can mend you.

MURELLUS What mean'st thou by that? Mend me, thou saucy fellow?

COBBLER   Why, sir, cobble you.

FLAVIUS     Thou art a cobbler, art thou?    20

The tradespeople celebrate Caesar's triumph over Pompey. The Tribunes accuse them of ingratitude to Pompey, who was once the people's favourite.

# Language in the play

## Rhetorical questions (in groups of four or five)

Murellus's lines 31–50 make much use of **rhetorical questions** (questions that do not need an answer). The questions are intended to influence the thoughts of the listeners and make them reflect on their actions.

**a** Share out the lines, making sure everyone has at least one rhetorical question. Practise speaking the lines, deciding where to speak harshly and where to speak softly. Surround another group and deliver the lines. Then they do the same to your group. Afterwards, talk together about the effect the lines have on the listeners.

**b** As you read on, keep a note of how many times rhetorical questions are used as a device to persuade a listening audience and what the effect of these questions might be.

# 1 Stop the party! (in large groups)

**a** Murellus and Flavius want to manipulate the common people and one way in which they do this is by using vivid language. They paint pictures with their words. In your group, read through Murellus's description of the crowd's reaction to Pompey (lines 36–46). Create a tableau (frozen picture) of this moment. Then discuss why Murellus chose to remind them of these previous celebrations.

**b** Ordinary Romans were deeply superstitious. Every action or decision was taken after consultation with the augurers, who performed rites and sacrifices to find out the will of the gods (see p. 171). Read the Tribunes' differing accounts of what the crowd should do next in lines 52–4 and 56–9. Decide how the Tribunes are playing on the crowd's superstition in these lines and swap your ideas with another group.

# 2 How do the common people react? (in pairs)

The common people exit at line 59 – but Shakespeare gives no clue as to their mood. Are they subdued, resentful, angry or something else?

• Improvise a conversation or write an exchange of text messages between two of the crowd after this brush with the furious Tribunes.

**awl** tool for piercing leather

**recover** resole and cure
**neat's leather** cattle hide
**gone** walked

**triumph** procession celebrating Caesar's victory over Pompey's sons in Spain in March 45 BC
**tributaries** conquered peoples forced to pay tax

**Pompey** a great Roman general (see p. 173)

**Tiber** river, sacred to Romans, that flows through Rome
**replication** echo
**attire** clothes
**cull out** pick, choose

**blood** blood relatives (Pompey's sons whom Caesar had defeated)

**intermit** prevent
**light on** fall upon

**Do kiss … of all** rises to the top of its banks

COBBLER    Truly, sir, all that I live by is with the awl. I meddle with no
tradesman's matters, nor women's matters; but withal I am indeed,
sir, a surgeon to old shoes: when they are in great danger I recover
them. As proper men as ever trod upon neat's leather have gone upon
my handiwork.    25

FLAVIUS    But wherefore art not in thy shop today?
Why dost thou lead these men about the streets?

COBBLER    Truly, sir, to wear out their shoes, to get myself into more work.
But indeed, sir, we make holiday to see Caesar and to rejoice in his
triumph.    30

MURELLUS    Wherefore rejoice? What conquest brings he home?
What tributaries follow him to Rome
To grace in captive bonds his chariot wheels?
You blocks, you stones, you worse than senseless things!
O you hard hearts, you cruel men of Rome,    35
Knew you not Pompey? Many a time and oft
Have you climbed up to walls and battlements,
To towers and windows, yea, to chimney tops,
Your infants in your arms, and there have sat
The livelong day, with patient expectation,    40
To see great Pompey pass the streets of Rome.
And when you saw his chariot but appear
Have you not made an universal shout,
That Tiber trembled underneath her banks
To hear the replication of your sounds    45
Made in her concave shores?
And do you now put on your best attire?
And do you now cull out a holiday?
And do you now strew flowers in his way,
That comes in triumph over Pompey's blood?    50
Be gone!
Run to your houses, fall upon your knees,
Pray to the gods to intermit the plague
That needs must light on this ingratitude.

FLAVIUS    Go, go, good countrymen, and for this fault    55
Assemble all the poor men of your sort,
Draw them to Tiber banks, and weep your tears
Into the channel till the lowest stream
Do kiss the most exalted shores of all.

*Exeunt all the Commoners*

The Tribunes leave, intending to stop further celebration. Caesar comes to the Lupercal races, in which Antony is to run. He orders Antony to touch Calpurnia in the race to cure her infertility.

# 1 Caesar and the crowd – high and low (in threes)

Caesar does not appear in Scene 1. But the loyal Pompeyite Flavius makes clear in lines 67–8 that he plans to take all the decorations off Caesar's statues. He is also anxious that Caesar should not be allowed to 'soar above the view of men / And keep us all in servile fearfulness'. This bird image emphasises the sense of superiority that Flavius fears in Caesar.

- In your groups, make a list of all the words used by the Tribunes in this first scene to describe the 'lowness' of the common people.
- Then decide whether the Cobbler seems aptly described by these terms. In your view, is he likely to feel 'servile fearfulness'?

## Stagecraft

### Caesar's triumphal progress (in groups of six to eight)

Plan how Caesar's entrance and exit (lines 1–24) can be staged.

- How will you manage the Tribunes' exit at the end of the previous scene (to follow Caesar back on stage shortly afterwards)?
- How will you enact the stage direction at the start of this scene?
- What is the behaviour of the 'great crowd'?
- How do the different characters speak to, and about, Caesar?
- How does Caesar address his wife and how sensitive is he about her childlessness?
- What sort of person is the Soothsayer?
- How will you use music in the scene? (Consider Caesar's remark at line 16 and the 'Sennet' stage direction at line 24.)

Make your choices, and then present your version of lines 1–24.

▼ Comment on the atmosphere created by the entrance of Caesar in this production.

basest metal inferior natures (with wordplay on metal/mettle; lead, the basest metal, is inert but malleable)

Capitol Senate house or government building (see p. 172)

Disrobe the images pull decorations off the statues

ceremonies garlands, decorations

feast of Lupercal festival held on 15 February (see p. 172)

trophies arms or other spoils of war taken from the enemy

vulgar common people

Stand you ... sterile curse a runner's touch was said to cure infertile women

|           |                                                    |     |
|-----------|----------------------------------------------------|-----|
|           | See where their basest metal be not moved:         | 60  |
|           | They vanish tongue-tied in their guiltiness.       |     |
|           | Go you down that way towards the Capitol,          |     |
|           | This way will I. Disrobe the images                |     |
|           | If you do find them decked with ceremonies.        |     |
| MURELLUS  | May we do so?                                      | 65  |
|           | You know it is the feast of Lupercal.              |     |
| FLAVIUS   | It is no matter; let no images                     |     |
|           | Be hung with Caesar's trophies. I'll about         |     |
|           | And drive away the vulgar from the streets;        |     |
|           | So do you too, where you perceive them thick.      | 70  |
|           | These growing feathers plucked from Caesar's wing  |     |
|           | Will make him fly an ordinary pitch,               |     |
|           | Who else would soar above the view of men          |     |
|           | And keep us all in servile fearfulness.            |     |

*Exeunt*

# Act 1 Scene 2
## Rome   A street

*Enter* CAESAR, ANTONY *for the course,* CALPURNIA, *Portia,*
*Decius, Cicero,* BRUTUS, CASSIUS, CASCA, *a* SOOTHSAYER,
*[a great crowd following]; after them Murellus and Flavius*

|           |                                                    |     |
|-----------|----------------------------------------------------|-----|
| CAESAR    | Calpurnia.                                          |     |
| CASCA     | Peace ho, Caesar speaks.                            |     |
| CAESAR    | Calpurnia.                                          |     |
| CALPURNIA | Here, my lord.                                      |     |
| CAESAR    | Stand you directly in Antonio's way                 |     |
|           | When he doth run his course. Antonio.               |     |
| ANTONY    | Caesar, my lord.                                    | 5   |
| CAESAR    | Forget not in your speed, Antonio,                  |     |
|           | To touch Calpurnia, for our elders say              |     |
|           | The barren, touchèd in this holy chase,             |     |
|           | Shake off their sterile curse.                      |     |
| ANTONY    | I shall remember:                                   |     |
|           | When Caesar says, 'Do this', it is performed.       | 10  |

Caesar is warned to beware the Ides of March. He dismisses the warning, then leaves. Cassius remains with Brutus and accuses him of being unfriendly, but Brutus says he is troubled by private problems.

## 1 A break in the progress of Caesar (in small groups)

Shakespeare wrote most of his plays in **blank verse** – lines of ten syllables (see p. 188). Though shared between the Soothsayer and Caesar, line 18 is a regular blank verse line of ten syllables. Count them, and then count the syllables of other lines chosen at random.

Line 23 has only six syllables. These breaks often occur at moments of crucial importance. Shakespeare's actor must pause for four syllables (two 'beats') to think, to listen or to take action. How will Caesar, all eyes on him, play this moment of silence? The Ides, the fifteenth day of the month, are during the full moon, an unlucky time. No Roman will do business under the waning moon that follows. Today is the Ides of February, so the Ides of March are a month away.

- From 'What man', play lines 18–24, taking it in turns to be Caesar. Imagine what Caesar would be thinking at this moment.
- When you come to the pause at line 23, hold a thought of Caesar's in your head that the others in your group must try to guess.

## Themes

### Public versus private (in pairs)

With Caesar's exit, the focus shifts to Cassius and Brutus. One of the many themes explored throughout this play is the tension between what happens in public and what happens in private. Shakespeare often closely juxtaposes these two spheres of life. Caesar is publicly warned amongst 'a great crowd' in the first part of this scene. As quickly as Caesar dismisses the Soothsayer and moves on, the crowd disperses and the scene becomes more intimate. Cassius has noticed a cooling in his friendship with Brutus, and Brutus confesses that he is 'with himself at war'. Again, Shakespeare uses shortened lines (26 and 27) to allow the two men to pause reflectively at the start of their discussion.

- Take parts and read lines 25–47.
- Work together to put these lines into modern English and then write down this dialogue. Take care to use a tone and vocabulary that reflect their close friendship. Aim to tease out the meaning of Brutus's powerful phrase: 'with himself at war'.
- Read through this modern dialogue together and then share it with other pairs.

**press** crowd

**Ides of March** 15 March

**throng** crowd

**Sennet** formal, stately music played on wooden cornetts

**gamesome** fond of sports and frivolity

**hinder** get in the way of

**was wont** used to

**You bear ... Over** you are too cold and almost hostile to

**If ... upon myself** if I have turned away from you, it is to turn my troubles upon myself

**passions of some difference** conflicting emotions

**soil** discredit

**construe** interpret

**shows** signs

| | |
|---|---|
| CAESAR | Set on, and leave no ceremony out. |
| SOOTHSAYER | Caesar! |
| CAESAR | Ha? Who calls? |
| CASCA | Bid every noise be still – peace yet again! |
| CAESAR | Who is it in the press that calls on me? |

15

I hear a tongue shriller than all the music
Cry 'Caesar!' Speak, Caesar is turned to hear.

| | |
|---|---|
| SOOTHSAYER | Beware the Ides of March. |
| CAESAR |                      What man is that? |
| BRUTUS | A soothsayer bids you beware the Ides of March. |
| CAESAR | Set him before me, let me see his face. |

20

| | |
|---|---|
| CASSIUS | Fellow, come from the throng, look upon Caesar. |
| CAESAR | What say'st thou to me now? Speak once again. |
| SOOTHSAYER | Beware the Ides of March. |
| CAESAR | He is a dreamer, let us leave him. Pass. |

*Sennet. Exeunt [all but] Brutus and Cassius*

| | |
|---|---|
| CASSIUS | Will you go see the order of the course? |

25

| | |
|---|---|
| BRUTUS | Not I. |
| CASSIUS | I pray you, do. |
| BRUTUS | I am not gamesome: I do lack some part |

Of that quick spirit that is in Antony.
Let me not hinder, Cassius, your desires;

30

I'll leave you.

| | |
|---|---|
| CASSIUS | Brutus, I do observe you now of late: |

I have not from your eyes that gentleness
And show of love as I was wont to have.
You bear too stubborn and too strange a hand

35

Over your friend that loves you.

| | |
|---|---|
| BRUTUS |                         Cassius, |

Be not deceived. If I have veiled my look
I turn the trouble of my countenance
Merely upon myself. Vexèd I am
Of late with passions of some difference,

40

Conceptions only proper to myself,
Which give some soil, perhaps, to my behaviours.
But let not therefore my good friends be grieved
(Among which number, Cassius, be you one)
Nor construe any further my neglect

45

Than that poor Brutus, with himself at war,
Forgets the shows of love to other men.

## Characters

### Brutus and Cassius (in pairs)

The relationship between these two men is crucial to the development of the play.

- Cassius is at pains to point out how much he values Brutus. One of you reads through Cassius's speeches and emphasises each word in praise of Brutus. The other writes these words down. You could start a Character file at this point for all your notes relating to the characters.
- Brutus is clearly suspicious of Cassius. Look at line 63. Swap over and the other person reads the same speeches but emphasises any word that might make Brutus wary of Cassius's motives. These words should be written down, too.
- Reflect upon the speeches and your lists and decide whether Brutus is right to question Cassius's motives at this point.

## Stagecraft

### A big moment – off stage

Read through lines 78–84. Why do you think Shakespeare decided to have this moment take place off stage so the audience would hear it but not see it? It would, after all, make a great public spectacle.

▶ Comment on the relationship between Brutus and Cassius (with the sword) at this moment.

**By means whereof** as a result of which (mistake)

**cogitations** thoughts

**just** true

**shadow** reflection

**respect** repute

**yoke** state of slavery

**glass** mirror

**jealous on** suspicious of

**a common laughter** a laughing-stock, figure of fun

**stale** devalue

**scandal** defame

**profess myself** offer friendship

**the rout** the common rabble

*Flourish* fanfare of trumpets

| CASSIUS | Then, Brutus, I have much mistook your passion, |
| | By means whereof this breast of mine hath buried |
| | Thoughts of great value, worthy cogitations. | 50 |
| | Tell me, good Brutus, can you see your face? |
| BRUTUS | No, Cassius, for the eye sees not itself |
| | But by reflection, by some other things. |
| CASSIUS | 'Tis just, |
| | And it is very much lamented, Brutus, | 55 |
| | That you have no such mirrors as will turn |
| | Your hidden worthiness into your eye |
| | That you might see your shadow. I have heard |
| | Where many of the best respect in Rome |
| | (Except immortal Caesar), speaking of Brutus | 60 |
| | And groaning underneath this age's yoke, |
| | Have wished that noble Brutus had his eyes. |
| BRUTUS | Into what dangers would you lead me, Cassius, |
| | That you would have me seek into myself |
| | For that which is not in me? | 65 |
| CASSIUS | Therefore, good Brutus, be prepared to hear. |
| | And since you know you cannot see yourself |
| | So well as by reflection, I, your glass, |
| | Will modestly discover to yourself |
| | That of yourself which you yet know not of. | 70 |
| | And be not jealous on me, gentle Brutus, |
| | Were I a common laughter, or did use |
| | To stale with ordinary oaths my love |
| | To every new protester. If you know |
| | That I do fawn on men and hug them hard | 75 |
| | And after scandal them, or if you know |
| | That I profess myself in banqueting |
| | To all the rout, then hold me dangerous. |

*Flourish and shout*

| BRUTUS | What means this shouting? I do fear the people |
| | Choose Caesar for their king. |
| CASSIUS | Ay, do you fear it? | 80 |
| | Then must I think you would not have it so. |
| BRUTUS | I would not, Cassius, yet I love him well. |
| | But wherefore do you hold me here so long? |
| | What is it that you would impart to me? |

Brutus demands that Cassius come to the point. Cassius proclaims that no man of honour should submit to Caesar. He is a mortal but behaves as if he were a god.

# Characters

## Brutus (in pairs)

Cassius has talked a great deal and Brutus is keen for him to come to the point. Briefly he outlines his principles in lines 85–9. Take it in turns to read through the lines until they are familiar. Decide where you think the emphasis should be placed. Then consider the lines from two perspectives:

- Why do you think Shakespeare wrote these lines? Discuss to what extent this seems like a character manifesto (explanation) and whether or not it might have been more effective to demonstrate these qualities in Brutus through his actions.
- Why do you think Brutus says these lines? After all, we know that Cassius knows him well. What effect do you think Brutus wants his words to have on Cassius?

# Language in the play

## What difference does rhetoric make? (in fours)

The art of **rhetoric** (see pp. 185–6) was taught in schools in Rome. This involved learning methods and techniques to make language more memorable, often in order to be more persuasive or credible when making a speech. Rhetoric should in a sense be 'invisible', as the speaker wants the effect of the speech to be significant without the methods being evident.

In his speech opposite, Cassius aims to reveal Caesar's human frailty to Brutus, but not in an obvious way. In order to gauge how the rhetoric works, try the following activity:

- One person prepares a reading of Cassius's speech from line 66. Three others prepare to be the silent Brutus.
- Once the preparation is done, Cassius delivers his speech. Everyone is in character, and acts out their responses.
- Do the same again, but this time, whenever one of the Brutuses thinks Cassius is being particularly persuasive, they should raise their hand. The speech stops and Brutus explains why the word, phrase or sentence has that effect. Don't worry about technical terms at this point, just try to get a feel for the effect of the language. Cassius can comment on his own language, too, but only after Brutus has had his say.

**indifferently** with unconcern
**speed** cause to succeed or prosper

**outward favour** external appearance

**as lief** rather

**chafing with** battering against

**Accoutred** dressed

**buffet it** hit against it

**stemming** battling against
**hearts of controversy** excited by the competition

**Aeneas** legendary founder of Rome (see p. 171)

**Anchises** Aeneas's father

If it be aught toward the general good,                                  85
Set honour in one eye and death i'th'other
And I will look on both indifferently.
For let the gods so speed me as I love
The name of honour more than I fear death.

CASSIUS   I know that virtue to be in you, Brutus,                       90
As well as I do know your outward favour.
Well, honour is the subject of my story:
I cannot tell what you and other men
Think of this life, but for my single self
I had as lief not be as live to be                                       95
In awe of such a thing as I myself.
I was born free as Caesar, so were you;
We both have fed as well, and we can both
Endure the winter's cold as well as he.
For once, upon a raw and gusty day,                                     100
The troubled Tiber chafing with her shores,
Caesar said to me, 'Dar'st thou, Cassius, now
Leap in with me into this angry flood
And swim to yonder point?' Upon the word,
Accoutred as I was, I plungèd in                                        105
And bade him follow; so indeed he did.
The torrent roared, and we did buffet it
With lusty sinews, throwing it aside
And stemming it with hearts of controversy.
But ere we could arrive the point proposed,                            110
Caesar cried, 'Help me, Cassius, or I sink!'
Ay, as Aeneas, our great ancestor,
Did from the flames of Troy upon his shoulder
The old Anchises bear, so from the waves of Tiber
Did I the tired Caesar. And this man                                   115
Is now become a god, and Cassius is
A wretched creature and must bend his body
If Caesar carelessly but nod on him.
He had a fever when he was in Spain,
And when the fit was on him I did mark                                  120
How he did shake. 'Tis true, this god did shake,
His coward lips did from their colour fly,

Brutus thinks the offstage shouts mean honours for Caesar. Cassius mocks Caesar's greatness and tries to spur Brutus to action by reminding him that his qualities rank equally with Caesar's.

# Language in the play
## Rhetoric continues – take the speech apart (in pairs)

If Cassius's last speech has been a rhetorical success, he will have made Brutus question Caesar's qualities and ambitions. In this speech he seeks to build on that.

**a** Read through the speech (lines 135–61) together and decide what Cassius's purpose is.

**b** Pick out the rhetorical techniques he uses to make his point. It may be helpful to make a copy of the speech on a large piece of paper so that you can identify the different techniques and then annotate the text. Look out for the following and highlight them on your copy of the speech:

- Rhetorical questions. Remember, these are questions that do not require an answer. Listeners are assumed to answer them themselves, reaching the conclusion the speaker wants them to reach.
- Powerful **imagery**: **similes** or **metaphors** (see p. 184), which create a persuasive picture or comparison in the mind of the listener.
- **Repetition** of words or phrases for emphasis (see p. 187). For example, how many times and where do the words 'man' or 'men' appear in this speech? Why?
- **Antithesis** – this is the opposition of words or phrases to each other (see p. 187). This technique tends to highlight contrast between one thing or person and another.
- **Exclamations**: an outburst of emotion. They are usually more planned than they appear.

**c** Afterwards, annotate the speech in any other ways you find helpful to bring out its persuasive qualities.

# Stagecraft

Except for his apprehensive response to the offstage shouts for Caesar, Brutus says nothing during Cassius's long speech.

- In your Director's Journal, write notes for the actor playing Brutus, indicating how he uses movement and gesture at key points to signal his character's feelings. You may have had practice as the silent Brutus during Cassius's previous speech.

**So get the start of** outstrip
**bear the palm** win the victor's trophy

**Colossus** giant statue (see p. 172)

**conjure** call up spirits
**start** startle so as to raise

**great flood** biblical flood that engulfed the entire world

**walks** tracts of land

**a Brutus once** Lucius Junius Brutus, the traditional founder of the Roman Republic
**brooked** tolerated

And that same eye whose bend doth awe the world
Did lose his lustre. I did hear him groan,
Ay, and that tongue of his that bade the Romans                    125
Mark him and write his speeches in their books,
'Alas', it cried, 'give me some drink, Titinius',
As a sick girl. Ye gods, it doth amaze me
A man of such a feeble temper should
So get the start of the majestic world                             130
And bear the palm alone.

*Shout. Flourish*

BRUTUS      Another general shout!
I do believe that these applauses are
For some new honours that are heaped on Caesar.

CASSIUS      Why, man, he doth bestride the narrow world      135
Like a Colossus, and we petty men
Walk under his huge legs and peep about
To find ourselves dishonourable graves.
Men at some time are masters of their fates:
The fault, dear Brutus, is not in our stars                        140
But in ourselves, that we are underlings.
Brutus and Caesar: what should be in that 'Caesar'?
Why should that name be sounded more than yours?
Write them together, yours is as fair a name;
Sound them, it doth become the mouth as well;                      145
Weigh them, it is as heavy; conjure with 'em,
'Brutus' will start a spirit as soon as 'Caesar'.
Now in the names of all the gods at once,
Upon what meat doth this our Caesar feed
That he is grown so great? Age, thou art shamed!                   150
Rome, thou hast lost the breed of noble bloods!
When went there by an age since the great flood
But it was famed with more than with one man?
When could they say, till now, that talked of Rome,
That her wide walks encompassed but one man?                       155
Now is it Rome indeed and room enough
When there is in it but one only man.
O, you and I have heard our fathers say
There was a Brutus once that would have brooked
Th'eternal devil to keep his state in Rome                         160
As easily as a king.

Brutus says he will think about what Cassius has said. Caesar returns, looking angry. He confides to Antony that he is suspicious of Cassius.

## 1 Brutus the 'son of Rome'

To a true aristocrat, honour is more important than life, as Brutus has already said at lines 85–9. He reinforces that view at lines 172–5. As a staunch Republican, he will resist any tyranny that might result from Caesar's becoming king.

* Put the word HONOUR in the middle of a sheet of paper and write a definition of it. Collect around it ideas, quotations and actions drawn from this scene so far. Brutus's honour and that of the other conspirators will be tested as the play progresses. This will be useful preparation for the 'Themes' activity on page 24.

### Write about it

#### Caesar's secret police (in pairs)

Imagine that you are Caesar's intelligence agents. You have shadowed Brutus and Cassius through lines 25–177 and bugged their conversation, in order to make a report on them. Examine their words with care and consider how they looked and acted as they spoke the most important parts of their conversation.

* Make your report to Caesar. The report might include: a series of bullet-point notes; a list of words and phrases that are particularly incriminating; a conclusion explaining how dangerous you think they are and why; and a photograph of Brutus and Cassius conspiring.

▼ Which line might Caesar (left) be speaking to Antony here?

**nothing jealous** not at all doubtful
**aim** guess

**moved** urged

**meet** appropriate

**villager** (i.e. not a Roman citizen)

TRAIN attendants

**chidden** scolded
**Cicero** great Republican orator (see p. 171)
**ferret** (this animal's eyes are red, thus angry)
**crossed in conference** opposed in debate

**Sleek-headed** agreeable, free of deep thoughts

**well given** friendly

| BRUTUS | That you do love me, I am nothing jealous; | |
| | What you would work me to, I have some aim. | |
| | How I have thought of this, and of these times, | |
| | I shall recount hereafter. For this present, | 165 |
| | I would not (so with love I might entreat you) | |
| | Be any further moved. What you have said | |
| | I will consider; what you have to say | |
| | I will with patience hear and find a time | |
| | Both meet to hear and answer such high things. | 170 |
| | Till then, my noble friend, chew upon this: | |
| | Brutus had rather be a villager | |
| | Than to repute himself a son of Rome | |
| | Under these hard conditions as this time | |
| | Is like to lay upon us. | 175 |
| CASSIUS | I am glad that my weak words | |
| | Have struck but thus much show of fire from Brutus. | |

*Enter* CAESAR *and his* TRAIN

| BRUTUS | The games are done and Caesar is returning. | |
| CASSIUS | As they pass by, pluck Casca by the sleeve | |
| | And he will (after his sour fashion) tell you | 180 |
| | What hath proceeded worthy note today. | |
| BRUTUS | I will do so. But look you, Cassius, | |
| | The angry spot doth glow on Caesar's brow | |
| | And all the rest look like a chidden train: | |
| | Calpurnia's cheek is pale, and Cicero | 185 |
| | Looks with such ferret and such fiery eyes | |
| | As we have seen him in the Capitol, | |
| | Being crossed in conference by some senators. | |
| CASSIUS | Casca will tell us what the matter is. | |
| CAESAR | Antonio. | 190 |
| ANTONY | Caesar. | |
| CAESAR | Let me have men about me that are fat, | |
| | Sleek-headed men and such as sleep a-nights. | |
| | Yond Cassius has a lean and hungry look, | |
| | He thinks too much: such men are dangerous. | 195 |
| ANTONY | Fear him not, Caesar, he's not dangerous, | |
| | He is a noble Roman and well given. | |

Caesar tells Antony that Cassius is restless, brooding and dangerous. He then departs. Casca confides to Brutus and Cassius that Caesar refused a crown three times at the races.

## 1 Caesar in the hot-seat (in sixes)

**a** Experiment with different ways of speaking everything Caesar says in lines 192–214. For example, is Caesar utterly confident and self-assured (he insists twice that he does not personally fear Cassius) or is he unsure of himself and secretly fearful of Cassius? Why do you think Shakespeare adds the detail about Caesar's deafness at line 213?

**b** Put Caesar in the 'hot-seat'. One of the group plays Caesar, and the others surround him to ask questions about Cassius, what happened at the Lupercal games and what it is like to have the top job.

## Characters
### Cassius – 'Would he were fatter!'

**a** In your Director's Journal, make a list of each description of Cassius in lines 192–214 (for example 'a lean and hungry look'). Note down what these phrases tell us about his character. Have a go at sketching a likeness of him.

**b** Use your list to identify a modern actor (on film, television or stage) who you think would play Cassius well.

## 2 The people respond to Caesar (in large groups)

**a** Quickly read through lines 220–76, in which Casca reports what has happened at the Lupercal games. Concentrate on how the crowd (Casca calls it a 'rabblement', line 240) responds to Caesar, especially when Caesar thrice declines the offer of a crown.

**b** Write down all the words and phrases that Casca uses to describe the common people, and what those words suggest about Casca's attitude to them.

**c** Stage this reported scene up to line 276 as a mime. You may find it easier to choose a director who can allocate parts and who can help to shape the rhythm of the scene. There is much scope for involvement from those playing the members of the crowd: they can be getting on with eating, chatting or whatever they feel like at first, before they begin to sense the importance of the event that is unfolding in front of them.

**spare** lean

**sort** manner

**chanced** happened
**sad** serious and sullen

**fell** began

**marry** why, to be sure

**gentle** noble, kind, refined

| | | |
|---|---|---|
| CAESAR | Would he were fatter! But I fear him not. | |
| | Yet if my name were liable to fear | |
| | I do not know the man I should avoid | 200 |
| | So soon as that spare Cassius. He reads much, | |
| | He is a great observer, and he looks | |
| | Quite through the deeds of men. He loves no plays, | |
| | As thou dost, Antony, he hears no music; | |
| | Seldom he smiles, and smiles in such a sort | 205 |
| | As if he mocked himself and scorned his spirit | |
| | That could be moved to smile at any thing. | |
| | Such men as he be never at heart's ease | |
| | Whiles they behold a greater than themselves, | |
| | And therefore are they very dangerous. | 210 |
| | I rather tell thee what is to be feared | |
| | Than what I fear: for always I am Caesar. | |
| | Come on my right hand, for this ear is deaf, | |
| | And tell me truly what thou think'st of him. | |

*Sennet. Exeunt Caesar and his train*

| | | |
|---|---|---|
| CASCA | You pulled me by the cloak, would you speak with me? | 215 |
| BRUTUS | Ay, Casca, tell us what hath chanced today | |
| | That Caesar looks so sad. | |
| CASCA | Why, you were with him, were you not? | |
| BRUTUS | I should not then ask, Casca, what had chanced. | |
| CASCA | Why, there was a crown offered him, and being offered him he put it by with the back of his hand thus, and then the people fell a-shouting. | 220 |
| BRUTUS | What was the second noise for? | |
| CASCA | Why, for that too. | |
| CASSIUS | They shouted thrice; what was the last cry for? | 225 |
| CASCA | Why, for that too. | |
| BRUTUS | Was the crown offered him thrice? | |
| CASCA | Ay, marry, was't, and he put it by thrice, every time gentler than other; and at every putting-by mine honest neighbours shouted. | |
| CASSIUS | Who offered him the crown? | 230 |
| CASCA | Why, Antony. | |
| BRUTUS | Tell us the manner of it, gentle Casca. | |

Casca describes how Caesar had an epileptic fit after Antony offered him the crown. After that, Caesar offered his bared throat for the crowd to cut.

## Themes

### Life, death and honour (in fours)

Romans believed that to be honourable, you must hold life lightly: 'there are conditions on which life is not worth having', as Aristotle the Greek philosopher said. Cassius and other major characters wilfully endanger or offer to give up their lives on many occasions, as Caesar does here when he 'offered them his throat to cut'.

- The status of the concept of honour varies in different cultures. In your group, discuss what honour means in your culture. It may help to think of actions that would be considered honourable and to think of people who have acted honourably. Create a list of five points about honour and be ready to contribute to a class discussion on the topic.

## Write about it

### Caesar offered the crown! (in fours)

You are a team of journalists sent out to cover the dramatic events at the Lupercal games for a newspaper report. Decide who you want to interview, which angle to take on the events (are you pro- or anti-Caesar at this point?) and which details you will highlight. How will you assess Antony's actions? Will you include details of Caesar's condition, or would it be more sensible not to? You could include photographs if you want to act out part of the scene and then photograph it. Put together your report and display it. How have other groups covered the same event?

## 1 Caesar's epilepsy (in pairs)

Casca reports (lines 246–7) that Caesar had what sounds like an epileptic fit in the market-place.

**a** Research epilepsy in your school library or on the Internet. Then discuss what you think this detail adds to the portrait of Caesar that Shakespeare is building up in this scene.

**b** Look back and list any other health conditions, disabilities or physical weaknesses that Caesar is reported to have. Note down who mentioned each one and speculate on their possible motives for making the point at that time.

**fain** gladly

**loath** unwilling

**chopped** chapped, roughened

**swounded** fainted

**the falling sickness** epilepsy

**Marry** indeed
**plucked me ope** opened
**doublet** jacket
**And I ... of any occupation** if I had been a man of trade
**at a word** at his word
**if I would not ... rogues** if I had not believed him I should be sent to hell with the evil doers
**infirmity** illness (i.e. his epilepsy)
**wenches** young women

| CASCA | I can as well be hanged as tell the manner of it. It was mere foolery, I did not mark it. I saw Mark Antony offer him a crown – yet 'twas not a crown neither, 'twas one of these coronets – and, as I told you, he put it by once; but for all that, to my thinking he would fain have had it. Then he offered it to him again; then he put it by again; but to my thinking he was very loath to lay his fingers off it. And then he offered it the third time; he put it the third time by, and still as he refused it, the rabblement hooted, and clapped their chopped hands, and threw up their sweaty nightcaps, and uttered such a deal of stinking breath because Caesar refused the crown that it had, almost, choked Caesar, for he swounded and fell down at it. And for mine own part I durst not laugh for fear of opening my lips and receiving the bad air. | 235 240 |
|---|---|---|
| CASSIUS | But soft, I pray you; what, did Caesar swound? | 245 |
| CASCA | He fell down in the market-place, and foamed at mouth, and was speechless. | |
| BRUTUS | 'Tis very like, he hath the falling sickness. | |
| CASSIUS | No, Caesar hath it not, but you, and I, And honest Casca, we have the falling sickness. | 250 |
| CASCA | I know not what you mean by that, but I am sure Caesar fell down. If the tag-rag people did not clap him and hiss him according as he pleased and displeased them, as they use to do the players in the theatre, I am no true man. | |
| BRUTUS | What said he when he came unto himself? | 255 |
| CASCA | Marry, before he fell down, when he perceived the common herd was glad he refused the crown, he plucked me ope his doublet and offered them his throat to cut. And I had been a man of any occupation, if I would not have taken him at a word I would I might go to hell among the rogues. And so he fell. When he came to himself again, he said if he had done or said anything amiss, he desired their worships to think it was his infirmity. Three or four wenches where I stood cried, 'Alas, good soul', and forgave him with all their hearts. But there's no heed to be taken of them: if Caesar had stabbed their mothers they would have done no less. | 260 265 |
| BRUTUS | And after that he came thus sad away? | |
| CASCA | Ay. | |
| CASSIUS | Did Cicero say anything? | |
| CASCA | Ay, he spoke Greek. | |
| CASSIUS | To what effect? | 270 |

Cassius invites Casca to supper. Brutus invites Cassius to his house. Cassius, alone, tells how he will turn Brutus against Caesar.

# Ἑλληνικῶς μοι ἦν

## 1 Conspirators as future rulers – the right stuff?
**(in pairs)**

Old-style Republicans educated their sons at home. Intellectuals like Cicero sent their sons to Athens. They believed the Greeks were culturally superior to the proud but uncultivated citizens of Rome. Some argued that gentry (high-status persons) would be corrupted by mixing with inferior people at school and should have home tutors.

**a** Talk together about whether you believe it is best 'That noble minds keep ever with their likes'. Does mixing with other people corrupt or benefit those born with high status?

**b** Casca is introduced to Brutus as the sort of man Cassius wants to recruit for the conspiracy, but Brutus seems doubtful about him. Has the shrewd Cassius misjudged how they might get on together? What might Brutus be thinking about Casca and Cassius during the pause at the end of line 291?

## Characters
### Cassius's and Brutus's private thoughts (in pairs)

Cassius's **soliloquy** (a speech delivered by a character who is 'thinking aloud' and usually alone on stage) in lines 297–311 reveals his true thoughts about the noble Brutus and the way Brutus's mind can be 'seduced' into conspiring against Caesar.

**a** Take it in turns to try different readings of Cassius's speech and settle on one version that you think appropriately conveys Cassius's state of mind and his scheming intentions.

**b** What is Cassius saying about Brutus's character in lines 298–9? Why do you think he chooses to make this point using this particular metaphor?

**c** Imagine that Shakespeare had given Brutus his own soliloquy, in which he reflects on the events of this scene. Write it in modern English and then perform it to the class.

---

**and** if

**it was Greek to me**
Cicero speaks Greek but Casca does not understand Greek.

**scarves** (possibly ribbons)

**sup** dine

**quick mettle** a lively character

**tardy form**
appearance of stupidity

**gives men stomach**
makes men inclined

**honourable metal** noble qualities

**bear me hard** dislike me

**humour** influence

**several hands**
different handwritings

**tending** referring

**glancèd at** mentioned in passing

**seat him sure** make sure he is safe and secure

CASCA        Nay, and I tell you that, I'll ne'er look you i'th'face again. But those that understood him smiled at one another and shook their heads; but for mine own part it was Greek to me. I could tell you more news too. Murellus and Flavius, for pulling scarves off Caesar's images, are put to silence. Fare you well. There was more foolery yet, 275 if I could remember it.

CASSIUS      Will you sup with me tonight, Casca?

CASCA        No, I am promised forth.

CASSIUS      Will you dine with me tomorrow?

CASCA        Ay, if I be alive, and your mind hold, and your dinner worth the 280 eating.

CASSIUS      Good, I will expect you.

CASCA        Do so. Farewell both.                                          *Exit*

BRUTUS       What a blunt fellow is this grown to be!
             He was quick mettle when he went to school.                   285

CASSIUS      So is he now in execution
             Of any bold or noble enterprise,
             However he puts on this tardy form.
             This rudeness is a sauce to his good wit,
             Which gives men stomach to digest his words                  290
             With better appetite.

BRUTUS       And so it is. For this time I will leave you.
             Tomorrow if you please to speak with me,
             I will come home to you; or if you will,
             Come home to me and I will wait for you.                     295

CASSIUS      I will do so. Till then, think of the world.      *Exit Brutus*
             Well, Brutus, thou art noble; yet I see
             Thy honourable metal may be wrought
             From that it is disposed. Therefore it is meet
             That noble minds keep ever with their likes;                 300
             For who so firm that cannot be seduced?
             Caesar doth bear me hard, but he loves Brutus.
             If I were Brutus now and he were Cassius,
             He should not humour me. I will this night,
             In several hands, in at his windows throw,                   305
             As if they came from several citizens,
             Writings, all tending to the great opinion
             That Rome holds of his name, wherein obscurely
             Caesar's ambition shall be glancèd at.
             And after this let Caesar seat him sure,                     310
             For we will shake him, or worse days endure.    *Exit*

Casca meets Cicero and describes the natural and supernatural wonders he sees in the tempest which rages. Casca thinks they are bad omens.

# Stagecraft

### All change (in groups of five or six)

Shakespeare's scene changes can be very dramatic moments and often highlight major themes of the plays. Here, the crowds and daylight of Scene 2 give way to night, fierce storms and solitary frightened figures.

The challenge for your group is to decide how you will stage this scene up to line 40, bringing out the turbulence of the times in the following production settings:

- **The Globe Theatre in 1599** There seems little doubt that *Julius Caesar* was one of the first plays performed by Shakespeare's own company at the newly built Globe Theatre. There were no stage lights and very basic sound effects. How would you maximise the drama of this scene within these theatrical constraints?
- **A contemporary theatre** Most modern societies are much more sceptical of signs and supernatural events than the Romans were. Discuss how you would persuade your audience of the sheer terror the Romans would have felt as their world was turned upside down. Would there be any merit in transferring the scene to a modern apocalyptic setting?
- **On film** You have all sorts of special effects at your disposal. Make the most of the freedom of the film medium to draw up your ideas for conveying a convincing night of terror.

Write up these three sets of ideas in your Director's Journal.

## 1 Prodigies on the wall (whole class in five groups)

Five prodigies (extraordinary things or events) are described by Casca (lines 15–32). Imagine they took place in your neighbourhood yesterday.

- For a wall display, each group should take a single prodigy and report it, filled out with vivid details, interviews and comments from people you know. You can add illustrations. One person in the group should be an augurer (an interpreter of signs or portents). In their part of the display, they should explain what the gods are using the prodigy to tell the people. Perhaps the augurer writes a horoscope column!

**sway** kingdom, dominion

**rived** split

**exalted** raised

**saucy** insolent, defiant

**sensible of** feeling

**Against** beside
**glazed upon** stared at
**annoying** harming
**drawn** assembled
**ghastly** causing terror

**prodigies** wondrous sights (interpreted as omens of the future)
**conjointly** together, in conjunction
**portentous** ominous, hugely important
**climate** region of the earth

# Act 1 Scene 3
## Rome   A street   Night

*Thunder and lightning. Enter [from opposite sides]* CASCA *and*
CICERO

| | |
|---|---|
| CICERO | Good even, Casca, brought you Caesar home? |
| | Why are you breathless, and why stare you so? |
| CASCA | Are not you moved when all the sway of earth |
| | Shakes like a thing unfirm? O Cicero, |

I have seen tempests when the scolding winds      5
Have rived the knotty oaks, and I have seen
Th'ambitious ocean swell, and rage, and foam,
To be exalted with the threatening clouds;
But never till tonight, never till now,
Did I go through a tempest dropping fire.      10
Either there is a civil strife in heaven,
Or else the world, too saucy with the gods,
Incenses them to send destruction.

CICERO    Why, saw you anything more wonderful?

CASCA    A common slave – you know him well by sight –      15
Held up his left hand, which did flame and burn
Like twenty torches joined, and yet his hand,
Not sensible of fire, remained unscorched.
Besides – I ha' not since put up my sword –
Against the Capitol I met a lion      20
Who glazed upon me and went surly by
Without annoying me. And there were drawn
Upon a heap a hundred ghastly women,
Transformèd with their fear, who swore they saw
Men, all in fire, walk up and down the streets.      25
And yesterday the bird of night did sit
Even at noon-day upon the market-place,
Hooting and shrieking. When these prodigies
Do so conjointly meet let not men say,
'These are their reasons, they are natural',      30
For I believe they are portentous things
Unto the climate that they point upon.

Cicero warns Casca that omens can be misinterpreted. Cassius enters, bare-chested. He welcomes the tempest and despises Casca's fear.

## 1 Cicero and Casca – conspirators? (in pairs)

Cicero and Casca's opening exchange shows a contrast in their respective characters. Cicero is calm, seeing nothing extraordinary in the storm's power, carefully avoiding political discussion. Casca is disturbed, deeply affected by the omens of the storm that he has seen, and anxious that they signify threat to Rome.

**a** Take parts and read lines 1–40. How will you bring out the different personalities and viewpoints of the two men?

**b** This is Cicero's last appearance in the play; Brutus later sees him as an unsuitable member of the conspiracy and rejects him, while Casca is accepted. Discuss how actors might play these two roles to highlight the contrasting fates of the two men.

## 2 The world through Cassius's eyes (in pairs)

It is hard to imagine more different reactions to the storm than those of fearful Casca, who we know from line 19 is carrying a sword, and Cassius, who says that he has been walking about offering his bare chest to the storm. Shakespeare is showing us an extreme contrast.

**a** Read lines 41–71. Aim to bring out the differences between the two men in the tone of voice you choose.

**b** Consider the contrast between the reactions of Cassius and Casca by picking out words and phrases from their speeches and putting them into a chart like the one below. Words and phrases that suggest a rational response go in one column, those that suggest an emotional response go in the other, and the speaker's name goes on the left. What observations can you make about the characters of the two men by looking at your finished chart?

| Character | Rational | Emotional |
|-----------|----------|-----------|
| Cassius | 'known the earth' | |
| Casca | | 'fear and tremble' |
| | | |
| | | |
| | | |

strange disposèd disturbed

thus unbracèd
with doublet undone
thunderstone thunderbolt
cross forked

tempt provoke

astonish terrify

want lack

from quality and kind
depart from their true natures
calculate reckon

| | |
|---|---|
| CICERO | Indeed, it is a strange-disposèd time. |
| | But men may construe things after their fashion |
| | Clean from the purpose of the things themselves. 35 |
| | Comes Caesar to the Capitol tomorrow? |
| CASCA | He doth, for he did bid Antonio |
| | Send word to you he would be there tomorrow. |
| CICERO | Good night then, Casca. This disturbèd sky |
| | Is not to walk in. |
| CASCA | Farewell, Cicero. 40 |

*Exit Cicero*

*Enter* CASSIUS

| | |
|---|---|
| CASSIUS | Who's there? |
| CASCA | A Roman. |
| CASSIUS | Casca, by your voice. |
| CASCA | Your ear is good. Cassius, what night is this! |
| CASSIUS | A very pleasing night to honest men. |
| CASCA | Who ever knew the heavens menace so? |
| CASSIUS | Those that have known the earth so full of faults. 45 |
| | For my part I have walked about the streets, |
| | Submitting me unto the perilous night, |
| | And, thus unbracèd, Casca, as you see, |
| | Have bared my bosom to the thunderstone; |
| | And when the cross blue lightning seemed to open 50 |
| | The breast of heaven, I did present myself |
| | Even in the aim and very flash of it. |
| CASCA | But wherefore did you so much tempt the heavens? |
| | It is the part of men to fear and tremble |
| | When the most mighty gods by tokens send 55 |
| | Such dreadful heralds to astonish us. |
| CASSIUS | You are dull, Casca, and those sparks of life |
| | That should be in a Roman you do want, |
| | Or else you use not. You look pale, and gaze, |
| | And put on fear, and cast yourself in wonder 60 |
| | To see the strange impatience of the heavens. |
| | But if you would consider the true cause |
| | Why all these fires, why all these gliding ghosts, |
| | Why birds and beasts from quality and kind, |
| | Why old men, fools, and children calculate, 65 |

Cassius hints that the tempest is a warning that should rouse the people of Rome. Casca tells him that outside Italy, Caesar will be king. Death will free me from such oppression, riddles Cassius.

# Language in the play

## Cassius and the art of persuasion (in pairs)

Once again, Cassius shows himself to be a powerful orator. He is out to recruit Casca to his cause. He is successful: by line 119, Casca is saying, 'I will set this foot of mine as far / As who goes farthest.' How has Cassius achieved this?

Taking parts, read carefully through lines 72–130. Follow Cassius's persuasive techniques by answering the following questions:

**a** In which lines does Cassius link Caesar to the strange events of the night?

**b** What is his view of Caesar's stature?

**c** Why does he not name Caesar?

**d** Why does he say Romans are grown 'womanish'?

**e** Look carefully at Cassius's speech beginning at line 89. Cassius says that he has a plan to make sure he never has to live under the reign of Caesar the king. What is that plan and how does having it make Cassius feel?

**f** The use of lists is a favourite rhetorical device. What is the effect of the list in lines 93–4?

**g** How does Casca's speech beginning at line 100 show that Cassius's persuasion is beginning to work?

**h** Cassius's speech beginning at line 103 is an especially clever piece of rhetoric. Looking carefully at his use of rhetorical questions, metaphors and his seeming change of attitude to Caesar, comment on how the speech works.

**i** It is clear the speech is well crafted, so why does he ask, 'But, O grief, / Where hast thou led me?' (lines 111–12)?

**j** What test does Cassius offer Casca at the end of this speech?

**k** How can you tell from Casca's language from line 116 onwards that he now has no doubts about joining Cassius?

**l** Twice in Cassius's speech beginning at line 120, he describes what they are about to embark on as highly dangerous. Identify where he does this.

**m** Explain the effect created by the **juxtaposition** (putting together) of the words 'honourable' and 'dangerous'.

**n** How does Cassius link the conspiracy to the events of the night?

**ordinance**
proper required behaviour

**preformèd faculties**
inborn qualities

**state** state of affairs

**prodigious**
supernaturally threatening

**thews** muscles

**woe the while** alas for these times

**yoke** bondage, slavery

**sufferance** long suffering

**bondman** slave

Why all these things change from their ordinance,
Their natures, and preformèd faculties,
To monstrous quality – why, you shall find
That heaven hath infused them with these spirits
To make them instruments of fear, and warning          70
Unto some monstrous state.
Now could I, Casca, name to thee a man
Most like this dreadful night,
That thunders, lightens, opens graves, and roars
As doth the lion in the Capitol –          75
A man no mightier than thyself, or me,
In personal action, yet prodigious grown
And fearful, as these strange eruptions are.

CASCA     'Tis Caesar that you mean, is it not, Cassius?

CASSIUS     Let it be who it is, for Romans now          80
Have thews and limbs like to their ancestors'.
But, woe the while, our fathers' minds are dead
And we are governed with our mothers' spirits;
Our yoke and sufferance show us womanish.

CASCA     Indeed, they say the senators tomorrow          85
Mean to establish Caesar as a king,
And he shall wear his crown by sea and land,
In every place save here in Italy.

CASSIUS     I know where I will wear this dagger then:
Cassius from bondage will deliver Cassius.          90
Therein, ye gods, you make the weak most strong;
Therein, ye gods, you tyrants do defeat.
Nor stony tower, nor walls of beaten brass,
Nor airless dungeon, nor strong links of iron,
Can be retentive to the strength of spirit;          95
But life, being weary of these worldly bars,
Never lacks power to dismiss itself.
If I know this, know all the world besides,
That part of tyranny that I do bear
I can shake off at pleasure.

*Thunder still*

CASCA                 So can I,          100
So every bondman in his own hand bears
The power to cancel his captivity.

Stung by Cassius's words, Casca commits himself to Caesar's overthrow. Cassius tells him of other conspirators he has recruited. One of them, Cinna, enters looking for Cassius.

## Stagecraft

### Embedded information

You might have noticed a lack of settings and stage directions in this play. Those that appear at the start of each scene were not included by Shakespeare but were added later by different editors of the play.

- Read through lines 131–8 and find the staging instructions that Shakespeare embedded within the script. In your Director's Journal, draw up a chart with two columns. Put the quotation in one column and in the other column, write down what sort of staging or movement it suggests.

▼ The conspirators wait for Cassius at Pompey's Porch. What feelings do you think these actors are trying to convey?'

**hinds** deer/menial servants

**fleering** sneering
**Be factious** form a rebel group
**griefs** grievances

**Pompey's Porch** the doorway into Pompey's theatre
**the complexion of the element** condition of the sky
**In favour's like** looks like

**Stand close** remain concealed
**gait** footsteps

**incorporate / To** committed to supporting

| | |
|---|---|
| CASSIUS | And why should Caesar be a tyrant then? |
| | Poor man, I know he would not be a wolf |
| | But that he sees the Romans are but sheep; |
| | He were no lion, were not Romans hinds. |
| | Those that with haste will make a mighty fire |
| | Begin it with weak straws. What trash is Rome, |
| | What rubbish and what offal, when it serves |
| | For the base matter to illuminate |
| | So vile a thing as Caesar? But, O grief, |
| | Where hast thou led me? I perhaps speak this |
| | Before a willing bondman, then I know |
| | My answer must be made. But I am armed, |
| | And dangers are to me indifferent. |
| CASCA | You speak to Casca, and to such a man |
| | That is no fleering tell-tale. Hold, my hand. |
| | Be factious for redress of all these griefs, |
| | And I will set this foot of mine as far |
| | As who goes farthest. |
| CASSIUS | There's a bargain made. |
| | Now know you, Casca, I have moved already |
| | Some certain of the noblest-minded Romans |
| | To undergo with me an enterprise |
| | Of honourable dangerous consequence. |
| | And I do know by this they stay for me |
| | In Pompey's Porch. For now, this fearful night, |
| | There is no stir or walking in the streets, |
| | And the complexion of the element |
| | In favour's like the work we have in hand, |
| | Most bloody, fiery, and most terrible. |

*Enter* CINNA

| | |
|---|---|
| CASCA | Stand close a while, for here comes one in haste. |
| CASSIUS | 'Tis Cinna, I do know him by his gait. |
| | He is a friend. Cinna, where haste you so? |
| CINNA | To find out you. Who's that? Metellus Cimber? |
| CASSIUS | No, it is Casca, one incorporate |
| | To our attempts. Am I not stayed for, Cinna? |
| CINNA | I am glad on't. What a fearful night is this! |
| | There's two or three of us have seen strange sights. |

105

110

115

120

125

130

135

Cassius orders Cinna to leave letters for Brutus in places where he will find them. Cassius says Brutus will join the conspirators tonight. They leave to join the other conspirators and go to Brutus's house.

## 1 Unspoken thoughts (in threes)

Cinna's dramatic and hasty arrival signals the gathering momentum of the conspiracy.

**a** Take parts and act out lines 131–41 with breathless speed, but emphasise the pause at the end of line 140.

**b** Talk about what is not said, but what is probably in the men's minds.

## Stagecraft

### Why include a tempest? (in eights)

Shakespeare often wrote or made changes in consultation with his actors. His main source for *Julius Caesar* was Plutarch's *Lives of the Noble Grecians and Romans* (see p. 166). In Plutarch's text there is only one paragraph describing the prodigies, and no tempest.

Some people today do not like 'historical facts' to be changed when made into films. Similarly, in Shakespeare's day, some people objected to the liberties taken by dramatists.

• Imagine that Shakespeare's actors meet a group of such objectors in a tavern after the opening night. Divide into two groups (actors and objectors) and plan a discussion in which you argue about whether or not Shakespeare should have inserted Scene 3, which does not advance the plot in any way. Prepare for the argument by listing justifications for, and objections to, inventing or changing historical events in plays. Then act out your discussion.

## Characters

### Brutus (in threes)

There are many ways for a dramatist to establish character. Obviously how that character acts and what they say are important, but just as important in establishing their role and characteristics is what others say about them. Here, right at the end of Act 1, and just before Brutus's soliloquy in his orchard, revealing his innermost thoughts, Shakespeare has the conspirators make clear why Brutus's support is so important to them.

**a** Take parts and read from line 140 to the end of the scene together. Remember your meeting and business are top secret.

**b** In character, take it in turns to explain to the others in modern English why you think Brutus's support is vital.

**praetor** chief magistrate (Brutus's official title)

**Repair** go

**hie** hasten, hurry
**bestow** put

**ere** before

**countenance** face or support
**alchemy** the ancient science that sought to turn base metals into gold
**conceited** imagined, understood

36

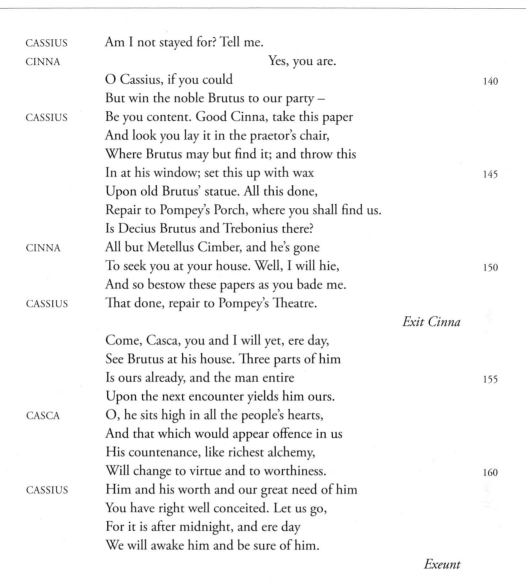

| CASSIUS | Am I not stayed for? Tell me. |
|---|---|
| CINNA | Yes, you are. |

O Cassius, if you could                                          140
But win the noble Brutus to our party –

CASSIUS        Be you content. Good Cinna, take this paper
And look you lay it in the praetor's chair,
Where Brutus may but find it; and throw this
In at his window; set this up with wax                          145
Upon old Brutus' statue. All this done,
Repair to Pompey's Porch, where you shall find us.
Is Decius Brutus and Trebonius there?

CINNA        All but Metellus Cimber, and he's gone
To seek you at your house. Well, I will hie,                    150
And so bestow these papers as you bade me.

CASSIUS        That done, repair to Pompey's Theatre.

                                                 *Exit Cinna*

Come, Casca, you and I will yet, ere day,
See Brutus at his house. Three parts of him
Is ours already, and the man entire                             155
Upon the next encounter yields him ours.

CASCA        O, he sits high in all the people's hearts,
And that which would appear offence in us
His countenance, like richest alchemy,
Will change to virtue and to worthiness.                        160

CASSIUS        Him and his worth and our great need of him
You have right well conceited. Let us go,
For it is after midnight, and ere day
We will awake him and be sure of him.

                                                 *Exeunt*

# Looking back at Act 1
## Activities for groups or individuals

## 1 A head for power?

One of the reasons for the continued appeal of this play is its examination of the nature of power.

- Discuss the personal qualities you would look for in a great leader. Find a picture of a real leader you admire, or draw a head to represent your ideal leader, and write these qualities around it. How many of these qualities does Caesar appear to have by the end of Act 1? Find an image of Caesar and write his qualities around it.

## 2 Caesar passes

There are twelve speaking parts in Act 1 other than Caesar. Cast yourselves in as many of these parts as there are people in your group, and choose one or two lines from the script to sum up what your character thinks of Caesar. Line up with expectant smiles. As you imagine Caesar passing in slow motion, say your line(s) about him, adding gestures and facial expressions. The rest of the class should try to identify who is playing whom.

## 3 Time for a speech

Cassius is highly persuasive. As we have seen, he has many clever rhetorical techniques at his disposal.

- Look back to your work on Cassius's speeches on pages 16, 18 and 32 and take inspiration. Choose a topic that you feel passionate about. Write a speech to persuade others that your point of view is the right one and include as many rhetorical techniques as you can. Deliver the speech to the class.

## 4 Caesar at the Lupercal

Royalty in Shakespeare's day copied the traditions of the Roman triumph. On special occasions, they paraded through the streets in a procession of elaborate floats.

a  Design a float that Caesar might have used at the Lupercal festival (see p. 172), emphasising his triumph and the protection of Rome from evil.

b  Queen Elizabeth I was often greeted at the gate of a stately home or a city with a poem that had been written for the occasion. Write a poem to welcome Caesar to the games.

## 5 What do we know about Cassius?

What do you make of Cassius? Brutus's close friend seems to be the instigator of the conspiracy and the character who dominates the first act. He has a deep hatred of Caesar that is never really explained.

- Write a profile of Cassius based on his language, his behaviour and what others have said about him in Act 1. Feel free to speculate about his motives, but make it clear what is speculation and what is drawn from the text.

## 6 What is a true Roman?

This is a key concept in the play and Shakespeare uses Brutus and Cassius to establish it. It is crucial that this idea is familiar to the audience before the deliberations of Act 2.

- Look back at Act 1 Scene 2, lines 150–75 and Act 1 Scene 3, lines 103–15. Using the views expressed there and your reflections on them, write your answer to the question 'What is a true Roman?' Remember to use quotations in support of your points.

## 7 The Soothsayer

Every producer must decide how to present the Soothsayer. He is sometimes played as a kind of outsider to the society in which the political drama is taking place.

- In small groups, discuss your own ideas for the Soothsayer. Decide first whether your staging will be in modern or traditional dress. The photographs opposite may help you. Then sketch out your own costume design for the Soothsayer.

39

Night. In his orchard, Brutus sends Lucius to light his study. He decides that Caesar must die to prevent him from using his new power wrongly.

## Stagecraft
### Public to private (in pairs)

Shakespeare retains a night-time setting for the opening of Act 2, but moves from public space (a Roman street) to a private one (Brutus's orchard). Brutus's lines 1–3 also draw attention to the thematic importance of light and darkness in the play (Lucius's name is close to the Latin word *lux*, meaning 'light', and he is sent to fetch light for Brutus's study).

* Work together to design a set for the opening of this scene in Brutus's orchard to be staged in a modern theatre. Sketch your design and show clearly how you would use lighting effects for lines 1–10. Add the annotated sketch to your Director's Journal.

## 1  Brutus: making his mind up (whole class)

Brutus's soliloquy charts the seesawing of his anguished thoughts as he considers the reasons why Caesar should be killed.

* First, choose a student to play Brutus. Then divide up his speech (lines 10–34) into 'sense units' (sometimes a phrase, sometimes a line or so) and allocate these to the other members of the class. Whilst Brutus is seated in the centre of the room, the others should, in turn, whisper their language extracts into Brutus's ear. Repeat the process several times, varying the volume and tone.
* Afterwards, put Brutus in the hot-seat and ask him about the impression made upon him by the thoughts of his own 'conscience'. Which words or arguments made a particular impression?

## Language in the play
### Snakes and ladders

Brutus uses two key images to describe the threat he imagines that Caesar poses. The first compares Caesar to an adder (a poisonous snake) and then a serpent; the other suggests that his ambition is like the process of his climbing a ladder.

* Find the specific images that Shakespeare creates. What do they suggest a) about Caesar and b) about Brutus's attitude to him?

**I cannot … day** looking at the stars doesn't tell me how close daybreak is
**I would it were my fault to** I wish I could

**taper** candle

**spurn at** attack
**general** common good
**would** desires to

**craves wary walking** requires treading carefully

**disjoins** separates

**affections** emotions
**swayed** dominated
**proof** experience
**lowliness** humble behaviour
**upmost round** top rung

**base degrees** earlier humble way of life

**prevent** act in anticipation
**quarrel** concern (about Caesar)
**Will bear no colour** cannot be justified
**Fashion it thus** argue it this way
**augmented** were it to grow

# Act 2 Scene 1
## Brutus' orchard   Night

*Enter* BRUTUS *in his orchard*

BRUTUS   What, Lucius, ho!
I cannot by the progress of the stars
Give guess how near to day. Lucius, I say!
I would it were my fault to sleep so soundly.
When, Lucius, when? Awake, I say! What, Lucius!          5

*Enter* LUCIUS

LUCIUS   Called you, my lord?
BRUTUS   Get me a taper in my study, Lucius.
When it is lighted, come and call me here.
LUCIUS   I will, my lord.                                *Exit*
BRUTUS   It must be by his death. And for my part        10
I know no personal cause to spurn at him
But for the general. He would be crowned:
How that might change his nature, there's the question.
It is the bright day that brings forth the adder
And that craves wary walking. Crown him that,          15
And then I grant we put a sting in him
That at his will he may do danger with.
Th'abuse of greatness is when it disjoins
Remorse from power. And to speak truth of Caesar,
I have not known when his affections swayed            20
More than his reason. But 'tis a common proof
That lowliness is young ambition's ladder,
Whereto the climber-upward turns his face;
But when he once attains the upmost round
He then unto the ladder turns his back,                25
Looks in the clouds, scorning the base degrees
By which he did ascend. So Caesar may.
Then lest he may, prevent. And since the quarrel
Will bear no colour for the thing he is,
Fashion it thus: that what he is, augmented,           30
Would run to these and these extremities.

Lucius brings Brutus one of Cassius's letters. It strengthens Brutus's resolve to kill Caesar. Lucius reports that tomorrow is 15 March – the Ides of March.

## Write about it

### Cryptic letters (in pairs)

Lucius delivers a letter to Brutus that he has found dropped through his window. This letter gets Brutus's attention because its meaning is not clear. It is one among many ('Such instigations'), all apparently by different writers, but all in fact written by Cassius.

- Each of you, in role as Cassius, writes a letter to Brutus, prompting him to action. (Look back to pages 16, 18 and 32 for analysis of the way Cassius uses the language of persuasion.) Swap letters and comment on how persuasive and effective each one is.

## Characters

### Focus on Brutus (in fours, then by yourself)

It is the eve of the Ides of March. By the end of his second soliloquy (lines 44–58), Brutus has resolved to assassinate Caesar.

a  Share out Brutus's lines amongst the group. As you read through them, emphasise any shifts in tone (e.g. the movement between questions and commands). Show clearly how you think Brutus's mood gradually changes as he moves towards his final position.

b  Work individually to read Brutus's first soliloquy (lines 10–34), followed instantly by his second. Write down in your own words the stages of his argument, culminating in his intention to kill Caesar.

c  Finally, write a paragraph in your Character file about what you think of Brutus at this point in the play. How far do you think his arguments are credible or justifiable? Is he being too idealistic or unreasonable? Use references to justify all the points you make.

◀ **Describe how this actor has sought to convey Brutus's mental anguish as he considers Caesar's growing power and ambition.**

**serpent's** snake's
**as his kind** as is its nature
**mischievous** dangerous

**closet** private room
**flint** (for lighting the taper)

**exhalations** meteors

**redress** put it right

**instigations** calls to action

**piece it out** work it out

**Tarquin** (the last tyrant kings of Rome; see p. 1)
**entreated** urged
**If the redress will follow** if you give me your backing
**thou receivest … full petition** you will get everything you ask for
**at** from
**March … days** it's the morning of 15 March

**whet** incite

And therefore think him as a serpent's egg
(Which, hatched, would as his kind grow mischievous)
And kill him in the shell.

*Enter* LUCIUS

| | | |
|---|---|---|
| LUCIUS | The taper burneth in your closet, sir. | 35 |

Searching the window for a flint, I found
This paper, thus sealed up, and I am sure
It did not lie there when I went to bed.

*Gives him the letter*

BRUTUS      Get you to bed again, it is not day.

Is not tomorrow, boy, the Ides of March?        40

LUCIUS      I know not, sir.

BRUTUS      Look in the calendar and bring me word.

LUCIUS      I will, sir.                                          *Exit*

BRUTUS      The exhalations whizzing in the air

Give so much light that I may read by them.     45

*Opens the letter and reads*

'Brutus, thou sleep'st. Awake, and see thyself!
Shall Rome, etc. Speak, strike, redress!'
'Brutus, thou sleep'st. Awake!'
Such instigations have been often dropped
Where I have took them up.                             50
'Shall Rome, etc.' Thus must I piece it out:
Shall Rome stand under one man's awe? What, Rome?
My ancestors did from the streets of Rome
The Tarquin drive when he was called a king.
'Speak, strike, redress!' Am I entreated         55
To speak and strike? O Rome, I make thee promise,
If the redress will follow, thou receivest
Thy full petition at the hand of Brutus.

*Enter* LUCIUS

LUCIUS      Sir, March is wasted fifteen days.

*Knock within*

BRUTUS      'Tis good. Go to the gate, somebody knocks.    60

[*Exit Lucius*]

Since Cassius first did whet me against Caesar
I have not slept.

Brutus describes how it feels to have made up one's mind to do a fearful act. Lucius reports the arrival of the disguised conspirators. Brutus muses that conspiracy must always hide its nature.

# Themes

## Appearance versus reality (in pairs)

The contrast between how things appear on the surface and what they are really like beneath is evident in all of Shakespeare's plays.

a Take parts and read aloud lines 72–85. Identify all the images that describe things being concealed or hidden. Write a sentence about each one, explaining how the image works to establish a contrast between appearance and reality.

b Choose one of the images to present as a tableau. Show it to other groups for them to guess which image you are portraying.

c Brutus views as shameful the need to hide his true thoughts and feelings now the conspiracy is underway. Write a short paragraph about what his choice of language suggests about his attitude to deception.

# Stagecraft

## Darkness versus light; movement versus inaction (in small groups)

Shakespeare deliberately contrasts the youthful innocence of Lucius with the dark, furtive thoughts of Brutus. The conspirators keep to the shadows with faces muffled, but Brutus feels the plotters will best 'mask' their feelings by hiding their true intentions in 'smiles and affability'.

a Imagine that you are directing a film version of the play. Focus on the start of this scene up to the conspirators' entrance (line 85). What colours and lighting would you use? Film noir (French for 'black film') uses light to hint at the state of mind of its characters. At what point would Brutus be in the shadows? When would he be in close-up? Discuss your ideas and then write up your notes in your Director's Journal.

b Using the opening 85 lines again, focus on all Lucius's entrances and exits. Talk together about the contrasts created by the constant movements of this character and how they are set against the motionless state of Brutus. Try to come up with two or three dramatic reasons why you think Shakespeare establishes this contrast. Share your best idea with the class.

**motion** impulse to do

**interim** time in between

**phantasma** nightmarish illusion

**genius … instruments** spirit and body

**in council** in debate with each other

**Like to** just like

**insurrection** uprising, civil war

**brother** brother-in-law

**mo** more

**discover** recognise

**mark of favour** distinguishing characteristics

**visage** face

**path** pursue your course of action

**native semblance** true appearance

**Erebus** the dark regions on the way to Hades (Roman hell)

**prevention** being thwarted

**we … rest** we are disturbing you

Between the acting of a dreadful thing
And the first motion, all the interim is
Like a phantasma or a hideous dream.                                    65
The genius and the mortal instruments
Are then in council, and the state of a man,
Like to a little kingdom, suffers then
The nature of an insurrection.

*Enter* LUCIUS

| | | |
|---|---|---|
| LUCIUS | Sir, 'tis your brother Cassius at the door, | 70 |
| | Who doth desire to see you. | |
| BRUTUS | Is he alone? | |
| LUCIUS | No, sir, there are mo with him. | |
| BRUTUS | Do you know them? | |
| LUCIUS | No, sir, their hats are plucked about their ears | |
| | And half their faces buried in their cloaks, | |
| | That by no means I may discover them | 75 |
| | By any mark of favour. | |
| BRUTUS | Let 'em enter. | |

[*Exit Lucius*]

They are the faction. O conspiracy,
Sham'st thou to show thy dang'rous brow by night,
When evils are most free? O then by day
Where wilt thou find a cavern dark enough                               80
To mask thy monstrous visage? Seek none, conspiracy,
Hide it in smiles and affability,
For if thou path, thy native semblance on,
Not Erebus itself were dim enough
To hide thee from prevention.                                          85

*Enter the conspirators,* CASSIUS, CASCA, DECIUS, CINNA,
METELLUS, *and* TREBONIUS

| | | |
|---|---|---|
| CASSIUS | I think we are too bold upon your rest. | |
| | Good morrow, Brutus, do we trouble you? | |
| BRUTUS | I have been up this hour, awake all night. | |
| | Know I these men that come along with you? | |
| CASSIUS | Yes, every man of them; and no man here | 90 |
| | But honours you, and every one doth wish | |

Brutus is introduced to the conspirators. After some secret words with Cassius, he shakes their hands but he rejects the suggestion that they should all swear an oath to kill Caesar.

## Stagecraft

### Watching the sun rise (in pairs)

**a** After line 100, Brutus and Cassius share a whispered and secret conversation. What do you think they talk about? Discuss possible ideas then work together to script their conversation in modern English.

**b** In your pairs, sketch a layout of the stage showing how all characters present (there are seven of them) are blocked (arranged on stage) between lines 100–112. Think carefully about the kind of relationship you want to show between the different conspirators.

**c** Whilst Brutus and Cassius talk out of earshot of the audience, Decius, Casca and Cinna contemplate the imminent sunrise. Remind yourself of the 'Stagecraft' activity on page 44, and think about how you would light this scene. What effects would you want to create?

**d** Why do you think Shakespeare chooses to include a passage of dialogue about the imminence of daybreak at this point?

**hither** here

**What … night?** what anxieties are keeping you awake?

**entreat** request

**fret** cut ornamental patterns into

**growing on** moving towards
**Weighing … year** considering how early in the year it is

## 1 Cassius's oath
### (in threes)

Cassius never gets to swear his resolution (line 113). Discuss what it might have been and write it down (in no more than two lines). Each group should share its version of Cassius's oath with the class. This will give you many ideas about Cassius and the conspiracy.

▶ Brutus (right) and Cassius: who holds the power?

**face** appearance
**sufferance** suffering
**betimes** immediately
**idle** empty

**by lottery** by chance

**kindle** ignite

**prick us** spur us on, incite us
**palter** say one thing and mean another
**honesty** honour
**engaged** pledged, promised
**fall** die

You had but that opinion of yourself
Which every noble Roman bears of you.
This is Trebonius.

BRUTUS                              He is welcome hither.

CASSIUS     This, Decius Brutus.

BRUTUS                              He is welcome too.                                          95

CASSIUS     This, Casca; this, Cinna; and this, Metellus Cimber.

BRUTUS      They are all welcome.
What watchful cares do interpose themselves
Betwixt your eyes and night?

CASSIUS     Shall I entreat a word?                                                            100

*They whisper*

DECIUS      Here lies the east, doth not the day break here?

CASCA       No.

CINNA       O, pardon, sir, it doth, and yon grey lines
That fret the clouds are messengers of day.

CASCA       You shall confess that you are both deceived.                                     105
Here, as I point my sword, the sun arises,
Which is a great way growing on the south,
Weighing the youthful season of the year.
Some two months hence, up higher toward the north
He first presents his fire, and the high east                                                  110
Stands, as the Capitol, directly here.

BRUTUS      [*Advancing with Cassius*] Give me your hands all over, one by one.

CASSIUS     And let us swear our resolution.

BRUTUS      No, not an oath! If not the face of men,
The sufferance of our souls, the time's abuse –                                                115
If these be motives weak, break off betimes,
And every man hence to his idle bed;
So let high-sighted tyranny range on,
Till each man drop by lottery. But if these
(As I am sure they do) bear fire enough                                                        120
To kindle cowards and to steel with valour
The melting spirits of women, then, countrymen,
What need we any spur but our own cause
To prick us to redress? What other bond
Than secret Romans that have spoke the word                                                    125
And will not palter? And what other oath
Than honesty to honesty engaged
That this shall be or we will fall for it?

## Characters

### Brutus's honour

Brutus uses his speech (lines 114–40) as a rallying cry to his fellow conspirators. To Brutus, the honour of their cause is all-important. A Roman's promise is binding and thus they do not need to swear an oath together to unite them in their enterprise.

a  Read carefully through his speech. Imagine that you have to give a presentation to a group of younger students about exactly what Brutus says, what it shows about his fundamental beliefs and principles, and how he uses words to persuade and inspire his listeners. Write the text of your presentation.

b  Look back at Brutus's language and behaviour so far in this scene. Produce a spider diagram of reasons why he is emerging as the natural leader of the conspirators. Link each point to evidence from the text.

## 1  Public relations (in small groups)

Metellus sees (line 145) that the conspirators have a public image problem, and so does Brutus (lines 162–83). In those lines, Brutus shows the conspirators how to think of their task in a high-minded, noble and honourable way. However, he does not show how to get the general public to think of the assassination in the same way.

•  You are a public relations firm sympathetic to the Republican cause. You have secretly been asked to prepare a presentation, using all modern forms of media at your disposal (blogs, social networking, posters, adverts and so on) to give an immediate explanation and justification of the campaign against Caesar. Put together a publicity package to convince everybody that Caesar poses a genuine threat to Rome and its traditions and values.

## 2  What to do about Antony? (in pairs)

Cassius urges that Antony ('A shrewd contriver') should be killed along with Caesar. Brutus believes Antony will pose no threat once Caesar is dead: 'Antony is but a limb of Caesar'. Brutus quickly wins the argument here, but imagine that Cassius later decides to take up the discussion again with Brutus and argue his point further. Write an exchange of emails between the two characters.

---

**cautelous** cautious, crafty
**carrions** people who are half dead

**even** steadfast, unwavering
**insuppressive mettle** irrepressible nature

**a several bastardy** an un-Roman act

**sound him** ask him, sound him out

**silver hairs** (Cicero's wisdom and maturity)
**purchase us** buy us

**no whit** not at all

**break with him** tell him anything

**meet** a good idea

**We shall … shrewd contriver** we shall find he's a scheming plotter
**means** capabilities
**improve** uses them well
**annoy** harm

**envy** wickedness
**but** just

Swear priests and cowards and men cautelous,
Old feeble carrions, and such suffering souls                                    130
That welcome wrongs: unto bad causes swear
Such creatures as men doubt. But do not stain
The even virtue of our enterprise,
Nor th'insuppressive mettle of our spirits,
To think that or our cause or our performance                                   135
Did need an oath, when every drop of blood
That every Roman bears, and nobly bears,
Is guilty of a several bastardy
If he do break the smallest particle
Of any promise that hath passed from him.                                        140

CASSIUS    But what of Cicero? Shall we sound him?
I think he will stand very strong with us.

CASCA      Let us not leave him out.

CINNA                          No, by no means.

METELLUS   O, let us have him, for his silver hairs
Will purchase us a good opinion                                                  145
And buy men's voices to commend our deeds.
It shall be said his judgement ruled our hands;
Our youths and wildness shall no whit appear,
But all be buried in his gravity.

BRUTUS     O, name him not, let us not break with him,                          150
For he will never follow anything
That other men begin.

CASSIUS                       Then leave him out.

CASCA      Indeed he is not fit.

DECIUS     Shall no man else be touched but only Caesar?

CASSIUS    Decius, well urged. I think it is not meet                           155
Mark Antony, so well beloved of Caesar,
Should outlive Caesar. We shall find of him
A shrewd contriver. And, you know, his means,
If he improve them, may well stretch so far
As to annoy us all, which to prevent,                                           160
Let Antony and Caesar fall together.

BRUTUS     Our course will seem too bloody, Caius Cassius,
To cut the head off and then hack the limbs –
Like wrath in death and envy afterwards –
For Antony is but a limb of Caesar.                                             165

Brutus says Caesar must be killed, not with spite, but with regret. Again, he overrules Cassius's fears about Antony. Cassius worries that superstition may keep Caesar at home.

# Language in the play
## The sacrifice of Caesar (in small groups)

'Let's be sacrificers, but not butchers', says Brutus.

**a** Try several group readings of Brutus's lines 162–80, taking a sentence each and then changing speaker. As you read, experiment with different tones that Brutus might employ to try to justify the conspirators' cause.

**b** Write down all Brutus's phrases that describe the act of killing Caesar (there may be up to ten such instances). In each case explain clearly the significance of the words he chooses. How far do you think he manages to justify or excuse the vicious act they are about to commit?

> **come by** get possession of
>
> **subtle** cunning
> **Stir up their servants** stir up our passions (i.e. the heart's 'servants')
> **chide 'em** reprimand them
> **make** make it seem as if
> **envious** malicious
> **purgers** healers

# Stagecraft
## The clock strikes three (in groups of three or four)

Brutus interrupts Cassius at line 185 and at line 192 the striking clock ends their discussion about whether Antony should also be killed.

- Talk together about the dramatic impact of the clock striking: it is 3 a.m. on the morning of the Ides of March.
- Discuss the way you would stage this moment in a modern production. What kind of 'striking' would you use to create the most powerful dramatic effect? How would you have Brutus, Cassius and Trebonius react as they listen?
- When you have settled on your ideas, try filming this dramatic moment accompanied by your chosen sound effects.

> **engrafted** deeply rooted
>
> **much he should** too much for him to do
> **fear** cause for fear

# 1 Conspirators caught in conspiracy (by yourself)

Imagine that you are one of Caesar's secret agents and, with or without Caesar's knowledge, you have bugged Brutus's house and listened in on this scene. Now with cast-iron proof of conspiracy, you must report your findings to Caesar. Write up your evidence, ensuring that all the information you collect is as factual and accurate as you can make it. Compare your version with those of other students to check the validity and detail of your report.

> **of late** lately
>
> **ceremonies / prodigies** omens
>
> **augurers** priests who 'foresaw' the future (see p. 171)
> **hold** keep him away

Let's be sacrificers, but not butchers, Caius.
We all stand up against the spirit of Caesar,
And in the spirit of men there is no blood.
O, that we then could come by Caesar's spirit
And not dismember Caesar! But, alas,                    170
Caesar must bleed for it. And, gentle friends,
Let's kill him boldly, but not wrathfully;
Let's carve him as a dish fit for the gods,
Not hew him as a carcass fit for hounds.
And let our hearts, as subtle masters do,               175
Stir up their servants to an act of rage
And after seem to chide 'em. This shall make
Our purpose necessary, and not envious;
Which so appearing to the common eyes,
We shall be called purgers, not murderers.              180
And for Mark Antony, think not of him,
For he can do no more than Caesar's arm
When Caesar's head is off.

CASSIUS                                Yet I fear him,
For in the engrafted love he bears to Caesar –

BRUTUS          Alas, good Cassius, do not think of him.    185
If he love Caesar, all that he can do
Is to himself – take thought and die for Caesar;
And that were much he should, for he is given
To sports, to wildness, and much company.

TREBONIUS      There is no fear in him, let him not die,     190
For he will live and laugh at this hereafter.
                        *Clock strikes*

BRUTUS          Peace, count the clock.

CASSIUS                                The clock hath stricken three.

TREBONIUS      'Tis time to part.

CASSIUS                        But it is doubtful yet
Whether Caesar will come forth today or no,
For he is superstitious grown of late,                  195
Quite from the main opinion he held once
Of fantasy, of dreams, and ceremonies.
It may be these apparent prodigies,
The unaccustomed terror of this night,
And the persuasion of his augurers                      200
May hold him from the Capitol today.

Decius promises to bring Caesar to the Capitol. The conspirators agree to meet at 8 a.m. at Caesar's house. They leave Brutus alone. Portia enters and Brutus questions why she has risen from her bed.

## 1 Justifying Brutus? (in pairs)

By the time the conspirators leave at line 228, Brutus has not only joined the conspiracy, he has taken charge of it.

**a** Find the three instances when Brutus overrules suggestions from Cassius and discuss how he achieves this.

**b** Remind yourself of the text up to line 233. Then draw up a table with two columns, headed 'Admirable decisions' and 'Questionable decisions'. Fill in the columns with details of the decisions Brutus makes. Discuss your findings and compare the kind of balance achieved.

### Write about it

#### Lucius the silent witness (by yourself)

Lucius has been off stage since line 76 of this scene. Since then the seven conspirators have gathered and made their plans.

- Imagine that Lucius has overheard key parts of their dialogue. Write up his thoughts as a secret diary entry in which he reflects on the conspiracy and speculates about what the future holds for him and his master. Look back at the earlier parts of the scene for clues about Lucius's character and his relationship with Brutus. Factor these into the 'voice' that you create for Lucius.

### Characters

#### Portia (in pairs)

*Julius Caesar* is dominated by men and male perspectives. The words of Portia, Brutus's wife, at line 233 mark the first speech by a woman in the play, apart from Calpurnia's 'Here, my lord' in Act 1 Scene 2.

- One of you has been cast as Portia in a new production of the play. In preparation for the role, you have asked for discussion time with your director. Plan for it by reading all Portia says in this scene before her exit at line 309. Make notes on key issues you want to discuss. For example, how do you think you should play your relationship with your husband, based on the evidence of the text? The other student is the director, who should prepare similarly.
- Run the meeting, resolve all contentious points and rehearse the episode. Another student can play Brutus if you want to work in threes.

**o'ersway him** persuade him otherwise

**unicorns ... toils** (these are all examples of how it was thought that animals could be trapped: unicorns got their horns stuck in trees; bears were captivated by looking into mirrors; elephants fell into covered pits; lions were caught in nets ['toils']). Why do you think Caesar loves to hear these tales?

**give his humour the true bent** make him think what we want him to think

**there** at Caesar's house

**uttermost** latest hour possible

**bear Caesar hard** hate Caesar

**rated** criticised

**by him** to his house

**fashion** work on

**put on** reveal, betray

**formal constancy** dignified behaviour

**figures** imaginings

52

| | |
|---|---|
| DECIUS | Never fear that. If he be so resolved |
| | I can o'ersway him, for he loves to hear |
| | That unicorns may be betrayed with trees, |
| | And bears with glasses, elephants with holes, 205 |
| | Lions with toils, and men with flatterers. |
| | But when I tell him he hates flatterers |
| | He says he does, being then most flatterèd. |
| | Let me work: |
| | For I can give his humour the true bent, 210 |
| | And I will bring him to the Capitol. |
| CASSIUS | Nay, we will all of us be there to fetch him. |
| BRUTUS | By the eighth hour, is that the uttermost? |
| CINNA | Be that the uttermost, and fail not then. |
| METELLUS | Caius Ligarius doth bear Caesar hard, 215 |
| | Who rated him for speaking well of Pompey. |
| | I wonder none of you have thought of him. |
| BRUTUS | Now, good Metellus, go along by him. |
| | He loves me well, and I have given him reasons. |
| | Send him but hither and I'll fashion him. 220 |
| CASSIUS | The morning comes upon's. We'll leave you, Brutus, |
| | And, friends, disperse yourselves, but all remember |
| | What you have said and show yourselves true Romans. |
| BRUTUS | Good gentlemen, look fresh and merrily: |
| | Let not our looks put on our purposes, 225 |
| | But bear it as our Roman actors do, |
| | With untired spirits and formal constancy. |
| | And so good morrow to you every one. |

*Exeunt [all but] Brutus*

| | |
|---|---|
| | Boy! Lucius! Fast asleep? It is no matter, |
| | Enjoy the honey-heavy dew of slumber. 230 |
| | Thou hast no figures nor no fantasies |
| | Which busy care draws in the brains of men, |
| | Therefore thou sleep'st so sound. |

*Enter* PORTIA

| | |
|---|---|
| PORTIA | Brutus, my lord. |
| BRUTUS | Portia! What mean you? Wherefore rise you now? |
| | It is not for your health thus to commit 235 |
| | Your weak condition to the raw cold morning. |

Portia tells Brutus how difficult he has been in recent days. He tells her he's sick. She asks why he is out of bed, insisting on the truth.

## 1 Watching Brutus (in small groups)

One or two of you read lines 237–51, where Portia describes what happened the previous night ('yesternight'), pausing briefly after each action. In those pauses, the other members of the group act out the scene without sound, as you might see it through an uncurtained window.

## 2 Portia and Brutus: marriage guidance (in pairs)

Portia is clearly troubled by the changes in her husband's behaviour. In lines 252–87, she catalogues a host of her concerns.

* First, read the lines together to pick up the details, and then enact a meeting between Portia and a marriage guidance counsellor (one of you is Portia, the other the counsellor) in which Portia seeks advice about how she should respond to these difficult times in her relationship with her husband. In preparation, you will need to decide just how in love with him she is, and to consider the time in which the play was set (and written), when the role of wives was very different to what you might expect today (see p. 180).
* Follow this by staging a second 'marriage guidance' meeting, this time between the counsellor and Brutus.
* After the meeting, work together to write up an account of what was discussed and what advice was given. This could be in the style of a formal report from the counsellor.

## Themes
### Sickness and disease

Sickness in different forms becomes an important dramatic element in the play. Already in this scene, Brutus, concerned about his wife's health, has referred to her 'weak condition' in the early morning air.

a Read Portia's lines 261–70. Collect examples of references to sickness and disease. Write down in modern English what each one means and what it suggests about the state of Brutus's mind.

b Why do you think the theme of sickness and disease comes to prominence in this scene? (Note there are two further examples on the next two pages.)

---

**Y'have** you have
**Stole** crept

**across** crossed

**wafture** wafting

**too much enkindled** too fierce
**an effect of humour** a sign of a passing mood

**shape** outward appearance
**condition** mind

**come by it** get it back

**physical** medically advisable
**unbracèd** with clothes undone
**humours** unhealthy moisture
**wholesome** healthy, comfortable
**dare** risk
**contagion** infection
**rheumy** moist and catarrh-making
**unpurgèd** unclean
**sick offence** harmful sickness

**charm** beg, entreat

**incorporate** unite, join

PORTIA Nor for yours neither. Y'have ungently, Brutus,
Stole from my bed; and yesternight at supper
You suddenly arose and walked about,
Musing and sighing, with your arms across,  240
And when I asked you what the matter was,
You stared upon me with ungentle looks.
I urged you further, then you scratched your head
And too impatiently stamped with your foot.
Yet I insisted, yet you answered not,  245
But with an angry wafture of your hand
Gave sign for me to leave you. So I did,
Fearing to strengthen that impatience
Which seemed too much enkindled, and withal
Hoping it was but an effect of humour  250
Which sometime hath his hour with every man.
It will not let you eat nor talk nor sleep;
And could it work so much upon your shape
As it hath much prevailed on your condition,
I should not know you, Brutus. Dear my lord,  255
Make me acquainted with your cause of grief.

BRUTUS I am not well in health, and that is all.

PORTIA Brutus is wise, and were he not in health
He would embrace the means to come by it.

BRUTUS Why, so I do. Good Portia, go to bed.  260

PORTIA Is Brutus sick? And is it physical
To walk unbracèd and suck up the humours
Of the dank morning? What, is Brutus sick?
And will he steal out of his wholesome bed
To dare the vile contagion of the night  265
And tempt the rheumy and unpurgèd air
To add unto his sickness? No, my Brutus,
You have some sick offence within your mind,
Which by the right and virtue of my place
I ought to know of. And upon my knees  270
I charm you, by my once commended beauty,
By all your vows of love, and that great vow
Which did incorporate and make us one,
That you unfold to me, your self, your half,

## 1 Portia's wound (in groups of four or five)

Portia makes a dramatic revelation at line 300: she has inflicted self-harm (a stab wound to her thigh). How Brutus responds to the news ('O ye gods, / Render me worthy of this noble wife') is a key moment in defining the depth of their relationship. Some productions use it to explore Brutus's tortured guilt and anguish; others suggest his words lack sincerity and that he is more preoccupied with the plot to assassinate Caesar.

**a** First, research the significance of this type of ritual act in Roman society in Caesar's time. Then discuss together the possible reasons for Portia committing this frightening deed. (For example, some see her capacity to 'bear' the wound 'with patience' as a mark of her love for her husband and as proof of her complete devotion to Brutus.)

**b** Why do you think Shakespeare chooses to reveal Portia's self-harm at this point in the play?

## 2 Brutus: speak the sub-text (in pairs)

Although later in the play (Act 2 Scene 4, line 9), it seems that Brutus did tell Portia the reasons for his behaviour, in this exchange with her he speaks very little (only nine lines between Portia's entrance and line 302).

• One of you reads aloud all of Brutus's words in this episode, pausing at the end of each line for the other to voice exactly what is in Brutus's mind.

▶ What does this photo suggest about the way in which Brutus and Portia relate to each other?

**heavy** so depressed
**resort to** a meeting with

**excepted** acceptable
**appertain** apply
**in sort or limitation** only within specific limits
**Dwell … suburbs** is my place on the fringes
**harlot** mistress, prostitute

**ruddy drops** blood

**Cato** a famous diehard Republican

**counsels** secrets
**constancy** trustworthiness

**partake** take possession of

**engagements** dealings
**construe** explain, tell
**All the … brows** all that is written in my sad face

|  | Why you are heavy and what men tonight | 275 |
|---|---|---|
|  | Have had resort to you, for here have been |  |
|  | Some six or seven who did hide their faces |  |
|  | Even from darkness. |  |

BRUTUS                      Kneel not, gentle Portia.

PORTIA    I should not need if you were gentle Brutus.
Within the bond of marriage, tell me, Brutus,       280
Is it excepted I should know no secrets
That appertain to you? Am I your self
But, as it were, in sort or limitation,
To keep with you at meals, comfort your bed,
And talk to you sometimes? Dwell I but in the suburbs    285
Of your good pleasure? If it be no more
Portia is Brutus' harlot, not his wife.

BRUTUS    You are my true and honourable wife,
As dear to me as are the ruddy drops
That visit my sad heart.                         290

PORTIA    If this were true, then should I know this secret.
I grant I am a woman, but withal
A woman that Lord Brutus took to wife.
I grant I am a woman, but withal
A woman well reputed, Cato's daughter.         295
Think you I am no stronger than my sex,
Being so fathered and so husbanded?
Tell me your counsels, I will not disclose 'em.
I have made strong proof of my constancy,
Giving myself a voluntary wound              300
Here, in the thigh. Can I bear that with patience
And not my husband's secrets?

BRUTUS                      O ye gods,
Render me worthy of this noble wife!

*Knock*

Hark, hark, one knocks. Portia, go in a while,
And by and by thy bosom shall partake        305
The secrets of my heart.
All my engagements I will construe to thee,
All the charactery of my sad brows.
Leave me with haste.

*Exit Portia*

Lucius, who's that knocks?

The sick Ligarius enters. Brutus asks for his help. Ligarius seems to find new strength in being part of the secret enterprise and swears blind obedience to Brutus.

# Themes

## More sickness and disease (in pairs)

**a** There are four separate instances of sickness in this scene:

- Brutus's concerns about Portia's health
- Brutus's declining psychological health (sleepless nights, troubled mind), which is contrasted with Lucius's restful innocence
- Portia's self-inflicted wound on her thigh
- Ligarius's bodily sickness, which is covered by a bandage ('kerchief').

Talk together about the different examples of sickness in this scene and then write a series of short paragraphs exploring the dramatic importance of each one. Why do you think there are so many overt references to sickness in this act?

**b** Ligarius's sickness miraculously disappears once he pledges himself to Brutus's cause.

- Take it in turns to be Ligarius and try different versions of lines 320–6, during which his transformation takes place. Can you present both his physical recovery and his strength of feeling for Brutus, the 'Soul of Rome'?
- Why do you think Shakespeare chooses to place this episode at the end of the scene?

# Write about it

## What lies ahead?

The scene begins with Brutus wrestling agonisingly with his conscience – and ends with a resolute Brutus becoming leader of the conspirators. A dramatic and symbolic roll of thunder seems to point to Caesar's death (this technique is called **foreshadowing**).

As Brutus exits, he cannot help his mind drifting ahead to what he hopes will be the outcome of that eventful day. In his private thoughts, what does he make of the plans, his fellow conspirators, the enormity of their actions, his wife and his responsibilities?

- Write a modern English dramatic monologue for Brutus to follow on from line 335.

---

**would** wishes to

**Vouchsafe good morrow** accept my greetings

**chose out** picked

**wear a kerchief** be ill (such a head-covering was commonly worn by the sick)

**healthful** healthy

**honourable loins** a noble family

**Thou … spirit** you have acted like an exorcist to bring back to life my deadened spirit

**strive with** challenge myself with

**whole** healthy

**Set on your foot** you go first

**it sufficeth** it's enough

*Enter* LUCIUS *and* LIGARIUS

| | | |
|---|---|---|
| LUCIUS | Here is a sick man that would speak with you. | 310 |
| BRUTUS | Caius Ligarius, that Metellus spake of. | |
| | Boy, stand aside. | |

[*Exit Lucius*]

Caius Ligarius, how?

| | |
|---|---|
| LIGARIUS | Vouchsafe good morrow from a feeble tongue. |
| BRUTUS | O, what a time have you chose out, brave Caius, |
| | To wear a kerchief! Would you were not sick! 315 |
| LIGARIUS | I am not sick if Brutus have in hand |
| | Any exploit worthy the name of honour. |
| BRUTUS | Such an exploit have I in hand, Ligarius, |
| | Had you a healthful ear to hear of it. |
| LIGARIUS | By all the gods that Romans bow before, 320 |
| | I here discard my sickness! |

[*He pulls off his kerchief*]

Soul of Rome,
Brave son, derived from honourable loins,
Thou, like an exorcist, hast conjured up
My mortifièd spirit. Now bid me run
And I will strive with things impossible, 325
Yea, get the better of them. What's to do?

| | |
|---|---|
| BRUTUS | A piece of work that will make sick men whole. |
| LIGARIUS | But are not some whole that we must make sick? |
| BRUTUS | That must we also. What it is, my Caius, |
| | I shall unfold to thee as we are going 330 |
| | To whom it must be done. |
| LIGARIUS | Set on your foot, |

And with a heart new fired I follow you
To do I know not what; but it sufficeth
That Brutus leads me on.

*Thunder*

| | |
|---|---|
| BRUTUS | Follow me then. |

*Exeunt*

Caesar tells how his wife Calpurnia has spoken of his murder in her sleep. She orders him to stay at home, telling of frightening portents of ill omen. Caesar is unmoved, declaring he will go out.

## Stagecraft

### The storm inside Caesar's house (in fours, then by yourself)

The first line of Scene 2 ('Nor heaven nor earth have been at peace tonight') makes it clear that the storm that ends Scene 1 carries across to the opening of this next domestic scene, this time inside Caesar's house.

**a** Together, work on a soundscape that could be used to accompany Caesar's lines 1–3. Think about what kind of 'storm noises' would best complement Caesar's troubled state of mind. Then have a go at recording Caesar's words accompanied by the soundscape you have designed.

**b** In your Director's Journal, write a paragraph on the dramatic effects created by the use of the storm and also the unnatural events that Calpurnia describes in the script opposite.

## 1 At home with Brutus and Caesar (in pairs)

**a** Remind yourselves briefly of Act 2 Scene 1, lines 233–309 (Brutus and Portia together). Then read through Act 2 Scene 2, lines 1–82 (Caesar and Calpurnia together). Act the two scenes out to another group.

**b** Discuss everything you notice about the ways in which Portia and Calpurnia behave with their husbands. Then create a Venn diagram, with 'Portia' in one circle and 'Calpurnia' in the other. Fill in the diagram with your observations about the two women. In what ways are they different? And in what ways similar?

## Write about it

### 'horrid sights' – two versions

Caesar's guards (the 'watch') witness some strange and supernatural events (lines 17–24).

- Imagine that you are the leader of that group. Write up in formal and accurate detail a report of exactly what you witness.
- Then, as another member of the group, take to a social networking site and describe in informal and much more personal, imaginative writing what you have seen and what you make of it.
- Compare the two texts and consider the different effects created.

*nightgown* dressing gown

**priests** (i.e. augurers)
**present** immediate
**success** the outcome (whether good or bad)

**stood on ceremonies** attached importance to omens
**fright** frighten
**Recounts** who is telling about
**watch** guards, night-watchmen
**whelpèd** given birth
**yawned and yielded up** opened and given up
**squadrons and right form** battle formations

**beyond all use** completely abnormal

**purposed** dictated

# Act 2 Scene 2
## Caesar's house   Early morning

*Thunder and lightning. Enter* JULIUS CAESAR *in his nightgown*

| | |
|---|---|
| CAESAR | Nor heaven nor earth have been at peace tonight. |
| | Thrice hath Calpurnia in her sleep cried out, |
| | 'Help ho, they murder Caesar!' Who's within? |

*Enter a* SERVANT

| | | |
|---|---|---|
| SERVANT | My lord? | |
| CAESAR | Go bid the priests do present sacrifice | 5 |
| | And bring me their opinions of success. | |
| SERVANT | I will, my lord. | *Exit* |

*Enter* CALPURNIA

| | | |
|---|---|---|
| CALPURNIA | What mean you, Caesar, think you to walk forth? | |
| | You shall not stir out of your house today. | |
| CAESAR | Caesar shall forth. The things that threatened me | 10 |
| | Ne'er looked but on my back; when they shall see | |
| | The face of Caesar they are vanishèd. | |
| CALPURNIA | Caesar, I never stood on ceremonies, | |
| | Yet now they fright me. There is one within, | |
| | Besides the things that we have heard and seen, | 15 |
| | Recounts most horrid sights seen by the watch. | |
| | A lioness hath whelpèd in the streets, | |
| | And graves have yawned and yielded up their dead; | |
| | Fierce fiery warriors fight upon the clouds | |
| | In ranks and squadrons and right form of war, | 20 |
| | Which drizzled blood upon the Capitol; | |
| | The noise of battle hurtled in the air, | |
| | Horses did neigh and dying men did groan, | |
| | And ghosts did shriek and squeal about the streets. | |
| | O Caesar, these things are beyond all use, | 25 |
| | And I do fear them. | |
| CAESAR | What can be avoided | |
| | Whose end is purposed by the mighty gods? | |
| | Yet Caesar shall go forth, for these predictions | |
| | Are to the world in general as to Caesar. | |

Although Caesar claims to have no fear of death and at first defies Calpurnia and the augurers, in the end their concerns prevail. He orders Decius to tell the Senate that Caesar will not come today.

# Write about it

## Calpurnia's fears for Caesar

It is the morning of the Ides of March. Calpurnia has dreamt all night of her husband's murder. Now she struggles to persuade Caesar to stay at home. She even offers him a way that he can use her as the excuse ('Call it my fear / That keeps you in the house'). Finally, at line 56, he agrees to her request.

- Write a short soliloquy or an aside for Calpurnia that could be spoken to the audience after line 56. In it, try to explore her deeper feelings about Caesar, her fears for him, and her relief that he has listened to her arguments.

# Characters

## Caesar: brave or foolish? (in pairs)

When Caesar first speaks to Calpurnia (lines 10–12), he insists that he will not be frightened into staying at home, in spite of any sense of danger that might be present. Even Calpurnia's description of the terrifying omens draws from him a firm belief that such portents are not directed at him specifically.

His famous line: 'Cowards die many times before their deaths' and an acceptance that death 'Will come when it will come' again show him resolute in the face of threat.

Finally, after the servant reports that the priests could find no heart in a sacrificed animal, Caesar puts his own gloss on that, too: he would be lacking 'heart' (courage) if he did not attend the Capitol.

- Consider each of these ideas in turn. Then make two columns on a piece of paper, one with the heading 'Brave', the other with the heading 'Foolish'. Add each detail to the appropriate column with a clear and detailed explanation of why you have put it there.

◀ How should Caesar respond to Calpurnia's pleas?

**blaze forth** announce

**in shame of cowardice** to shame cowardice

**a beast without a heart** like a cowardly animal

**Your wisdom … confidence** your self-confidence makes you behave rashly

**for thy humour** to keep you happy

**in very happy time** just at the right time

| | | |
|---|---|---|
| CALPURNIA | When beggars die there are no comets seen, | 30 |
| | The heavens themselves blaze forth the death of princes. | |
| CAESAR | Cowards die many times before their deaths, | |
| | The valiant never taste of death but once. | |
| | Of all the wonders that I yet have heard | |
| | It seems to me most strange that men should fear, | 35 |
| | Seeing that death, a necessary end, | |
| | Will come when it will come. | |

*Enter a* SERVANT

What say the augurers?

| | | |
|---|---|---|
| SERVANT | They would not have you to stir forth today. | |
| | Plucking the entrails of an offering forth, | |
| | They could not find a heart within the beast. | 40 |
| CAESAR | The gods do this in shame of cowardice. | |
| | Caesar should be a beast without a heart | |
| | If he should stay at home today for fear. | |
| | No, Caesar shall not. Danger knows full well | |
| | That Caesar is more dangerous than he: | 45 |
| | We are two lions littered in one day, | |
| | And I the elder and more terrible. | |
| | And Caesar shall go forth. | |
| CALPURNIA | Alas, my lord, | |
| | Your wisdom is consumed in confidence. | |
| | Do not go forth today. Call it my fear | 50 |
| | That keeps you in the house, and not your own. | |
| | We'll send Mark Antony to the Senate House | |
| | And he shall say you are not well today. | |
| | Let me, upon my knee, prevail in this. | |
| CAESAR | Mark Antony shall say I am not well, | 55 |
| | And for thy humour I will stay at home. | |

*Enter* DECIUS

| | | |
|---|---|---|
| | Here's Decius Brutus, he shall tell them so. | |
| DECIUS | Caesar, all hail! Good morrow, worthy Caesar, | |
| | I come to fetch you to the Senate House. | |
| CAESAR | And you are come in very happy time | 60 |
| | To bear my greeting to the senators | |
| | And tell them that I will not come today. | |
| | Cannot is false, and that I dare not, falser: | |
| | I will not come today. Tell them so, Decius. | |

Calpurnia suggests that Decius should say Caesar is sick. Caesar scorns the lie and describes Calpurnia's dream. Decius interprets it favourably and says the Senate intend to crown Caesar.

## Characters

### 'Caesar will not come' (in pairs)

Caesar gives Decius this message for the Senate, explaining why he will not attend the Capitol that day: 'The cause is in my will. I will not come: / That is enough to satisfy the Senate' (lines 71–2).

- Read these lines several times to each other until you arrive at your preferred version. Then look back at all that Caesar says in this scene and identify every occasion on which he refers to himself not as 'I' or 'me', but as 'Caesar' (even in conversation with his wife). There are more than ten such instances.
- Discuss what these details show about Caesar's character.

## 1 The dream interpreted in two ways (in two groups)

Both Republican conspirators and Caesarites could make use of Calpurnia's prophetic dream to justify or condemn Caesar's assassination after the event.

- One group focuses on Calpurnia's interpretation of the dream (lines 76–82). The other concentrates on Decius's explanation (lines 83–90). Each group produces a tableau of their version. Compare versions.

## Language in the play

### Blood ... and more blood

Calpurnia's dream features much blood: a statue 'with an hundred spouts' in Caesar's words; one 'spouting blood in many pipes' according to Decius.

- Create a striking drawing of Caesar's statue with its excesses of blood. Add around it all references to the word you have encountered so far: Pompey's blood (Act 1 Scene 1); Brutus speaking about the killing of Caesar (Act 2 Scene 1) and his reluctance to shed unnecessary blood in killing Antony; Portia's self-inflicted wound (Act 2 Scene 1); Calpurnia's ominous vision (the start of Act 2 Scene 2).
- Add all future references to blood as they appear. Look out specifically for those in Act 3!

**greybeards** old men

**stays me** keeps me

**lusty** healthy, strong

**all amiss** incorrectly

**tinctures ... cognisance**
Because Caesar is a martyr, relics dipped in his blood are holy; he can dispense colours or 'tinctures' that can be put on a coat of arms – recognition or 'cognisance' by a royal personage
**expounded** interpreted

**mock / Apt to be rendered** sarcastic remark likely to be made

**meet with** have

| CALPURNIA | Say he is sick. | |
|---|---|---|
| CAESAR | Shall Caesar send a lie? | 65 |
| | Have I in conquest stretched mine arm so far | |
| | To be afeard to tell greybeards the truth? | |
| | Decius, go tell them Caesar will not come. | |
| DECIUS | Most mighty Caesar, let me know some cause, | |
| | Lest I be laughed at when I tell them so. | 70 |
| CAESAR | The cause is in my will. I will not come: | |
| | That is enough to satisfy the Senate. | |
| | But for your private satisfaction, | |
| | Because I love you, I will let you know: | |
| | Calpurnia here, my wife, stays me at home. | 75 |
| | She dreamt tonight she saw my statue, | |
| | Which like a fountain with an hundred spouts | |
| | Did run pure blood, and many lusty Romans | |
| | Came smiling and did bathe their hands in it. | |
| | And these does she apply for warnings and portents | 80 |
| | And evils imminent, and on her knee | |
| | Hath begged that I will stay at home today. | |
| DECIUS | This dream is all amiss interpreted, | |
| | It was a vision fair and fortunate. | |
| | Your statue spouting blood in many pipes, | 85 |
| | In which so many smiling Romans bathed, | |
| | Signifies that from you great Rome shall suck | |
| | Reviving blood and that great men shall press | |
| | For tinctures, stains, relics, and cognisance. | |
| | This by Calpurnia's dream is signified. | 90 |
| CAESAR | And this way have you well expounded it. | |
| DECIUS | I have, when you have heard what I can say. | |
| | And know it now: the Senate have concluded | |
| | To give this day a crown to mighty Caesar. | |
| | If you shall send them word you will not come, | 95 |
| | Their minds may change. Besides, it were a mock | |
| | Apt to be rendered for someone to say, | |
| | 'Break up the Senate till another time, | |
| | When Caesar's wife shall meet with better dreams.' | |

Caesar finally resolves to go to the Senate. First the conspirators, then Antony arrive. Caesar offers wine while he prepares himself. The conspirators secretly confide their true intentions.

## 1 Decius the persuader (in threes)

Decius needs to persuade Caesar to go to the Capitol. Between lines 92 and 104 he marshals three arguments that suggest Caesar should attend.

- Read his lines to each other several times and identify the three elements of Decius's strategy. Then rank them in order: based on your knowledge of Caesar, which is the most important in changing Caesar's mind? Compare your ideas with those of other groups.

**my dear … proceeding** my concern for your future career

**reason … is liable** my love for you is greater than my judgement

**robe** Roman toga

## Characters

### Antony: setting the stage for the future

Prior to his vital role in Act 3, Antony has a shadowy and insubstantial part. Here he is given just five words to make an impact and remind the audience of his loyalty to, and respect for, Caesar – attributes that will be crucial later in the play. He has only five lines in total in the first two acts.

- Find all of Antony's lines so far. Write a short paragraph about what they have in common and what they show about Antony.

**ague** fever

**lean** thin

## Themes

### Appearance versus reality (in threes)

The final dramatic episode of the scene is often used in performance to highlight the difference between the easy and assured public confidence of Caesar and the secret scheming of the conspirators. Caesar wants to share wine with his 'Good friends' (line 126); Trebonius's and Brutus's 'asides' both make clear to the audience that appearing to be Caesar's friend is nothing like actually being one.

a Write an extension of both of the asides mentioned above, in which you explore in greater detail what Trebonius and Brutus each feels about the prospect of betraying Caesar's friendship. (Note that Brutus gives a clue to his feelings by using the word 'earns', which at the time meant 'grieves'.)

b Create a tableau of the final moment of the scene, exploring the contrast between the three men's attitudes.

**revels long a-nights** parties until late

**notwithstanding** nevertheless

**prepare within** (presumably prepare the wine; see line 126)

**every like … same** being 'like friends' is not the same as being true friends

**earns** grieves

If Caesar hide himself, shall they not whisper,                    100
'Lo, Caesar is afraid'?
Pardon me, Caesar, for my dear dear love
To your proceeding bids me tell you this,
And reason to my love is liable.

CAESAR      How foolish do your fears seem now, Calpurnia!          105
I am ashamèd I did yield to them.
Give me my robe, for I will go.

*Enter* BRUTUS, *Ligarius, Metellus, Casca,* TREBONIUS, *Cinna, and* PUBLIUS

And look where Publius is come to fetch me.

PUBLIUS     Good morrow, Caesar.

CAESAR                                 Welcome, Publius.
What, Brutus, are you stirred so early too?          110
Good morrow, Casca. Caius Ligarius,
Caesar was ne'er so much your enemy
As that same ague which hath made you lean.
What is't o'clock?

BRUTUS                        Caesar, 'tis strucken eight.

CAESAR      I thank you for your pains and courtesy.          115

*Enter* ANTONY

See, Antony, that revels long a-nights,
Is notwithstanding up. Good morrow, Antony.

ANTONY      So to most noble Caesar.

CAESAR      [*To Calpurnia*]          Bid them prepare within,

[*Exit Calpurnia*]

I am to blame to be thus waited for.
Now, Cinna, now, Metellus. What, Trebonius,          120
I have an hour's talk in store for you.
Remember that you call on me today;
Be near me that I may remember you.

TREBONIUS   Caesar, I will. [*Aside*] And so near will I be
That your best friends shall wish I had been further.          125

CAESAR      Good friends, go in and taste some wine with me,
And we, like friends, will straightway go together.

BRUTUS      [*Aside*] That every like is not the same, O Caesar,
The heart of Brutus earns to think upon.

*Exeunt*

Artemidorus reads out the warning he intends to give Caesar. Sending Lucius to the Capitol, Portia confides how she can hardly hide her worries.

# Characters

## Focus on Artemidorus (in small groups)

This is Artemidorus's first appearance in the play, and we will see him only once more (in Act 3 Scene 1).

a  Talk together about what Artemidorus adds to the dramatic structure of Act 2. Think about why Shakespeare might have given him this scene to himself, coming after the scenes involving the conspirators and then Caesar. What, for example, does he say about Caesar and how does that affect your view of the plans to assassinate him? What do you think is the importance of Artemidorus's final two lines? What is Shakespeare suggesting about the conspiracy? (You might look ahead to the start of Act 3 Scene 1 to find out what happens when he tries to give his warning letter to Caesar.)

b  Imagine you are Artemidorus. Take each of the conspirators named in your paper and put together a dossier of evidence that supports your suspicions about them. Your dossier could be a combination of witness statements, interviews, filmed or taped evidence and covert photographs. Perhaps you even have an informer amongst the conspirators! You can use your classmates to help 'stage' some of this evidence or adapt pictures and photographs from magazines. You can make up details, but keep close to the spirit of the play. Remember that you have signed the paper and your evidence may come up in court.

**bent** directed

**security ... conspiracy** overconfidence leaves you open to plots against you

**Thy lover** your loyal friend

**suitor** petitioner

**laments** is sad

**virtue ... emulation** virtuous men are never beyond the reach of envious rivals

**contrive** conspire, plot

# 1  Portia's agitation

Portia, like her husband Brutus in Act 2 Scene 1, has troubled thoughts jostling in her mind. Her confidential aside (lines 6–9) suggests that she is desperate to speak of something and finds it incredibly hard to restrain herself.

•  What do you think is on her mind? It seems to involve sending Lucius on an errand to the Capitol. Read quickly through to the end of the scene for possible clues and then make notes on your ideas. Pool your responses as a class.

**Ere** before

**constancy** self-control

**'tween** between

**might** strength

**keep counsel** keep a secret or keep quiet

**Art thou here yet?** are you still here?

# Act 2 Scene 3
## Rome   A street

*Enter* ARTEMIDORUS [*reading a paper*]

ARTEMIDORUS 'Caesar, beware of Brutus, take heed of Cassius, come not near Casca, have an eye to Cinna, trust not Trebonius, mark well Metellus Cimber, Decius Brutus loves thee not, thou hast wronged Caius Ligarius. There is but one mind in all these men, and it is bent against Caesar. If thou beest not immortal look about you: security gives way to conspiracy. The mighty gods defend thee!    5

>                                                  Thy lover,
>                                                  Artemidorus.'

    Here will I stand till Caesar pass along,
    And as a suitor will I give him this.
    My heart laments that virtue cannot live    10
    Out of the teeth of emulation.
    If thou read this, O Caesar, thou mayst live;
    If not, the fates with traitors do contrive.    *Exit*

# Act 2 Scene 4
## Rome   A street

*Enter* PORTIA *and* LUCIUS

PORTIA     I prithee, boy, run to the Senate House.
    Stay not to answer me but get thee gone.
    Why dost thou stay?

LUCIUS               To know my errand, madam.

PORTIA     I would have had thee there and here again
    Ere I can tell thee what thou shouldst do there.    5
    [*Aside*] O constancy, be strong upon my side,
    Set a huge mountain 'tween my heart and tongue!
    I have a man's mind, but a woman's might.
    How hard it is for women to keep counsel! –
    Art thou here yet?

LUCIUS               Madam, what should I do?    10
    Run to the Capitol, and nothing else?
    And so return to you, and nothing else?

Portia sends Lucius to report back to her what Brutus says and does. The Soothsayer foresees harm to Caesar, but crowds make his warning difficult to deliver.

## 1 Listening to the wind (in pairs)

Sometimes, when listening for an all-important sound – the door, the telephone, a car – we can't concentrate on anything else and seem forgetful and distracted.

**a** Whisper lines 10–20. Leave a long listening pause at the end of line 16 and the start of line 20. One of you can make sound effects.

**b** Both of you are Portia, straining to hear sounds from the Capitol. As you listen, whisper your suspicions, hopes and fears for what this moment means to your life.

**c** Gather Portia's thoughts into a poem, in which every line starts 'Listen. In the wind I hear …'.

## 2 The power of the Soothsayer (in pairs)

**a** Act out lines 21–46, thinking hard about why Portia nearly faints after speaking to the Soothsayer. Does the Soothsayer recognise Portia as the wife of one of the conspirators?

**b** Write a short paragraph on the role of the Soothsayer in this scene. Consider everything he says about Caesar (e.g. 'I shall beseech him to befriend himself'). How fearful is he of what might happen?

**c** Write notes for the actor playing the Soothsayer about how to deliver his lines in this scene. What actions or gestures should accompany his words?

### Characters
#### Last look at Portia

Portia's line 46 is her final line in the play. In confessing that she finds it hard to keep quiet (line 9), she displays gender stereotyping – prevalent in Shakespeare's time, but often problematic to a modern audience. In lines 39–46, as her anxiety grows, the audience is left to wonder how much she knows about Brutus's plans. What does she mean when she says: 'The heavens speed thee in thine enterprise!'?

- On page 52 you were invited to consider Portia's role in Act 2 Scene 1 (the only other scene in which she appears). As Portia, plan your rehearsal notes for a follow-up meeting with your director to work through this scene. How will you deal with the issues raised above and what final impression will you seek to make on your audience?

**press to him** crowd round him

**rumour** tumult, confusion
**fray** battle
**Sooth** truly

**suit** petition

**beseech him** plead with him

**chance** happen

**praetors** justice administrators

**more void** more empty

**commend me** give my best wishes
**merry** in good spirits
*severally* in different directions

| | |
|---|---|
| PORTIA | Yes, bring me word, boy, if thy lord look well, |
| | For he went sickly forth, and take good note |
| | What Caesar doth, what suitors press to him. 15 |
| | Hark, boy, what noise is that? |
| LUCIUS | I hear none, madam. |
| PORTIA | Prithee listen well: |
| | I heard a bustling rumour, like a fray, |
| | And the wind brings it from the Capitol. |
| LUCIUS | Sooth, madam, I hear nothing. 20 |

*Enter the* SOOTHSAYER

| | |
|---|---|
| PORTIA | Come hither, fellow, which way hast thou been? |
| SOOTHSAYER | At mine own house, good lady. |
| PORTIA | What is't o'clock? |
| SOOTHSAYER | About the ninth hour, lady. |
| PORTIA | Is Caesar yet gone to the Capitol? |
| SOOTHSAYER | Madam, not yet. I go to take my stand 25 |
| | To see him pass on to the Capitol. |
| PORTIA | Thou hast some suit to Caesar, hast thou not? |
| SOOTHSAYER | That I have, lady, if it will please Caesar |
| | To be so good to Caesar as to hear me: |
| | I shall beseech him to befriend himself. 30 |
| PORTIA | Why, know'st thou any harm's intended towards him? |
| SOOTHSAYER | None that I know will be, much that I fear may chance. |
| | Good morrow to you. Here the street is narrow: |
| | The throng that follows Caesar at the heels, |
| | Of senators, of praetors, common suitors, 35 |
| | Will crowd a feeble man almost to death. |
| | I'll get me to a place more void, and there |
| | Speak to great Caesar as he comes along. *Exit* |
| PORTIA | I must go in. [*Aside*] Ay me, how weak a thing |
| | The heart of woman is! O Brutus, 40 |
| | The heavens speed thee in thine enterprise! |
| | Sure the boy heard me. Brutus hath a suit |
| | That Caesar will not grant. O, I grow faint. – |
| | Run, Lucius, and commend me to my lord, |
| | Say I am merry. Come to me again 45 |
| | And bring me word what he doth say to thee. |

*Exeunt* [*severally*]

# Looking back at Act 2
## Activities for groups or individuals

## 1 Loyalties

In Scene 1 Brutus's loyalty is divided between Caesar, Cassius, Portia and himself.

- Work in four groups, each taking responsibility for one of these characters. Each group prepares the case for why its character has a claim to Brutus's loyalty.

- Each group has one minute to present its case beginning: 'You owe me loyalty because …'. Which character can make the strongest case?

## 2 The world through whose eyes?

Identify who you think is the more important character in each of the four scenes in Act 2. Write a short paragraph for each, saying what the character thinks about the events unfolding in Rome.

## 3 Focusing on female perspectives …

Act 2 is the only act to give a real insight into the domestic lives of Portia and Calpurnia.

**a** Imagine you are researching a radio programme on the lifestyles of important Roman wives and you have arranged an interview with the two women. Script their contributions, making clear their attitudes to their husbands. Then record your interviews.

In Elizabethan times, women were subject to rules of patriarchy, which meant that they were not allowed the freedom and responsibility that many women would reasonably expect today. Calpurnia's attempts to influence her husband's public actions are dismissed by Caesar: 'How foolish do your fears seem now, Calpurnia! / I am ashamèd I did yield to them'. Shakespeare seems to stereotype Portia by giving her the line: 'How hard it is for women to keep counsel'.

**b** As a group, discuss how a modern production of the play might deal with the potential problems of the presentation of the two Roman wives. (Refer to the activities you did earlier in the act.)

## 4 … and a male perspective

For a TV documentary programme, you plan to focus on Brutus and Caesar at home – the personal lives of the politicians. Arrange and film a television-style interview with the two men. Play the interviews back to the class for observation and comment.

## 5 To cut or not to cut

Some argue that the final two scenes of Act 2 are very brief and add nothing significant to the action. In pairs, one of you argues for cutting the scenes (giving all suitable reasons for doing so). The other argues for their retention (again with justifications).

## 6 What do you think Shakespeare made of Caesar?

Act 2 makes it clear that Caesar's days are numbered – and within the first few lines of the next scene he is dead!

**a** Remind yourself of how Shakespeare presented Caesar in Act 1. Then create a character map of him for Act 2 that reflects how Shakespeare consolidates and enhances his main characteristics. Put his name in the middle of a sheet of paper and group around it all key quotations and references from Act 2.

**b** Use all your research to help you write an essay on Shakespeare's presentation of Caesar in this act and how far you think he is sympathetic to Caesar.

## 7 Lucius and Artemidorus: casting the parts

Look back through Act 2 Scenes 1 and 4 (Lucius) and Act 2 Scene 3 (Artemidorus) for the contributions of these two minor characters. As a director you have to cast these small parts.

- Write a short 'casting brief' for each character, making it clear what significant qualities you are looking for in the actors who will take on these roles.

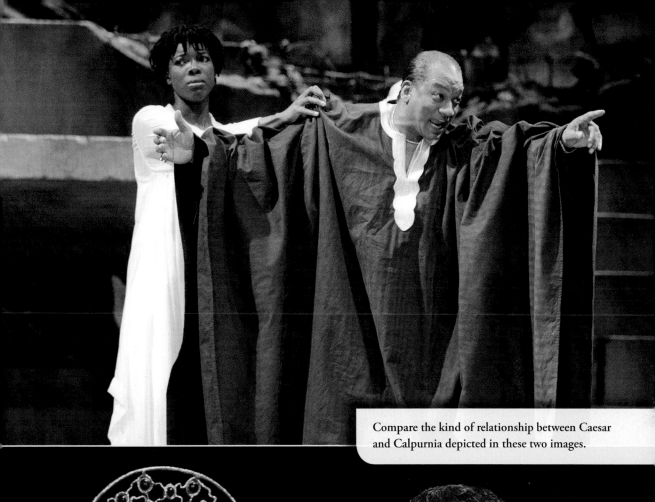

Compare the kind of relationship between Caesar and Calpurnia depicted in these two images.

73

## Stagecraft

### Caesar enters the Capitol

At least fifteen characters enter to the sound of trumpets.

- Make an enlarged sketch of the Globe Theatre, using the picture above to help you. On it, work out where everyone is at line 18, bearing in mind the change from street to Capitol at line 12. (For a description of Caesar's walk to the Capitol read Act 2 Scene 4, lines 34–6.)

## 1 What is your picture of Caesar? (in threes)

Caesar's words in lines 1–26 can be delivered in different ways in order to signal key aspects of his character moments before his death. Some critics see line 8 as pivotal. How does Caesar show that he is ignoring Artemidorus through his actions here?

- Try different readings of lines 1, 8 and 10. Then settle on the versions that work best.
- Present them to other groups and explain your choices.

## 2 Raising the tension (in pairs)

At the start of this act, Shakespeare continues to increase the dramatic tension surrounding the conspiracy.

- In your pairs, discuss and then list the ways in which he does this in the script opposite. Take time to consider the length of the lines, on whom the action focuses and whether any of the characters act out of character at this point.
- Swap and discuss your list with others.

---

**schedule** paper, document

**touches** concerns

**Sirrah, give place** get out of the way, man

*Caesar enters the Capitol, the rest following* the exact details of Elizabethan staging are unclear, but it is known that at the Globe Theatre there was a 'discovery space' at the rear of the stage; which may have been used as the Senate House; the area in front may have been used as the street.

**makes to** moves towards
**sudden** quick

**turn back** come back alive

**be constant** keep your nerve

# Act 3 Scene 1
## Rome   The Capitol

*Flourish. Enter* CAESAR, BRUTUS, CASSIUS, CASCA, DECIUS,
METELLUS, TREBONIUS, CINNA, ANTONY, *Lepidus,*
ARTEMIDORUS, PUBLIUS, [POPILLIUS, *Ligarius,] and the*
SOOTHSAYER

| | |
|---|---|
| CAESAR | The Ides of March are come. |
| SOOTHSAYER | Ay, Caesar, but not gone. |
| ARTEMIDORUS | Hail, Caesar! Read this schedule. |
| DECIUS | Trebonius doth desire you to o'er-read |
| | (At your best leisure) this his humble suit. |
| ARTEMIDORUS | O Caesar, read mine first, for mine's a suit |
| | That touches Caesar nearer. Read it, great Caesar. |
| CAESAR | What touches us ourself shall be last served. |
| ARTEMIDORUS | Delay not, Caesar, read it instantly. |
| CAESAR | What, is the fellow mad? |
| PUBLIUS | Sirrah, give place. |
| CASSIUS | What, urge you your petitions in the street? |
| | Come to the Capitol. |

*[Caesar enters the Capitol, the rest following]*

| | |
|---|---|
| POPILLIUS | I wish your enterprise today may thrive. |
| CASSIUS | What enterprise, Popillius? |
| POPILLIUS | Fare you well. |

*[Leaves him and joins Caesar]*

| | |
|---|---|
| BRUTUS | What said Popillius Lena? |
| CASSIUS | He wished today our enterprise might thrive. |
| | I fear our purpose is discoverèd. |
| BRUTUS | Look how he makes to Caesar, mark him. |
| CASSIUS | Casca, be sudden, for we fear prevention. |
| | Brutus, what shall be done? If this be known |
| | Cassius or Caesar never shall turn back, |
| | For I will slay myself. |
| BRUTUS | Cassius, be constant. |
| | Popillius Lena speaks not of our purposes, |
| | For look he smiles, and Caesar doth not change. |
| CASSIUS | Trebonius knows his time, for look you, Brutus, |
| | He draws Mark Antony out of the way. |

*[Exeunt Antony and Trebonius]*

5

10

15

20

25

Repeal my brother's banishment, Metellus begs Caesar. Brutus and Cassius support him and get nearer to Caesar. Caesar adamantly refuses them all.

## 1 Focus on Caesar's behaviour (in fours)

- In quick succession read aloud Metellus Cimber's speech at line 33, Brutus's speech at line 52 (with Caesar's response) and Cassius's speech at line 55. Do this several times, giving everyone the chance to be Caesar.

- Now look closely at Caesar's two long speeches (beginning at lines 35 and 58) and talk together about how well he copes with the three senators' successive pleas to repeal Publius Cimber's banishment.

- Follow this up by discussing what sort of a leader Caesar presents himself as at this point. How does this suit the conspirators' intentions? Remember that Caesar drank wine with some of these people before leaving for the Capitol.

## 2 Caesar – dramatic irony (in pairs)

**Dramatic irony** occurs when the audience knows more than a character does. Here the audience knows what is about to happen to Caesar. Caesar thinks that he is going to show off his supreme power, having put aside his fear of coming to the Capitol.

**a** Analyse in detail Caesar's simile in lines 60–2 and discuss the dramatic irony in the light of what is about to happen.

**b** Make a note in your Director's Journal outlining the directions you would give to the actor playing Caesar at this point. Which words should he emphasise and how should he stand? Would you advise any gestures to accompany these three lines?

▼ **How close is this Caesar (right) to your view of him at this point in the play?**

**presently prefer** immediately offer
**addressed** ready to begin

**puissant** powerful

**couchings** bowings down

**turn preordinance … children** make a children's game of long-established laws
**Be not fond** be not so foolish
**true quality** stability or firmness

**cur** dog

**repealing** recall from banishment

**freedom of** permission for

**enfranchisement** release (from banishment)

**resting** unchanging
**fellow** equal
**firmament** sky

| DECIUS | Where is Metellus Cimber? Let him go |
| | And presently prefer his suit to Caesar. |
| BRUTUS | He is addressed, press near and second him. |
| CINNA | Casca, you are the first that rears your hand. | 30 |
| CAESAR | Are we all ready? What is now amiss |
| | That Caesar and his Senate must redress? |
| METELLUS | Most high, most mighty, and most puissant Caesar, |
| | Metellus Cimber throws before thy seat |
| | An humble heart. |
| CAESAR | I must prevent thee, Cimber. | 35 |
| | These couchings and these lowly courtesies |
| | Might fire the blood of ordinary men |
| | And turn preordinance and first decree |
| | Into the law of children. Be not fond |
| | To think that Caesar bears such rebel blood | 40 |
| | That will be thawed from the true quality |
| | With that which melteth fools – I mean sweet words, |
| | Low-crookèd curtsies, and base spaniel fawning. |
| | Thy brother by decree is banishèd: |
| | If thou dost bend, and pray, and fawn for him, | 45 |
| | I spurn thee like a cur out of my way. |
| | Know Caesar doth not wrong, nor without cause |
| | Will he be satisfied. |
| METELLUS | Is there no voice more worthy than my own |
| | To sound more sweetly in great Caesar's ear | 50 |
| | For the repealing of my banished brother? |
| BRUTUS | I kiss thy hand, but not in flattery, Caesar, |
| | Desiring thee that Publius Cimber may |
| | Have an immediate freedom of repeal. |
| CAESAR | What, Brutus? |
| CASSIUS | Pardon, Caesar! Caesar, pardon! | 55 |
| | As low as to thy foot doth Cassius fall |
| | To beg enfranchisement for Publius Cimber. |
| CAESAR | I could be well moved, if I were as you; |
| | If I could pray to move, prayers would move me. |
| | But I am constant as the northern star, | 60 |
| | Of whose true-fixed and resting quality |
| | There is no fellow in the firmament. |

Having declared himself the world's only constant man, Caesar is stabbed to death. Brutus tries to reassure all who flee, but the conspirators are left alone in the Senate.

## 1 The assassination (in sevens)

Brutus said, 'Let's be sacrificers, but not butchers' (Act 2 Scene 1, line 166), but the conspirators probably kill Caesar in a variety of ways.

- Each person chooses which conspirator to play. Think about which part of Caesar's body he might choose to stab, and the style in which he would stab. Notice that Brutus is the last to attack.
- Carefully stage the assassination. Then, without words, present it to the class in slow motion.

## Themes

### Love and friendship (in pairs)

Caesar's death line '*Et tu, Brute?* – Then fall, Caesar!' suggests Caesar's bewilderment at what is happening. Literally translated, the first three words mean 'Even you, Brutus?' Some argue that his friend's betrayal is as mortally wounding as Brutus's blade.

**a** Discuss the dramatic effect of these three words. How would Caesar's death have been different without them?

**b** Take turns to create a 'snapshot' of Caesar at the moment of his death. Concentrate on facial expression and gesture. Hold your pose for a few seconds for your partner to look at.

## Write about it

### What does Publius think?

Publius, an old senator, silently witnesses the assassination of his leader and is dumbstruck at the turn of events. Brutus is concerned that Publius is 'affrighted' and tries to reassure him.

- Imagine that you are Publius. As the conspirators usher you away, you reflect on the amazing events that have just unfolded. How will you respond to the assassins' chant: 'Liberty! Freedom! Tyranny is dead!'? Do you believe Brutus when he says 'There is no harm intended to your person'?
- Either write a diary entry describing what you have witnessed and heard today, making it as vivid as you can, or do as Brutus says – 'So, tell them, Publius' (line 91). Write the speech you would make to the people to reassure them that the conspirators intend them no harm.

**apprehensive** quick to learn

**holds ... rank** keeps to his position

**Olympus** the Greek mountain home of the gods

**bootless** in vain, without effect

**common pulpits** public speaking platforms

**Ambition's debt** what was due to Caesar for being ambitious

**confounded** confused, amazed

**mutiny** uproar, confusion

**Stand fast together** get ready to defend ourselves

**standing** organising resistance

**your age** you as an old man

**abide** pay the penalty for

The skies are painted with unnumbered sparks,
They are all fire, and every one doth shine;
But there's but one in all doth hold his place.                      65
So in the world: 'tis furnished well with men,
And men are flesh and blood, and apprehensive;
Yet in the number I do know but one
That unassailable holds on his rank,
Unshaked of motion, and that I am he                                 70
Let me a little show it, even in this:
That I was constant Cimber should be banished,
And constant do remain to keep him so.

CINNA          O Caesar –

CAESAR                    Hence! Wilt thou lift up Olympus?

DECIUS         Great Caesar –

CAESAR                       Doth not Brutus bootless kneel?          75

CASCA          Speak hands for me!

                              *They stab Caesar*

CAESAR         *Et tu, Brute?* – Then fall, Caesar!        *Dies*

CINNA          Liberty! Freedom! Tyranny is dead!
               Run hence, proclaim, cry it about the streets.

CASSIUS        Some to the common pulpits, and cry out,              80
               'Liberty, freedom, and enfranchisement!'

BRUTUS         People and senators, be not affrighted,
               Fly not, stand still! Ambition's debt is paid.

CASCA          Go to the pulpit, Brutus.

DECIUS                             And Cassius too.

BRUTUS         Where's Publius?                                      85

CINNA          Here, quite confounded with this mutiny.

METELLUS       Stand fast together lest some friend of Caesar's
               Should chance –

BRUTUS         Talk not of standing. Publius, good cheer,
               There is no harm intended to your person,             90
               Nor to no Roman else. So tell them, Publius.

CASSIUS        And leave us, Publius, lest that the people,
               Rushing on us, should do your age some mischief.

BRUTUS         Do so, and let no man abide this deed
               But we the doers.                                     95

                         [*Exeunt all but the conspirators*]

Trebonius reports panic outside. The conspirators prepare to depart to proclaim themselves liberators, their daggers and forearms ritually bloodied. They halt as Antony's servant enters, bringing his master's message.

# 1 'let us bathe our hands in Caesar's blood'
**(in small groups)**

The photograph below shows how a 2005 production at the Barbican staged the moments following Caesar's assassination. Cassius stands at the back with his dagger out; Brutus is beside him.

a Talk together about the different thoughts and emotions that these conspirators express as they stoop to smear their hands and weapons in Caesar's blood. How many of them appear excited by Brutus's proclamation that their actions have brought 'Peace, freedom, and liberty!'?

b What is the dramatic impact of this moment?

## Characters
### Judging Brutus

Brutus seems to take charge after the assassination. He deals with Publius and then urges the conspirators to 'bathe our hands in Caesar's blood'.

- Step into role as director. Re-read Brutus's speech at lines 103–10. How do you judge Brutus here? Is this a good decision or one that he may live to regret?
- With your judgement and what you know of Brutus in the play so far in mind, write notes in your Director's Journal advising the actor who plays Brutus how to deliver this speech.
- Include a note about how Brutus should react when he hears Antony's description of him in line 126 delivered by the servant.

*Enter* TREBONIUS

| | |
|---|---|
| CASSIUS | Where is Antony? |
| TREBONIUS | Fled to his house amazed. |
| | Men, wives, and children stare, cry out, and run |
| | As it were doomsday. |
| BRUTUS | Fates, we will know your pleasures. |
| | That we shall die we know: 'tis but the time, |
| | And drawing days out, that men stand upon. |
| CASCA | Why, he that cuts off twenty years of life |
| | Cuts off so many years of fearing death. |
| BRUTUS | Grant that, and then is death a benefit. |
| | So are we Caesar's friends, that have abridged |
| | His time of fearing death. Stoop, Romans, stoop, |
| | And let us bathe our hands in Caesar's blood |
| | Up to the elbows and besmear our swords. |
| | Then walk we forth, even to the market-place, |
| | And waving our red weapons o'er our heads |
| | Let's all cry, 'Peace, freedom, and liberty!' |
| CASSIUS | Stoop then and wash. How many ages hence |
| | Shall this our lofty scene be acted over |
| | In states unborn and accents yet unknown! |
| BRUTUS | How many times shall Caesar bleed in sport, |
| | That now on Pompey's basis lies along |
| | No worthier than the dust! |
| CASSIUS | So oft as that shall be, |
| | So often shall the knot of us be called |
| | The men that gave their country liberty. |
| DECIUS | What, shall we forth? |
| CASSIUS | Ay, every man away. |
| | Brutus shall lead, and we will grace his heels |
| | With the most boldest and best hearts of Rome. |

*Enter a* SERVANT

| | |
|---|---|
| BRUTUS | Soft, who comes here? A friend of Antony's. |
| SERVANT | Thus, Brutus, did my master bid me kneel, |
| | Thus did Mark Antony bid me fall down, |
| | And, being prostrate, thus he bade me say: |
| | Brutus is noble, wise, valiant, and honest; |
| | Caesar was mighty, bold, royal, and loving. |

100

105

110

115

120

125

## 1 Send in the servant (in pairs)

**a** Analyse the servant's speech (lines 123–37) closely for deliberately vague
or misleading phrases, especially about Brutus and Caesar. For example,
what is the impact of having 'say' at the start of lines 128 and 129?

**b** Discuss why Mark Antony decided to send a servant with this message
for Brutus and the conspirators.

## 2 Antony – a lesson in sincerity? (in small groups)

Before Mark Antony's entrance, Cassius says: 'my misgiving still / Falls
shrewdly to the purpose.' Antony confronts Caesar's killers while their
hands are still covered in his blood (Shakespeare departed from his source
material to include this moment; see p. 166). He is quick to declare his
reverence for Caesar and to suggest that he would willingly die alongside
his former leader. But is he telling the truth?

**a** How would you have Antony enter after line 146? Brutus is keen to
welcome him. How does Antony respond?

**b** One of you reads Antony's lines 148–63, emphasising all references to
blood and death. The others, as blood-soaked assassins, listen closely
to his words. Afterwards, talk together about the emotive qualities of
Antony's speech. Is Antony speaking from the heart, or does he want
to make the conspirators squirm? Discuss your ideas and collect
evidence to justify your conclusions.

**c** Consider Antony's motives for offering to die now.

**d** Make notes in your Director's Journal under the heading 'Antony',
summing up your observations about him and his motives at this point.

▼ What is going on in this photo? Antony
is in the foreground.

---

**vouchsafe** grant, permit

**this untrod state** these
unprecedented circumstances

**presently** at once

**fears** distrusts

**my misgiving … purpose**
my suspicions always turn out
to be close to the truth

**measure** extent, size

**rank** rotten or diseased

**bear me hard** hate me

**purpled** (Antony says Caesar's
blood is the colour of royalty)

**Live** if I should live

**apt to die** ready, willing to die

**mean of death** way of dying

**cut off** killed

|  | Say I love Brutus, and I honour him; |  |
|--|--|--|
|  | Say I feared Caesar, honoured him, and loved him. |  |
|  | If Brutus will vouchsafe that Antony | 130 |
|  | May safely come to him and be resolved |  |
|  | How Caesar hath deserved to lie in death, |  |
|  | Mark Antony shall not love Caesar dead |  |
|  | So well as Brutus living, but will follow |  |
|  | The fortunes and affairs of noble Brutus | 135 |
|  | Through the hazards of this untrod state |  |
|  | With all true faith. So says my master Antony. |  |
| BRUTUS | Thy master is a wise and valiant Roman, |  |
|  | I never thought him worse. |  |
|  | Tell him, so please him come unto this place, | 140 |
|  | He shall be satisfied and by my honour |  |
|  | Depart untouched. |  |
| SERVANT | I'll fetch him presently. | *Exit Servant* |
| BRUTUS | I know that we shall have him well to friend. |  |
| CASSIUS | I wish we may. But yet have I a mind |  |
|  | That fears him much, and my misgiving still | 145 |
|  | Falls shrewdly to the purpose. |  |

*Enter* ANTONY

| BRUTUS | But here comes Antony. Welcome, Mark Antony! |  |
|--|--|--|
| ANTONY | O mighty Caesar! Dost thou lie so low? |  |
|  | Are all thy conquests, glories, triumphs, spoils |  |
|  | Shrunk to this little measure? Fare thee well! | 150 |
|  | I know not, gentlemen, what you intend, |  |
|  | Who else must be let blood, who else is rank. |  |
|  | If I myself, there is no hour so fit |  |
|  | As Caesar's death's hour, nor no instrument |  |
|  | Of half that worth as those your swords made rich | 155 |
|  | With the most noble blood of all this world. |  |
|  | I do beseech ye, if you bear me hard, |  |
|  | Now, whilst your purpled hands do reek and smoke, |  |
|  | Fulfil your pleasure. Live a thousand years, |  |
|  | I shall not find myself so apt to die: | 160 |
|  | No place will please me so, no mean of death, |  |
|  | As here by Caesar, and by you cut off, |  |
|  | The choice and master spirits of this age. |  |

Brutus claims that pity for Rome killed Caesar. Brutus loves Antony and loved Caesar. Antony shakes the conspirators' hands, but fears this act of friendship wrongs Caesar.

## Characters

### Brutus and Cassius – two different politicians (in pairs)

a One of you reads Brutus's lines 164–76; the other reads Cassius's lines 177–8. Afterwards, talk together about how differently the two conspirators treat Antony. Make a list of the contrasting points that emerge.

b Discuss the following question: Do Brutus and Cassius respond to Antony in ways you would expect? After talking about this in pairs, pool your answers in a class discussion.

## 1 Outward action, secret thoughts (in eights)

At the end of Act 3 Scene 1 we have no doubt about Antony's intentions towards the conspirators, regardless of how he behaves towards them here.

- In order to explore Antony's reaction to each conspirator and theirs to him at this point, first rehearse lines 184–9. Each conspirator, although they do not speak, should think carefully about how they will react to being greeted by Antony, who was a friend of Caesar. Do they trust him? Who has the power in this encounter? How awkward is it having your hand shaken when it's covered in blood?

- Then read the lines through again, freezing the action after each greeting. Antony and then the conspirator being greeted should express how they really feel at this point. Try to bring out the tension of the moment as much as you can, as well as the contrast between appearance and reality.

## Write about it

### Conspirators – why so many?

Apart from Brutus and Cassius, we do not see the seven conspirators again. Write a short paragraph in answer to the following questions:

- Why do you think Shakespeare decided to have so many conspirators, only to focus on two of them after Act 3?
- Do the other conspirators (not Brutus and Cassius) have individual characteristics? Give evidence for your view.

**pitiful** full of pity

**pity … pity** pity for Rome's suffering extinguished pity for Caesar

**leaden points** (i.e. soft and harmless)

**Our arms … do receive you in** we welcome you like a brother despite our savage appearance

**voice** vote, influence

**dignities** positions of influence

**credit** honour, reputation

**conceit me** think of me

**dearer** more keenly

**corse** corpse

**close / In terms of friendship** make a deal

| | |
|---|---|
| BRUTUS | O Antony, beg not your death of us. |
| | Though now we must appear bloody and cruel, 165 |
| | As by our hands and this our present act |
| | You see we do, yet see you but our hands |
| | And this the bleeding business they have done. |
| | Our hearts you see not, they are pitiful; |
| | And pity to the general wrong of Rome – 170 |
| | As fire drives out fire, so pity pity – |
| | Hath done this deed on Caesar. For your part, |
| | To you our swords have leaden points, Mark Antony; |
| | Our arms in strength of malice, and our hearts |
| | Of brothers' temper, do receive you in 175 |
| | With all kind love, good thoughts, and reverence. |
| CASSIUS | Your voice shall be as strong as any man's |
| | In the disposing of new dignities. |
| BRUTUS | Only be patient till we have appeased |
| | The multitude, beside themselves with fear, 180 |
| | And then we will deliver you the cause |
| | Why I, that did love Caesar when I struck him, |
| | Have thus proceeded. |
| ANTONY | I doubt not of your wisdom. |
| | Let each man render me his bloody hand. |
| | First, Marcus Brutus, will I shake with you; 185 |
| | Next, Caius Cassius, do I take your hand; |
| | Now, Decius Brutus, yours; now yours, Metellus; |
| | Yours, Cinna; and, my valiant Casca, yours; |
| | Though last, not least in love, yours, good Trebonius. |
| | Gentlemen all – alas, what shall I say? 190 |
| | My credit now stands on such slippery ground |
| | That one of two bad ways you must conceit me, |
| | Either a coward or a flatterer. |
| | That I did love thee, Caesar, O, 'tis true. |
| | If then thy spirit look upon us now, 195 |
| | Shall it not grieve thee dearer than thy death |
| | To see thy Antony making his peace, |
| | Shaking the bloody fingers of thy foes – |
| | Most noble – in the presence of thy corse? |
| | Had I as many eyes as thou hast wounds, 200 |
| | Weeping as fast as they stream forth thy blood, |
| | It would become me better than to close |
| | In terms of friendship with thine enemies. |

## Language in the play

### 'That I did love thee, Caesar' (in small groups)

Even though the conspirators look on, Antony is effusive in declaring his love for Caesar.

**a** Work through lines 194–210. What is the effect of Antony directly addressing the dead Caesar as 'Julius' and his repetition of the word 'here' three times.

**b** Antony's words resonate with two image patterns: blood and hunting. Caesar's wounds are like eyes that weep with blood, and Caesar the man is described as a hunted animal (a 'hart' is a deer, but it is also a pun suggesting the word 'heart' to his audience). Work through the details of the deer image and decide what impression of Caesar Antony is aiming to give his audience by using it.

**c** Talk together about what you think Antony's intentions are in speaking as he does in lines 194–210 and then list them.

## 1 Brutus gives Antony satisfaction (in pairs)

Antony asks the conspirators to 'give me reasons / Why and wherein Caesar was dangerous' (lines 221–2). But Brutus never does explain his actions to Antony.

- Imagine Brutus has decided to offer Antony an explanation of the conspirators' actions. Improvise that conversation between them.

## 2 Antony – one final request (in pairs)

In lines 227–30, Antony requests that he be allowed to 'Produce his [Caesar's] body to the market-place' and speak like a 'friend' at his funeral. This is a crucial moment and it provokes differing responses in Brutus and Cassius. Cassius urgently takes Brutus aside at line 231 to talk in confidence with him.

- Take parts and read Brutus and Cassius's brief private conversation (lines 231–43). Afterwards, talk about what the lines reveal about the two men's characters. If you kept notes of your answers to the 'Characters' activity on page 84, add to them.

---

**bayed** hunted and cornered

**hart** (see 'Language' box)

**Signed in thy spoil** marked with bits of your flesh and blood

**Lethe** river of the underworld

**cold modesty** being very restrained

**compact** agreement

**pricked** marked down, listed

**full of good regard** sound

**suitor** one who requests something

**in the order of** as part of

|  | Pardon me, Julius! Here wast thou bayed, brave hart, | |
|--|--|--|
|  | Here didst thou fall, and here thy hunters stand, | 205 |
|  | Signed in thy spoil and crimsoned in thy Lethe. | |
|  | O world! Thou wast the forest to this hart, | |
|  | And this indeed, O world, the heart of thee. | |
|  | How like a deer strucken by many princes | |
|  | Dost thou here lie! | 210 |
| CASSIUS | Mark Antony – | |
| ANTONY |               Pardon me, Caius Cassius, | |
|  | The enemies of Caesar shall say this; | |
|  | Then, in a friend, it is cold modesty. | |
| CASSIUS | I blame you not for praising Caesar so, | |
|  | But what compact mean you to have with us? | 215 |
|  | Will you be pricked in number of our friends, | |
|  | Or shall we on and not depend on you? | |
| ANTONY | Therefore I took your hands, but was indeed | |
|  | Swayed from the point by looking down on Caesar. | |
|  | Friends am I with you all, and love you all, | 220 |
|  | Upon this hope, that you shall give me reasons | |
|  | Why and wherein Caesar was dangerous. | |
| BRUTUS | Or else were this a savage spectacle. | |
|  | Our reasons are so full of good regard | |
|  | That were you, Antony, the son of Caesar | 225 |
|  | You should be satisfied. | |
| ANTONY |                That's all I seek, | |
|  | And am, moreover, suitor that I may | |
|  | Produce his body to the market-place, | |
|  | And in the pulpit, as becomes a friend, | |
|  | Speak in the order of his funeral. | 230 |
| BRUTUS | You shall, Mark Antony. | |
| CASSIUS |             Brutus, a word with you. | |
|  | [*Aside to Brutus*] You know not what you do. Do not consent | |
|  | That Antony speak in his funeral. | |
|  | Know you how much the people may be moved | |
|  | By that which he will utter? | |
| BRUTUS | [*Aside to Cassius*]        By your pardon, | 235 |
|  | I will myself into the pulpit first | |
|  | And show the reason of our Caesar's death. | |

Antony is given permission to speak at Caesar's funeral after Brutus, but not to blame the conspirators. Left alone with Caesar's body, Antony prophesies horrific civil war.

## Themes

### Love and friendship (in pairs)

It is worth exploring the dramatic impact of Antony's crucial soliloquy, spoken over the mutilated body of his friend. Cassius's suspicions about the potential threat posed by Antony prove correct. Now alone, Antony reveals his true feelings about Caesar's murder and the men who killed him.

- Share out the lines and read through Antony's soliloquy (lines 254–75). Find words in it that convey what he truly feels about a) Caesar, b) his murderers and c) revenge. Write them down.
- Now look back through the earlier part of the scene, starting at Antony's entrance after line 146. Compare his 'soliloquy' thoughts and feelings with those he speaks openly to the conspirators. In what ways are they similar and why? In what ways are they very different?

## 1 Nightmare voices (in large groups)

Work out how you can present Antony's soliloquy to create the maximum horror. Use all your voices, sometimes speaking together, sometimes separately or individually. You can repeat or echo words; emphasise sound patterns and rhythms; build to a crescendo; fade to nothing and become suddenly loud or suddenly soft. There is no need to stick to words: you can make rhythmic, threatening noises or other sounds that the words suggest. By putting people in different parts of the room you can get quadraphonic sound.

▶ **Would you consider staging Antony's soliloquy like this? Give your reasons either way.**

JULIUS CAESAR ACT 3 SCENE 1

|  | What Antony shall speak, I will protest |  |
|---|---|---|
|  | He speaks by leave and by permission, |  |
|  | And that we are contented Caesar shall | 240 |
|  | Have all true rites and lawful ceremonies. |  |
|  | It shall advantage more than do us wrong. |  |
| CASSIUS | [*Aside to Brutus*] I know not what may fall, I like it not. |  |
| BRUTUS | Mark Antony, here take you Caesar's body. |  |
|  | You shall not in your funeral speech blame us, | 245 |
|  | But speak all good you can devise of Caesar |  |
|  | And say you do't by our permission, |  |
|  | Else shall you not have any hand at all |  |
|  | About his funeral. And you shall speak |  |
|  | In the same pulpit whereto I am going, | 250 |
|  | After my speech is ended. |  |
| ANTONY | Be it so, |  |
|  | I do desire no more. |  |
| BRUTUS | Prepare the body then and follow us. |  |

*Exeunt [all but] Antony*

| ANTONY | O, pardon me, thou bleeding piece of earth, |  |
|---|---|---|
|  | That I am meek and gentle with these butchers! | 255 |
|  | Thou art the ruins of the noblest man |  |
|  | That ever livèd in the tide of times. |  |
|  | Woe to the hand that shed this costly blood! |  |
|  | Over thy wounds now do I prophesy – |  |
|  | Which like dumb mouths do ope their ruby lips | 260 |
|  | To beg the voice and utterance of my tongue – |  |
|  | A curse shall light upon the limbs of men: |  |
|  | Domestic fury and fierce civil strife |  |
|  | Shall cumber all the parts of Italy; |  |
|  | Blood and destruction shall be so in use | 265 |
|  | And dreadful objects so familiar |  |
|  | That mothers shall but smile when they behold |  |
|  | Their infants quartered with the hands of war, |  |
|  | All pity choked with custom of fell deeds; |  |
|  | And Caesar's spirit, ranging for revenge, | 270 |
|  | With Ate by his side come hot from hell, |  |
|  | Shall in these confines with a monarch's voice |  |
|  | Cry havoc and let slip the dogs of war, |  |
|  | That this foul deed shall smell above the earth |  |
|  | With carrion men groaning for burial. | 275 |

Octavius's servant reports his master's approach. Antony suggests that Octavius waits until the people's mood has been tested. In the market-place, Brutus and Cassius prepare to speak.

## 1 The day that Caesar was killed (in small groups)

**a** Discuss in your groups any dramatic or significant event in your lifetime that made it feel as if time had come to a standstill. It could be a personal or a political event.

**b** Imagine how ordinary Romans might have felt on hearing of Caesar's death. Write a report to send to Octavius Caesar (Julius Caesar's nephew and heir) about the mood of the city after the assassination. Begin with Antony's words at line 288: 'Here is a mourning Rome, a dangerous Rome'.

## 2 Great speeches (in small groups)

Some of the greatest oratory (public speaking) that Shakespeare wrote is in Act 3 Scene 2. Brutus's and Mark Antony's speeches (lines 13–39 and lines 65–242) have to be read aloud and listened to in their entirety for their art to be fully appreciated.

- Two or three of you read the speeches aloud, taking a sentence each in turn while the rest listen closely without following the script. Leave out the plebeians' lines.
- Then swap over. After each speech, discuss how it felt when you spoke it and how it felt when you listened to it.

### Write about it

#### Cassius's speech to the people

At line 10 of Act 3 Scene 2, Cassius leaves to speak to half the crowd in another street.

- Look back at how Cassius speaks in Act 1 Scenes 2 and 3 and write the speech he might have delivered to the crowd. The Elizabethan lesson in **rhetoric** on page 92 will help you. You could also look at the ways in which Brutus (line 13) and Antony (line 65) begin their speeches to the crowd in this scene.
- Your class could be the crowd to whom you deliver the speech. They will no doubt want to ask you questions having heard your speech.

---

Octavius Caesar (see Activity 1)

**Passion** intense emotion

**seven leagues** about twenty-one miles
**Post back** hurry back

**Hie hence** get you gone

**try** discover
**take / The cruel issue** react to the savage actions

**the which** (i.e. the outcome of Antony's testing of the crowd)

PLEBEIANS ordinary people, workers
**be satisfied** be given an explanation
**audience** a hearing
**part** divide

*Enter Octavio's* SERVANT

|  | You serve Octavius Caesar, do you not? | |
| --- | --- | --- |
| SERVANT | I do, Mark Antony. | |
| ANTONY | Caesar did write for him to come to Rome. | |
| SERVANT | He did receive his letters, and is coming, | |
|  | And bid me say to you by word of mouth – | 280 |

[*Seeing the body*]

O Caesar!

| ANTONY | Thy heart is big, get thee apart and weep. | |
| --- | --- | --- |
|  | Passion, I see, is catching, for mine eyes, | |
|  | Seeing those beads of sorrow stand in thine, | |
|  | Began to water. Is thy master coming? | 285 |
| SERVANT | He lies tonight within seven leagues of Rome. | |
| ANTONY | Post back with speed and tell him what hath chanced. | |
|  | Here is a mourning Rome, a dangerous Rome, | |
|  | No Rome of safety for Octavius yet: | |
|  | Hie hence and tell him so. Yet stay awhile, | 290 |
|  | Thou shalt not back till I have borne this corse | |
|  | Into the market-place. There shall I try | |
|  | In my oration how the people take | |
|  | The cruel issue of these bloody men, | |
|  | According to the which thou shalt discourse | 295 |
|  | To young Octavius of the state of things. | |
|  | Lend me your hand. | |

*Exeunt* [*with Caesar's body*]

# Act 3 Scene 2
## Rome   The market-place

*Enter* BRUTUS *and Cassius with the* PLEBEIANS

| ALL | We will be satisfied! Let us be satisfied! | |
| --- | --- | --- |
| BRUTUS | Then follow me and give me audience, friends. | |
|  | Cassius, go you into the other street | |
|  | And part the numbers. | |
|  | Those that will hear me speak, let 'em stay here; | 5 |

Brutus addresses the people. He says he loved Rome's freedom more than Caesar. The crowd accepts it. Antony enters with Caesar's corpse.

# Language in the play

## An Elizabethan lesson in rhetoric (in threes)

Rhetoric is the art of discourse, public speaking and debate. An Elizabethan textbook on rhetoric would typically divide up a speech like this:

> *exordium* **(introduction)** to gain the attention and approval of the hearers
>
> *narratio* **(development)** so that listeners may fully understand the matter being discussed
>
> *confirmatio* **(evidence)** proofs, arguments and reasons, illustrated by quotations
>
> *confutatio* **(dealing with objections)** consideration of what objections may be raised and how to answer them
>
> *conclusio* **(summing up)** a short recapitulation of the point(s).

**a** Find these five sections in lines 13–39 of Brutus's speech (they are very clear) and lines 65–242 of Antony's speech (perhaps less clear). Try reading out loud one of Brutus's sections, then the corresponding one of Antony. Note contrasts in technique, thought and behaviour.

**b** Identify and comment upon any other persuasive techniques Brutus uses in his speech – for example repetitions and echoes, balanced sentences, rhetorical questions and flattering his audience. How do you respond? Are you persuaded?

# Stagecraft

## Enter Mark Antony with Caesar's body

Antony likes plays and, in Act 3 Scene 1, demonstrates what a good actor he is himself!

- Imagine you are Antony, and plan your big entrance. Think carefully about: your appearance (blood?); how you relate to the corpse (would you touch it?); the corpse itself and its presentation ('coffin' at line 98?); and finally where to enter and where to stand while Brutus speaks.
- Present your ideas to the class. This could be in the form of a short talk, or you could act as director and another class member could act out your ideas as you explain them.

---

**renderèd** put forward

**severally** separately

**last** end of my address
**lovers / lover** dear friend(s)
**have respect … honour** bear in mind I am a man of honour
**Censure me** judge me
**your senses** your reason

**base** lowborn
**bondman** slave
**rude** ignorant, uncivilised

**The question of** the facts of
**enrolled** recorded
**extenuated** played down
**enforced** heavily emphasised

|  | Those that will follow Cassius, go with him; |  |
|---|---|---|
|  | And public reasons shall be renderèd |  |
|  | Of Caesar's death. |  |
| 1 PLEBEIAN | I will hear Brutus speak. |  |
| 2 PLEBEIAN | I will hear Cassius and compare their reasons |  |
|  | When severally we hear them renderèd. | 10 |

[*Exit Cassius with some of the Plebeians*]

[*Brutus goes into the pulpit*]

3 PLEBEIAN The noble Brutus is ascended, silence!

BRUTUS Be patient till the last.

Romans, countrymen, and lovers, hear me for my cause, and be silent that you may hear. Believe me for mine honour, and have respect to mine honour that you may believe. Censure me in your wisdom, and awake your senses that you may the better judge. If there be any in this assembly, any dear friend of Caesar's, to him I say that Brutus' love to Caesar was no less than his. If then that friend demand why Brutus rose against Caesar, this is my answer: not that I loved Caesar less, but that I loved Rome more. Had you rather Caesar were living, and die all slaves, than that Caesar were dead, to live all freemen? As Caesar loved me, I weep for him; as he was fortunate, I rejoice at it; as he was valiant, I honour him; but, as he was ambitious, I slew him. There is tears for his love, joy for his fortune, honour for his valour, and death for his ambition. Who is here so base that would be a bondman? If any, speak, for him have I offended. Who is here so rude that would not be a Roman? If any, speak, for him have I offended. Who is here so vile that will not love his country? If any, speak, for him have I offended. I pause for a reply.

15

20

25

ALL None, Brutus, none.

30

BRUTUS Then none have I offended. I have done no more to Caesar than you shall do to Brutus. The question of his death is enrolled in the Capitol, his glory not extenuated wherein he was worthy, nor his offences enforced for which he suffered death.

*Enter* MARK ANTONY [*and others*] *with Caesar's body*

Here comes his body, mourned by Mark Antony, who, though he had no hand in his death, shall receive the benefit of his dying, a place in the commonwealth, as which of you shall not? With this I depart: that, as I slew my best lover for the good of Rome, I have the same dagger for myself when it shall please my country to need my death.

35

[*Comes down*]

Hailed as a new leader, Brutus asks the crowd to hear Antony out. In the pulpit, Antony at first seems to reflect the anti-Caesar mood of the crowd.

## Characters

### Brutus's errors (in pairs)

Brutus's speech is very well received by the crowd. However, he then makes several errors of judgement.

- Read lines 45–53. Decide what Brutus's errors are.
- One of you steps into role as Brutus and the other interrogates him about his mistakes.

## Stagecraft

### Antony takes centre stage (in sixes)

Brutus descends from the pulpit to a hero's reception from the crowd. The third plebeian even shouts, 'Let him be Caesar'! But before Antony can begin his funeral oration, he must subdue the raucous, pro-Brutus crowd.

- Take parts (you will need four plebeians, Brutus and Antony). Start at the moment when Brutus comes down from the speaker's platform. Read through all the lines until Antony begins his speech at line 65.
- Now work out how you would stage this part of the scene. You will need to show how the mood of the plebeians changes and how Antony gradually subdues them in order to begin his address. Act it out!

## 1 The speaker's skill (whole class)

Antony, in his funeral oration (lines 65–99), uses many of the persuasive techniques that Brutus employed earlier. Amongst other strategies he: asks for his listeners' attention; explains his purpose; acknowledges and flatters Brutus; praises Caesar; shows his own distress.

**a** One person reads Antony's speech. The others line up on the opposite side of the room. Each time Antony uses one of the techniques listed, the others take a step towards him and call out the technique used.

**b** Between lines 65 and 151 of Antony's speech you will find five or six key words (such as ambition/ambitious) emphasised and repeated seven to fifteen times each. Find at least three of these words and work out what effects the repetitions have. Contribute your findings to a class discussion.

| | | |
|---|---|---|
| ALL | Live, Brutus, live, live! | 40 |
| 1 PLEBEIAN | Bring him with triumph home unto his house. | |
| 2 PLEBEIAN | Give him a statue with his ancestors. | |
| 3 PLEBEIAN | Let him be Caesar. | |
| 4 PLEBEIAN |       Caesar's better parts | |
| | Shall be crowned in Brutus. | |
| 1 PLEBEIAN |         We'll bring him to his house | |
| | With shouts and clamours. | |
| BRUTUS |       My countrymen – | 45 |
| 2 PLEBEIAN | Peace, silence, Brutus speaks! | |
| 1 PLEBEIAN |       Peace ho! | |
| BRUTUS | Good countrymen, let me depart alone, | |
| | And, for my sake, stay here with Antony. | |
| | Do grace to Caesar's corpse, and grace his speech | |
| | Tending to Caesar's glories, which Mark Antony | 50 |
| | (By our permission) is allowed to make. | |
| | I do entreat you, not a man depart, | |
| | Save I alone, till Antony have spoke.      *Exit* | |
| 1 PLEBEIAN | Stay ho, and let us hear Mark Antony. | |
| 3 PLEBEIAN | Let him go up into the public chair, | 55 |
| | We'll hear him. Noble Antony, go up. | |
| ANTONY | For Brutus' sake, I am beholding to you. | |
| |      *[Goes into the pulpit]* | |
| 4 PLEBEIAN | What does he say of Brutus? | |
| 3 PLEBEIAN |        He says for Brutus' sake | |
| | He finds himself beholding to us all. | |
| 4 PLEBEIAN | 'Twere best he speak no harm of Brutus here! | 60 |
| 1 PLEBEIAN | This Caesar was a tyrant. | |
| 3 PLEBEIAN |       Nay, that's certain: | |
| | We are blest that Rome is rid of him. | |
| 2 PLEBEIAN | Peace, let us hear what Antony can say. | |
| ANTONY | You gentle Romans – | |
| ALL |       Peace ho, let us hear him. | |
| ANTONY | Friends, Romans, countrymen, lend me your ears! | 65 |
| | I come to bury Caesar, not to praise him. | |
| | The evil that men do lives after them, | |
| | The good is oft interrèd with their bones: | |
| | So let it be with Caesar. The noble Brutus | |
| | Hath told you Caesar was ambitious; | 70 |
| | If it were so, it was a grievous fault, | |
| | And grievously hath Caesar answered it. | |

While appearing to agree with Brutus's portrait of Caesar, Antony rejects it in reality by listing Caesar's virtues. The crowd becomes uncertain, swayed by Antony's grief.

## Stagecraft

### Staging Antony's funeral oration

Step into role as director. By now the plebeians and the audience have heard quite a lot of speeches and there are more to come. It is crucial that they do not lose interest at this point, so they need something interesting to look at, to complement the challenging speeches they will hear. It is also important that this grand and public address is staged differently from Antony's more personal soliloquy (see p. 89).

- Remember Caesar's body is on the stage. Where would you place Antony in relation to it and why? Sketch out your staging ideas in your Director's Journal.
- Now consider the photographs below carefully. Decide which staging of the oration you prefer – you can choose your own! – and be prepared to justify your choice to the class.

**general coffers** public finances

**disprove** prove wrong, refute

**judgement** wisdom, good sense

**dear abide it** pay dearly for it

96

Here, under leave of Brutus and the rest –
For Brutus is an honourable man,
So are they all, all honourable men – 75
Come I to speak in Caesar's funeral.
He was my friend, faithful and just to me,
But Brutus says he was ambitious,
And Brutus is an honourable man.
He hath brought many captives home to Rome, 80
Whose ransoms did the general coffers fill;
Did this in Caesar seem ambitious?
When that the poor have cried, Caesar hath wept:
Ambition should be made of sterner stuff;
Yet Brutus says he was ambitious, 85
And Brutus is an honourable man.
You all did see that on the Lupercal
I thrice presented him a kingly crown,
Which he did thrice refuse. Was this ambition?
Yet Brutus says he was ambitious, 90
And sure he is an honourable man.
I speak not to disprove what Brutus spoke,
But here I am to speak what I do know.
You all did love him once, not without cause;
What cause withholds you then to mourn for him? 95
O judgement, thou art fled to brutish beasts,
And men have lost their reason! Bear with me,
My heart is in the coffin there with Caesar,
And I must pause till it come back to me.

| | |
|---|---|
| 1 PLEBEIAN | Methinks there is much reason in his sayings. 100 |
| 2 PLEBEIAN | If thou consider rightly of the matter, |
| | Caesar has had great wrong. |
| 3 PLEBEIAN |                    Has he, masters! |
| | I fear there will a worse come in his place. |
| 4 PLEBEIAN | Marked ye his words? He would not take the crown, |
| | Therefore 'tis certain he was not ambitious. 105 |
| 1 PLEBEIAN | If it be found so, some will dear abide it. |
| 2 PLEBEIAN | Poor soul, his eyes are red as fire with weeping. |
| 3 PLEBEIAN | There's not a nobler man in Rome than Antony. |
| 4 PLEBEIAN | Now mark him, he begins again to speak. |

Antony pleads that the plebeians must remain loyal to the conspirators, and that he must wrong Caesar by refusing to let them know how generous his will is to them. Read it! they shout.

## 1 'The will, the will, we will hear Caesar's will!'
**(in fours)**

This is perhaps Antony's masterstroke. So skilled at focusing his listeners' attention on a specific detail, in line 120 he 'just happens to' mention Caesar's will. He very probably does not have Caesar's will at this point (he sends Lepidus to fetch it from Caesar's house in Act 4 Scene 1, lines 7–9, having fled to his own house following the assassination), so this tactic is a con.

- Take parts and act out lines 120–54. Concentrate on the techniques Antony uses to 'work' his audience. How does he tease them?

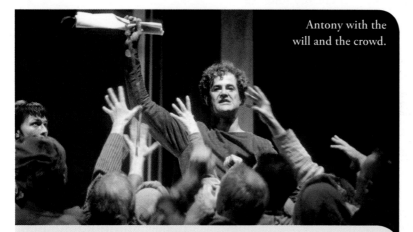
Antony with the will and the crowd.

## Language in the play
### Convincing the crowd (in small groups)

Antony is a skilled orator, but he does not have much time to bring the crowd around to his side. Brutus trusts him not to go beyond his remit of 'Tending to Caesar's glories'. He does, of course, but in subtle and carefully crafted ways.

- Draw up a table like the one below to help you keep track of where, how and to what effect Antony exceeds his brief.

| What does Antony say? | Rhetorical techniques used | Effect on crowd |
|---|---|---|
| He has Caesar's will (line 120) | Concentrates on specific detail | Whips up crowd frenzy |
| | | |
| | | |

- In your groups, look back to Antony's first speech ('Friends, Romans' line 65) and fill in your table with detail about it. Then turn to his speech opposite and do the same.

mutiny riot, disorder

closet private room
commons ordinary people

napkins handkerchiefs

issue children

o'ershot myself gone further than I meant

testament another word for will

98

| ANTONY | But yesterday the word of Caesar might | 110 |
| | Have stood against the world; now lies he there, | |
| | And none so poor to do him reverence. | |
| | O masters, if I were disposed to stir | |
| | Your hearts and minds to mutiny and rage, | |
| | I should do Brutus wrong and Cassius wrong, | 115 |
| | Who (you all know) are honourable men. | |
| | I will not do them wrong; I rather choose | |
| | To wrong the dead, to wrong myself and you, | |
| | Than I will wrong such honourable men. | |
| | But here's a parchment with the seal of Caesar, | 120 |
| | I found it in his closet, 'tis his will. | |
| | Let but the commons hear this testament – | |
| | Which, pardon me, I do not mean to read – | |
| | And they would go and kiss dead Caesar's wounds | |
| | And dip their napkins in his sacred blood, | 125 |
| | Yea, beg a hair of him for memory, | |
| | And, dying, mention it within their wills, | |
| | Bequeathing it as a rich legacy | |
| | Unto their issue. | |
| 4 PLEBEIAN | We'll hear the will. Read it, Mark Antony. | 130 |
| ALL | The will, the will, we will hear Caesar's will! | |
| ANTONY | Have patience, gentle friends, I must not read it. | |
| | It is not meet you know how Caesar loved you: | |
| | You are not wood, you are not stones, but men, | |
| | And, being men, hearing the will of Caesar, | 135 |
| | It will inflame you, it will make you mad. | |
| | 'Tis good you know not that you are his heirs, | |
| | For if you should, O, what would come of it? | |
| 4 PLEBEIAN | Read the will, we'll hear it, Antony. | |
| | You shall read us the will, Caesar's will! | 140 |
| ANTONY | Will you be patient? Will you stay awhile? | |
| | I have o'ershot myself to tell you of it. | |
| | I fear I wrong the honourable men | |
| | Whose daggers have stabbed Caesar, I do fear it. | |
| 4 PLEBEIAN | They were traitors. Honourable men! | 145 |
| ALL | The will! The testament! | |
| 2 PLEBEIAN | They were villains, murderers! The will, read the will! | |
| ANTONY | You will compel me then to read the will? | |

Obeying the crowd, Antony comes down to show them Caesar's corpse, starting with the dagger cuts in his cloak. The plebeians weep.

# 1 How well does Antony manipulate his audience? (in groups of three or four)

**a** Read Act 3 Scene 1 again closely and then write a precise account of what actually happened when Caesar was murdered. Compare it with Mark Antony's version in lines 160–80. What reason(s) are there to doubt the accuracy of Antony's account of the murder?

**b** Just as a jury has to weigh up the arguments of both the prosecuting and defending barristers to arrive at a fair verdict, see if you can spot how Antony colours his account to manipulate the crowd's emotions and show the conspirators in a bad light. Note down your observations.

**c** **Emotive language** is language that seeks to arouse powerful emotions such as fear, pity, anger and so on. Discuss and then write down three or four of the most emotive words or phrases that Antony uses, explaining how and why you think they spark such strong responses in the people watching and listening to him.

## Themes

### Death in detail

Having come down from the pulpit, Antony gathers the crowd around Caesar's body. Rather than immediately appealing to their love of Caesar and how they feel looking at his body, he uses the opportunity to focus on the very specific details of Caesar's cloak. Like Caesar, this cloak has known victory but it is now torn and covered in blood. At the end of the speech he questions why the crowd weeps to see 'Caesar's vesture wounded' when before them is his actual body ruined by the conspirators' actions. Thus he switches their focus to the body itself.

- Read the description of the torn cloak (lines 165–80) and then make a drawing of it. Annotate the drawing with details about the damage done to the cloak by the various conspirators (you can decide whether Caesar is still in it or not). It suits Antony's purposes to mention only three conspirators, but you can draw and write about the damage done by the others as well. Be as imaginative as possible. If the wounds were 'mouths' that could speak, what would they say about the conspirator who made them and his motives?

**far off** further off

**mantle** cloak

**Nervii** a fierce tribe in Gaul (brilliantly defeated by Caesar)

**rent** tear in the fabric

**envious** malicious

**steel** dagger

**As rushing out** as if it were rushing out

**unkindly** savagely, unnaturally

**most unkindest** most savage or unnatural

**base** pedestal

**flourished** waved its weapons in triumph

**dint** blow, force

**gracious** honourable

|  |  |  |
|---|---|---|
|  | Then make a ring about the corpse of Caesar |  |
|  | And let me show you him that made the will. | 150 |
|  | Shall I descend? And will you give me leave? |  |
| ALL | Come down. |  |
| 2 PLEBEIAN | Descend. |  |
| 3 PLEBEIAN | You shall have leave. |  |

*[Antony comes down from the pulpit]*

|  |  |  |
|---|---|---|
| 4 PLEBEIAN | A ring, stand round. | 155 |
| 1 PLEBEIAN | Stand from the hearse, stand from the body. |  |
| 2 PLEBEIAN | Room for Antony, most noble Antony. |  |
| ANTONY | Nay, press not so upon me, stand far off. |  |
| ALL | Stand back! Room, bear back! |  |
| ANTONY | If you have tears, prepare to shed them now. | 160 |
|  | You all do know this mantle. I remember |  |
|  | The first time ever Caesar put it on, |  |
|  | 'Twas on a summer's evening, in his tent, |  |
|  | That day he overcame the Nervii. |  |
|  | Look, in this place ran Cassius' dagger through; | 165 |
|  | See what a rent the envious Casca made; |  |
|  | Through this the well-belovèd Brutus stabbed, |  |
|  | And as he plucked his cursèd steel away, |  |
|  | Mark how the blood of Caesar followed it, |  |
|  | As rushing out of doors to be resolved | 170 |
|  | If Brutus so unkindly knocked or no, |  |
|  | For Brutus, as you know, was Caesar's angel. |  |
|  | Judge, O you gods, how dearly Caesar loved him! |  |
|  | This was the most unkindest cut of all. |  |
|  | For when the noble Caesar saw him stab, | 175 |
|  | Ingratitude, more strong than traitors' arms, |  |
|  | Quite vanquished him. Then burst his mighty heart, |  |
|  | And, in his mantle muffling up his face, |  |
|  | Even at the base of Pompey's statue |  |
|  | (Which all the while ran blood) great Caesar fell. | 180 |
|  | O, what a fall was there, my countrymen! |  |
|  | Then I, and you, and all of us fell down, |  |
|  | Whilst bloody treason flourished over us. |  |
|  | O, now you weep, and I perceive you feel |  |
|  | The dint of pity. These are gracious drops. | 185 |

There are cries of grief when Antony displays the body. When he cleverly praises Brutus's oratory over his own, the enraged crowd move to attack the conspirators.

## Stagecraft

### 'You blocks, you stones' / 'Good friends, sweet friends' (in large groups)

Remind yourself of how Murellus berates the crowd in Act 1 Scene1. Now Antony calls them his friends. The crowd has an important role in this play (see p. 182). It represents the people of Rome, whose support is essential to whoever will next govern the city. But how fickle is the crowd?

- One person is the director and holds a meeting with the actors to discuss the most effective way of using the crowd in Act 3. Improvise being members of an angry crowd and then a more positive and celebratory one. Consider whether or not the numbered plebeians have individual characteristics.
- Put your improvisation into action and read lines 186–249. Members of the crowd should stay in role throughout. Remember that Antony has worked them up after his speech about Caesar's mantle, but he is able to quieten them three times before their final angry explosion at the end of the scene.
- Finally come together as one very large group and act out the response of the crowd to Antony's 'Here was a Caesar! When comes such another?'

## Language in the play

### Blaming conspirators (in small groups)

Brutus let Antony speak on the condition 'You shall not in your funeral speech blame us' (Act 3 Scene 1, line 245).

- Imagine that by Scene 2, line 220, the conspirators have found out how Antony has roused the people. They send in a force to arrest him and disperse the crowd.
- Organise your group into lawyers for the prosecution and the defence at Antony's trial. The prosecution must prove that he *did* blame the conspirators, the defence that he did not. Both sides must look closely at the language of the speech. It may be helpful to look back at the work you did in Activity 1 on page 100.
- When you have prepared your arguments, join up with another group, choose a judge, lawyers and a jury, and run the trial. Finally, get the jury to sift the evidence and arrive at a verdict.

**vesture** clothing
**marred … with** ruined as you see by

**About!** let's go looking!

**private griefs** personal grievances

**Action** effective gestures
**utterance** good delivery
**right on** plainly

**ruffle up** stir up to rage

Kind souls, what weep you when you but behold
Our Caesar's vesture wounded? Look you here,
Here is himself, marred as you see with traitors.

1 PLEBEIAN   O piteous spectacle!

2 PLEBEIAN   O noble Caesar!                                                                190

3 PLEBEIAN   O woeful day!

4 PLEBEIAN   O traitors, villains!

1 PLEBEIAN   O most bloody sight!

2 PLEBEIAN   We will be revenged!

ALL          Revenge! About! Seek! Burn! Fire! Kill!                                        195
             Slay! Let not a traitor live!

ANTONY       Stay, countrymen.

1 PLEBEIAN   Peace there, hear the noble Antony.

2 PLEBEIAN   We'll hear him, we'll follow him, we'll die with him.

ANTONY       Good friends, sweet friends, let me not stir you up                            200
             To such a sudden flood of mutiny.
             They that have done this deed are honourable.
             What private griefs they have, alas, I know not,
             That made them do it. They are wise and honourable,
             And will no doubt with reasons answer you.                                     205
             I come not, friends, to steal away your hearts.
             I am no orator, as Brutus is,
             But – as you know me all – a plain blunt man
             That love my friend, and that they know full well
             That gave me public leave to speak of him.                                     210
             For I have neither wit, nor words, nor worth,
             Action, nor utterance, nor the power of speech
             To stir men's blood. I only speak right on.
             I tell you that which you yourselves do know,
             Show you sweet Caesar's wounds, poor, poor, dumb mouths,                        215
             And bid them speak for me. But were I Brutus,
             And Brutus Antony, there were an Antony
             Would ruffle up your spirits and put a tongue
             In every wound of Caesar, that should move
             The stones of Rome to rise and mutiny.                                         220

ALL          We'll mutiny.

1 PLEBEIAN                  We'll burn the house of Brutus.

3 PLEBEIAN   Away then, come, seek the conspirators.

Antony reveals how much Caesar's will left to the people. They swear vengeance on the conspirators and leave. Alone, Antony confides his satisfaction. Octavius's arrival is announced.

## Language in the play
### How did Antony do it?

Go back to the chart you began on page 98 and fill in the details for Antony's subsequent speeches.

## Themes
### Themes in focus (in small groups)

By this point in the play, all the main themes have been established. They are considered in more detail on pages 168–70.

- Choose and then write down in the middle of a large piece of paper one theme that runs through the play. Each group should choose a different theme. Already mentioned in 'Themes' boxes are:
  - death and attitudes towards it
  - public versus private life
  - sickness and disease
  - love and friendship
  - honour
  - what it is to be a Roman
- Using the charts you have drawn up to assess Antony's speeches (see pp. 98 and 104), as well as the notes you have made in your Director's Journal, cover your paper with ideas, references, quotations and thoughts about your theme.
- Either display the pieces of paper or pass them around for other groups to look at and discuss.

## 1 'Mischief, thou art afoot' (in pairs)

In lines 250–1, Antony makes it clear that he has deliberately worked the crowd in order to unleash their 'mischief'.

- Imagine that, with Octavius a day or so later, Antony reflects on his performance at Caesar's funeral. Improvise their conversation in which Antony runs through some of the highlights of his oration. Which strategies and ideas pleased him? Were there any surprises (either pleasant or unpleasant)? Did he feel that he accomplished all that he set out to?

**Wherein** in what respect

**several** individual
**drachmaes** silver coins

**walks** parks
**arbours** garden retreats

**common pleasures** public pleasure-grounds

**holy place** where the most sacred temples are
**brands** burning torches

**forms** benches
**windows** window shutters

| ANTONY | Yet hear me, countrymen, yet hear me speak. | |
| ALL | Peace ho, hear Antony, most noble Antony! | |
| ANTONY | Why, friends, you go to do you know not what. | 225 |
| | Wherein hath Caesar thus deserved your loves? | |
| | Alas, you know not! I must tell you then: | |
| | You have forgot the will I told you of. | |
| ALL | Most true. The will, let's stay and hear the will! | |
| ANTONY | Here is the will, and under Caesar's seal: | 230 |
| | To every Roman citizen he gives, | |
| | To every several man, seventy-five drachmaes. | |
| 2 PLEBEIAN | Most noble Caesar, we'll revenge his death! | |
| 3 PLEBEIAN | O royal Caesar! | |
| ANTONY | Hear me with patience. | 235 |
| ALL | Peace ho! | |
| ANTONY | Moreover, he hath left you all his walks, | |
| | His private arbours and new-planted orchards, | |
| | On this side Tiber; he hath left them you, | |
| | And to your heirs for ever – common pleasures, | 240 |
| | To walk abroad and recreate yourselves. | |
| | Here was a Caesar! When comes such another? | |
| 1 PLEBEIAN | Never, never! Come, away, away! | |
| | We'll burn his body in the holy place | |
| | And with the brands fire the traitors' houses. | 245 |
| | Take up the body. | |
| 2 PLEBEIAN | Go fetch fire! | |
| 3 PLEBEIAN | Pluck down benches! | |
| 4 PLEBEIAN | Pluck down forms, windows, anything! | |

*Exeunt Plebeians [with the body]*

| ANTONY | Now let it work. Mischief, thou art afoot, | 250 |
| | Take thou what course thou wilt! | |

*Enter* SERVANT

How now, fellow?

| SERVANT | Sir, Octavius is already come to Rome. | |
| ANTONY | Where is he? | |
| SERVANT | He and Lepidus are at Caesar's house. | |
| ANTONY | And thither will I straight to visit him. | 255 |

Octavius's servant reports that Brutus and Cassius have fled Rome. Cinna the poet is interrogated by the plebeians. Going where? Caesar's funeral. Friend or enemy? Friend.

## Characters

### Antony assessed (in threes)

In many of Shakespeare's plays, servants play a crucial role in overhearing important events or asides.

- One of you is a journalist covering the recent events in Rome. You have been asked to focus on Antony's role. You were present at both Brutus's and Antony's speeches in the market-place. You then manage to track down Octavius's and Antony's servants who are prepared to tell you that they overheard everything Antony said just before they entered at Act 3 Scene 1, line 276, and Scene 2, line 251. In your group improvise your conversation with the servants.
- How does what they tell you make you reassess what Antony said and did after the assassination? Write your exclusive report on 'the real Antony' for television or a newspaper.

## Write about it

This act is considered to be one of the most dramatic in all of Shakespeare's works. Think of the power shifts that have taken place: at the beginning of the act Caesar comes to the Capitol and shows how 'constant' he is, before being assassinated by the conspirators. They briefly hold power before it is taken from them by Antony, and Brutus and Cassius flee Rome.

- Write a detailed analysis of why this act is so dramatic. You could include discussion of: the nature of the events shown on stage, the use of dramatic irony (see p. 76), the use of language, the reversal of fortunes and the role the crowd plays.

## 1 The crowd again (in large groups)

Act 3 Scene 3 exemplifies the brutality that can take place following a political regime change.

- Prepare to act out the whole scene. Consider whether you want to experiment with locating the scene in another country and/or historical period and discuss why this might be worth doing. Then act it out, remembering that the crowd is at its most powerful and deadly.

**upon a wish** exactly as I hoped

**Are rid** have ridden

**Belike** presumably

**they had … moved them** they had news of how I had swayed the people

**tonight** last night

**things unluckily … fantasy** recent events weigh ominously on my mind

**forth of doors** out of doors

**directly** at once, to the point

**they are fools that marry** an Elizabethan proverb

**bear me a bang** get a blow from me

|  |  |
|---|---|
|  | He comes upon a wish. Fortune is merry, |
|  | And in this mood will give us anything. |
| SERVANT | I heard him say Brutus and Cassius |
|  | Are rid like madmen through the gates of Rome. |
| ANTONY | Belike they had some notice of the people, |
|  | How I had moved them. Bring me to Octavius. |

*Exeunt*

# Act 3 Scene 3
## Rome   A street

*Enter* CINNA THE POET, *and after him the* PLEBEIANS

CINNA THE POET   I dreamt tonight that I did feast with Caesar,
And things unluckily charge my fantasy.
I have no will to wander forth of doors,
Yet something leads me forth.

1 PLEBEIAN   What is your name? 5

2 PLEBEIAN   Whither are you going?

3 PLEBEIAN   Where do you dwell?

4 PLEBEIAN   Are you a married man or a bachelor?

2 PLEBEIAN   Answer every man directly.

1 PLEBEIAN   Ay, and briefly. 10

4 PLEBEIAN   Ay, and wisely.

3 PLEBEIAN   Ay, and truly, you were best.

CINNA THE POET   What is my name? Whither am I going? Where do I
dwell? Am I a married man or a bachelor? Then to answer every man
directly and briefly, wisely and truly. Wisely I say I am a bachelor. 15

2 PLEBEIAN   That's as much as to say they are fools that marry. You'll
bear me a bang for that, I fear. Proceed directly.

CINNA THE POET   Directly I am going to Caesar's funeral.

1 PLEBEIAN   As a friend or an enemy?

CINNA THE POET   As a friend. 20

2 PLEBEIAN   That matter is answered directly.

4 PLEBEIAN   For your dwelling – briefly.

CINNA THE POET   Briefly, I dwell by the Capitol.

3 PLEBEIAN   Your name, sir, truly.

260

**107**

Hearing his name, the common people accuse Cinna of conspiracy; he protests he's just a poet not a conspirator. They drag him off anyway, intending to burn the conspirators' houses.

## 1 What happened that day? (in eights)

Before and during World War II, many Germans were incited by the oratory of Adolf Hitler and became involved in acts of persecution that they later regretted.

**a**  Four of you are Plebeians 1–4 in old age, the other four a group of students who are investigating senior citizens' reminiscences about events surrounding Caesar's assassination. The plebeians describe the influence of Antony's oratory very fully, as well as how they now feel about their deeds that night. The students sharpen their memories with searching and detailed questions. Among other things, they want to know what happened to Cinna the poet – and why. Improvise their discussion.

**b**  If you were a student, write up a report of your findings. If you were a senior citizen, write your memoirs of the events you have just discussed.

**Pluck but** just tear
**turn him going** finish him off

## Stagecraft

### Arguing with the director again! (in fours)

The director wants to cut Act 3 Scene 3 (as he did Act 2 Scenes 3 and 4). As before, some of the actors want to keep it.

- One of you steps into role as director, with the support of one actor. The other two take the opposing view. Each side should put a good case together and then argue it.

CINNA THE POET  Truly, my name is Cinna.                                        25

1 PLEBEIAN  Tear him to pieces, he's a conspirator.

CINNA THE POET  I am Cinna the poet, I am Cinna the poet.

4 PLEBEIAN  Tear him for his bad verses, tear him for his bad verses.

CINNA THE POET  I am not Cinna the conspirator.

4 PLEBEIAN  It is no matter, his name's Cinna. Pluck but his name out of          30
his heart and turn him going.

3 PLEBEIAN  Tear him, tear him! Come, brands ho, firebrands! To
Brutus', to Cassius', burn all! Some to Decius' house, and some to
Casca's, some to Ligarius'! Away, go!

*Exeunt all the Plebeians [forcing out Cinna]*

# Looking back at Act 3
## Activities for groups or individuals

### 1 Newspaper billboards

Newsagents' billboards give very brief summaries of the news. Write three of them, one for each scene in Act 3. The billboards should reflect the key aspects of the action. Full sentences are not required.

### 2 The coffin and the cloak

Antony is a master at using visual objects to enhance his oratory. He makes striking references to Caesar's 'coffin' and to his 'mantle' (cloak).

- All producers have to decide how to display Caesar's corpse during the funeral speeches. Write some notes for the set designer and the props manager about your own ideas. Study the photographs opposite and on pages x, 96 and 179 for help.

### 3 Favourite lines

Act 3 contains some of Shakespeare's most memorable lines … and most eloquent persuasion. Select a handful of your own favourites and display them strikingly: a poster, a collage or a montage?

### 4 The crowd

Many productions seek to give the Roman crowd a dynamic and energetic presence. Some do this by having the common people dotted amongst the real audience. Some have used the audience as interactive participants in the funeral scene. The photo on page 111 (top right) shows the theatre audience mingling with cast members.

- Write two or three paragraphs summarising the strengths and weaknesses of this staging idea.
- What other ideas do you have for exploiting the crowd scenes?

### 5 A Caesar memorial and obituary

**a** Design a striking and impressive memorial to celebrate the life of your benefactor, Caesar. It is to be installed in the newly bequeathed gardens.

Present your finished idea or your work in progress as a series of sketches with explanation. Use the play to give you ideas: for example, Antony's funeral eulogies (Act 3 Scene 2), Calpurnia's dream (Act 2 Scene 2) and Cassius's references to Caesar as Colossus.

**b** Now write Caesar's obituary – a written memorial. Was he a good ruler or a tyrant? Decide on your target audience and consider what impression of Caesar you wish to convey.

### 6 Total coverage

Create your own newspaper coverage of the assassination of Caesar and subsequent events. You can include any newspaper pieces you may have already written, if appropriate. Decide whether your newspaper is a tabloid or a broadsheet and what its political bias is, who to interview, what to comment on and what to speculate about. Display your front page and other articles for others to see.

### 7 Honour and friendship

Look back at Brutus's important lines 85–9 in Act 1 Scene 2. Bearing in mind the discussions about honour and friendship you have already had, write your answer to the following question, making sure you back up your points with quotations:

- Did Brutus act honourably in becoming one of the conspirators who assassinated his friend Caesar?

### 8 Queen Elizabeth I and Julius Caesar

When a contemporary audience saw the assassination of Caesar on stage, thoughts of the attempts on the life of their queen would have come to mind (see p. 167).

- Research the parallels between the lives and reigns of these two leaders. Display your findings so that others can benefit from them.

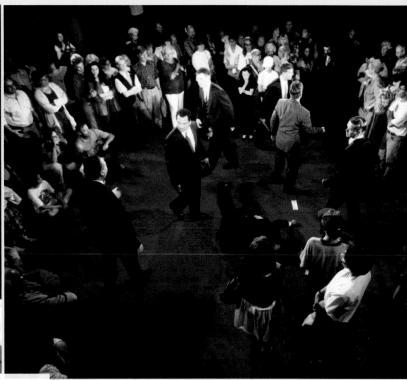

What are your views on the stagings of these dramatic moments from Act 3?

111

The Triumvirate organises a purge which includes family relatives. Antony shows contempt for Lepidus, and Octavius defends him.

# 1 Antony, Octavius and Lepidus: the Triumvirate
## (in threes)

As Act 4 begins, the audience is introduced to the Triumvirate ('three people') who each now rule one third of the Roman Empire – Europe, North Africa and Asia (comprising modern-day Turkey, Iran and Iraq).

**a** This opening scene often follows an interval, and many directors use the opportunity to quickly establish the significance and power of the three men who will now form the direct opposition to Brutus and Cassius. Working together, suggest ways in which a modern production (in traditional costume) might quickly achieve this. Add your strongest idea to a whole-class wall display.

**b** In many coalition groups, there can be an issue about how 'equal' the members are and who might begin to emerge as its natural leader. Take parts and read this short scene aloud to each other. Experiment with different tones, pitch and volume as you seek to give your character the edge on your rivals. Use your classmates as a live audience and get them to score your performance, awarding marks when they think you are clearly dominating your fellow rulers and taking them away when you seem to be losing influence. At the end of the reading, decide together who is emerging as the natural leader, and why.

## Characters

### A new view of Antony?

Antony and his partners now control Rome. Look closely at what he says and how he behaves in the first fifteen lines. Think, too, about the significance of his having the opening line of the act and any conclusions you have reached after the activity above.

- Make notes to add to your Character file on the kind of man Antony is now revealed to be. Justify your comments by referring to the text.
- Compare the latest depiction of Antony with your earlier judgements of him. What glimpses do you recall Shakespeare providing in Act 3 of the 'new' Antony that we see in this scene?

**pricked** identified or chosen

**spot** mark

**cut off … legacies** keep back some money from Caesar's will

**Or** either

**slight, unmeritable** insignificant, undeserving
**Meet** fit only
**threefold world** three-part Roman Empire (see Activity 1 opposite)
**voice** side
**proscription** condemning to death (see p. 173)

**divers … loads** blame for various things we have done

**where we will** where we intend
**turn him off** dismiss him
**empty** unburdened
**graze in commons** graze on common land

# Act 4 Scene 1
## Rome

*Enter* ANTONY, OCTAVIUS, *and* LEPIDUS

| | | |
|---|---|---|
| ANTONY | These many then shall die, their names are pricked. | |
| OCTAVIUS | Your brother too must die; consent you, Lepidus? | |
| LEPIDUS | I do consent. | |
| OCTAVIUS |             Prick him down, Antony. | |
| LEPIDUS | Upon condition Publius shall not live, | |
| | Who is your sister's son, Mark Antony. | 5 |
| ANTONY | He shall not live – look, with a spot I damn him. | |
| | But, Lepidus, go you to Caesar's house, | |
| | Fetch the will hither, and we shall determine | |
| | How to cut off some charge in legacies. | |
| LEPIDUS | What, shall I find you here? | 10 |
| OCTAVIUS | Or here or at the Capitol. | |

*Exit Lepidus*

| | | |
|---|---|---|
| ANTONY | This is a slight, unmeritable man, | |
| | Meet to be sent on errands; is it fit, | |
| | The threefold world divided, he should stand | |
| | One of the three to share it? | |
| OCTAVIUS |                   So you thought him | 15 |
| | And took his voice who should be pricked to die | |
| | In our black sentence and proscription. | |
| ANTONY | Octavius, I have seen more days than you, | |
| | And though we lay these honours on this man | |
| | To ease ourselves of divers slanderous loads, | 20 |
| | He shall but bear them as the ass bears gold, | |
| | To groan and sweat under the business, | |
| | Either led or driven, as we point the way; | |
| | And having brought our treasure where we will, | |
| | Then take we down his load and turn him off | 25 |
| | (Like to the empty ass) to shake his ears | |
| | And graze in commons. | |
| OCTAVIUS |               You may do your will, | |
| | But he's a tried and valiant soldier. | |

Antony compares Lepidus to his horse. He and Octavius prepare for war against Brutus and Cassius. In the next scene Brutus asks Pindarus to bring his master Cassius to discuss Cassius's suspected misdeeds.

# Language in the play

## Lepidus the 'ass' (in pairs)

Between lines 12 and 40, Antony uses powerful language to describe Lepidus. For example, he compares him to an 'ass' who should 'shake his ears / And graze in commons'.

- One of you is Antony. Read his speech aloud, pausing after the key images. The other is a staff officer in Mark Antony's army who has in the past entertained him and the rest of his staff by drawing satirical cartoon portraits of other commanders and senior officers. Using information from the script opposite, draw your cartoon portrait of the man Antony describes. Look at the political cartoon below for inspiration!

▶ **A 1936 cartoon by David Low, showing Adolf Hitler goose-stepping across the 'spineless leaders of democracy'.**

# 1 Antony and Octavius make plans (in pairs)

In line 45, Antony urges Octavius to join him in private to plan a response to Brutus and Cassius's gathering threat.

- Take parts as Antony and Octavius and script their conversation, basing their speaking styles and attitudes on the glimpses of their characterisation that Shakespeare provides in this scene.

# 2 Recruiting in Asia (in two groups of up to five each)

By the time Brutus and Cassius return to the stage in Act 4 Scene 2, they have raised large armies in Asia.

- One group of you is made up of Republican recruiting officers who try to explain why Brutus and Cassius must defeat Antony and Octavius. The others are Asians who challenge and ask questions. Assume that newspapers have kept the people of Asia well informed of recent events in Rome!

**provender** food

**wind** turn
**corporal** physical
**in some taste** to some extent

**Which ... his fashion**
(i.e. everything about him is second-hand and out of date)
**property** thing to be used
(as in theatre 'prop')
**Listen** listen to
**levying powers** raising troops
**straight make head**
immediately raise an army
**presently** straight away
**in counsel** in private
**covert** hidden or secret
**at the stake** in serious danger
(image from bear-baiting)
**bayed about with** surrounded by
(image from hunting)

**Sardis** town in modern Turkey

*Drum* the accompaniment for troops on the march

**In his own change** in his own right
**ill** incompetent, inadequate
**worthy** major

114

| | | |
|---|---|---|
| ANTONY | So is my horse, Octavius, and for that | |
| | I do appoint him store of provender. | 30 |
| | It is a creature that I teach to fight, | |
| | To wind, to stop, to run directly on, | |
| | His corporal motion governed by my spirit. | |
| | And, in some taste, is Lepidus but so: | |
| | He must be taught and trained and bid go forth, | 35 |
| | A barren-spirited fellow, one that feeds | |
| | On objects, arts, and imitations, | |
| | Which, out of use and staled by other men, | |
| | Begin his fashion. Do not talk of him | |
| | But as a property. And now, Octavius, | 40 |
| | Listen great things. Brutus and Cassius | |
| | Are levying powers; we must straight make head. | |
| | Therefore let our alliance be combined, | |
| | Our best friends made, our means stretched, | |
| | And let us presently go sit in counsel, | 45 |
| | How covert matters may be best disclosed | |
| | And open perils surest answerèd. | |
| OCTAVIUS | Let us do so, for we are at the stake | |
| | And bayed about with many enemies, | |
| | And some that smile have in their hearts, I fear, | 50 |
| | Millions of mischiefs. | |

*Exeunt*

# Act 4 Scene 2
## Brutus' camp near Sardis in Asia

*Drum. Enter* BRUTUS, LUCILIUS, [*Lucius,*] *and the army. Titinius
and* PINDARUS *meet them*

| | | |
|---|---|---|
| BRUTUS | Stand ho! | |
| LUCILIUS | Give the word ho, and stand! | |
| BRUTUS | What now, Lucilius, is Cassius near? | |
| LUCILIUS | He is at hand, and Pindarus is come | |
| | To do you salutation from his master. | 5 |
| BRUTUS | He greets me well. Your master, Pindarus, | |
| | In his own change or by ill officers, | |
| | Hath given me some worthy cause to wish | |
| | Things done undone, but if he be at hand | |
| | I shall be satisfied. | |

Lucilius, returned from Cassius, reports that Cassius is no longer as friendly as before. Cassius enters with his army and says Brutus has wronged him. Brutus urges him to speak quietly.

## Stagecraft

### 'Enter CASSIUS *and his powers*' (in fours)

Brutus's description of Cassius as 'A hot friend cooling' in line 19 makes it clear that there is friction between them. When Cassius enters with his military 'powers' at line 30, the tension is ratcheted up further.

- As a group, work out how to stage the arrival of Cassius and his followers to create maximum impact. Where will you position or 'block' the characters? How does Brutus deploy his soldiers? How do the men speak to each other? Use the picture of the Globe stage on page 74 if you wish. Focus on blocking from the stage direction '*Low march within*' after line 24 to line 42. Remember that Shakespeare's company is probably only about fifteen strong.

- If you have access to a hall or stage, join forces with one or more other groups in the class and try out your different ideas for this opening confrontation. Explore how you can add sound effects to create further impact.

- Decide which group's blocking combinations you like best and then rehearse and present your staging of the beginning of Brutus and Cassius's famous quarrel scene to the rest of the class.

▶ **What is this actor playing Brutus suggesting about the character's demeanour at this point in the play?**

**resolved** briefed (does the use of the word 'resolved' also suggest that Brutus hopes his mind will be put at rest?)

**instances** signs (of friendship)

**free** frank, open

**conference** conversation

**he hath used of old** he used to

**enforcèd** strained, forced

**hot at hand** keen to be off at first

**mettle** ability

*Low march within* quiet marching drumbeat backstage

**crests** heads

**jades** poor, inferior horses

**Sink in the trial** fail in the test

**horse in general** entire cavalry

**gently** slowly

**sober form** serious manner

**content** satisfied

**griefs** complaints

116

| | |
|---|---|
| PINDARUS | I do not doubt |
| | But that my noble master will appear |
| | Such as he is, full of regard and honour. |
| BRUTUS | He is not doubted. |

*[Brutus and Lucilius draw apart]*

BRUTUS                    A word, Lucilius,
How he received you; let me be resolved.

LUCILIUS    With courtesy and with respect enough,
But not with such familiar instances,
Nor with such free and friendly conference,
As he hath used of old.

BRUTUS                              Thou hast described
A hot friend cooling. Ever note, Lucilius,
When love begins to sicken and decay
It useth an enforcèd ceremony.
There are no tricks in plain and simple faith,
But hollow men, like horses hot at hand,
Make gallant show and promise of their mettle.

*Low march within*

But when they should endure the bloody spur
They fall their crests, and like deceitful jades
Sink in the trial. Comes his army on?

LUCILIUS    They mean this night in Sardis to be quartered.
The greater part, the horse in general,
Are come with Cassius.

*Enter* CASSIUS *and his powers*

BRUTUS                              Hark, he is arrived.
March gently on to meet him.

CASSIUS    Stand ho!

BRUTUS    Stand ho, speak the word along!

1 SOLDIER    Stand!

2 SOLDIER    Stand!

3 SOLDIER    Stand!

CASSIUS    Most noble brother, you have done me wrong.

BRUTUS    Judge me, you gods! Wrong I mine enemies?
And if not so, how should I wrong a brother?

CASSIUS    Brutus, this sober form of yours hides wrongs,
And when you do them –

BRUTUS                              Cassius, be content,
Speak your griefs softly, I do know you well.

10

15

20

25

30

35

40

Brutus and Cassius enter Brutus's tent for privacy. Inside, Brutus charges Cassius with greed and corruption. Cassius says that if such accusations came from anyone but Brutus, he would kill them.

## Stagecraft

### Quarrelling in private

In lines 43–7, Brutus urges that any heated discussion with Cassius should take place away from the watching soldiers ('in my tent').

- Sketch a set design that could quickly transform the public space of Brutus's camp (Scene 2) into the 'tent' of Scene 3. Notice that Lucilius and Titinius are instructed to 'guard our door', so they must be visible. Add your sketch to your Director's Journal.

## 1 Animated discussion? (in pairs)

Brutus and Cassius's quarrel holds the stage up to line 162 in a scene of strong emotion that must be carefully 'orchestrated' by the actors. Too loud and it will exhaust the audience; too restrained and it will not catch the passion of their exchange.

- Imagine you have a volume control calibrated 1–10, where normal conversation registers 4. Talk together about the scene and mark down volume levels at particular points. Remember that a big climax could be conveyed by silence, or intense emotion with a whisper.
- Record a dramatic part of the scene to match your planned version.

## Write about it

### Canvas walls have ears (in fours)

Brutus and Cassius's quarrel could decide the fate of the Republican cause, which can only succeed if they are allies.

**a** Two of you read aloud lines 1–123, pausing every so often so that the other two (as Lucilius and Titinius on guard, listening through the tent's thin walls) can reflect on what is being said and jot down their thoughts. Focus on the point where it comes dangerously near to a fight and how Brutus and Cassius manage to avoid it.

**b** Lucilius and Titinius should use their notes to help script a conversation between the two guards. The students playing Brutus and Cassius at the same time write a summary in modern English of their grievances against each other.

**c** Compare all perspectives of Brutus and Cassius's quarrel. Which man has the stronger case and who handles the quarrel better? Why?

**enlarge** explain fully

**charges** troops

**noted** publicly criticised

**praying on his side** siding with him

**slighted off** shamefully ignored

**every nice offence … comment** every trivial fault is criticised

**condemned to have** accused of

**itching palm** greed for money

**mart your offices** award jobs and positions

**honours this corruption** makes your financial corruption seem respectable

**chastisement** criticism, telling off

Before the eyes of both our armies here –
Which should perceive nothing but love from us –
Let us not wrangle. Bid them move away.                    45
Then in my tent, Cassius, enlarge your griefs
And I will give you audience.

CASSIUS                              Pindarus,
Bid our commanders lead their charges off
A little from this ground.

BRUTUS     Lucius, do you the like, and let no man            50
Come to our tent till we have done our conference.
Let Lucilius and Titinius guard our door.

*Exeunt [all but] Brutus and Cassius*

# Act 4 Scene 3
## In Brutus' tent

CASSIUS     That you have wronged me doth appear in this:
You have condemned and noted Lucius Pella
For taking bribes here of the Sardians,
Wherein my letters, praying on his side,
Because I knew the man, was slighted off.                    5

BRUTUS     You wronged yourself to write in such a case.

CASSIUS     In such a time as this it is not meet
That every nice offence should bear his comment.

BRUTUS     Let me tell you, Cassius, you yourself
Are much condemned to have an itching palm,                  10
To sell and mart your offices for gold
To undeservers.

CASSIUS                    I, an itching palm?
You know that you are Brutus that speaks this,
Or, by the gods, this speech were else your last.

BRUTUS     The name of Cassius honours this corruption,       15
And chastisement doth therefore hide his head.

CASSIUS     Chastisement?

BRUTUS     Remember March, the Ides of March remember:
Did not great Julius bleed for justice' sake?

Caesar was killed to stamp out corruption, says Brutus. Cassius claims greater experience as a soldier. Brutus scorns Cassius's bad temper.

# Language in the play

## The balance of power (in pairs)

When two characters quarrel, they often fire rhetorical questions (see pp. 185–6) at each other in order to score points and express indignation. There are three on the previous page and a further eleven in the script opposite.

- Take parts as Brutus and Cassius and claim your rhetorical questions. Practise speaking them aloud in a variety of ways in order to maximise their emotional impact. Then, whilst Cassius sits in the centre of the room Brutus should circle him, speaking only his questions to the silent Cassius. Swap positions so that Cassius gets his chance.
- Afterwards, talk about the effects created. It's a fair point to note that Brutus has more of the questions, but who has the more powerful ones? Why?

The rhythms of speech in this scene – as much as what is said – suggest the characters' strength or weakness. In addition, they suggest which character holds control over the dialogue at any one time.

- Read carefully from 'I am a soldier, I' (line 30) to line 42. In this passage you will find many short and broken lines. Where the pauses fall will be crucial to the balance between Brutus and Cassius. Try reading it in different ways and decide which sounds right. What do your pauses tell you about which character holds the balance of power at various points?

# Write about it

## The ghost of Caesar

Later in this scene (at line 274) the ghost of Caesar appears to Brutus (see p. 136 for more detail on the apparition).

- Imagine that prior to his appearance as a ghost, Caesar witnesses all that goes on between the conspirators. As Caesar, write your thoughts as you listen to the Republicans' discussion. What do you think about the behaviour and viewpoints of the two men who were so instrumental in your downfall? Do you have any sympathy? Try to match your style of writing to the Caesar that you defined earlier.

What villain touched his body, that did stab          20
And not for justice? What, shall one of us,
That struck the foremost man of all this world,
But for supporting robbers, shall we now
Contaminate our fingers with base bribes
And sell the mighty space of our large honours     25
For so much trash as may be graspèd thus?
I had rather be a dog and bay the moon
Than such a Roman.

CASSIUS        Brutus, bait not me,
I'll not endure it. You forget yourself
To hedge me in. I am a soldier, I,          30
Older in practice, abler than yourself
To make conditions.

BRUTUS        Go to, you are not, Cassius!

CASSIUS  I am.

BRUTUS  I say you are not.

CASSIUS  Urge me no more, I shall forget myself.     35
Have mind upon your health, tempt me no farther!

BRUTUS  Away, slight man!

CASSIUS  Is't possible?

BRUTUS      Hear me, for I will speak.
Must I give way and room to your rash choler?
Shall I be frighted when a madman stares?     40

CASSIUS  O ye gods, ye gods, must I endure all this?

BRUTUS  All this? Ay, more. Fret till your proud heart break.
Go show your slaves how choleric you are,
And make your bondmen tremble. Must I budge?
Must I observe you? Must I stand and crouch     45
Under your testy humour? By the gods,
You shall digest the venom of your spleen
Though it do split you. For, from this day forth,
I'll use you for my mirth, yea, for my laughter,
When you are waspish.

CASSIUS       Is it come to this?     50

BRUTUS  You say you are a better soldier:
Let it appear so, make your vaunting true
And it shall please me well. For mine own part
I shall be glad to learn of noble men.

Brutus shrugs off Cassius's temper but is angry that Cassius refused him gold for his troops. Cassius says friends should not magnify each other's faults.

## 1 Money! Different attitudes (in pairs)

The quarrel between Brutus and Cassius in Act 4 Scene 3 is primarily over money to pay their troops. Look at what Brutus says about the matter in lines 69–82, and then in lines 100–5, where Cassius reveals something of his attitude to money.

- Read the two speeches carefully several times. Make notes on what the characters actually say, and then talk together about how Shakespeare uses the issue of money to reveal the contrasting characters of Brutus and Cassius.
- Now look back to Act 3 Scene 2, lines 120–50, and Act 4 Scene 1, lines 7–27, to see what is revealed of Antony's attitude to money. Add further details to your notes.
- Finally, write a short paragraph comparing Antony's views with those of Brutus and Cassius.

## 2 Design a coin (in small groups)

In Caesar's time, Roman generals often owned their armies and had to pay them out of their own pockets. Generals often minted coins with their own 'heads and tails' on them. Like today's coins, they carried designs that symbolised something important to those who minted them.

- As a design consultancy, come up with a series of designs for coin 'tails' for Brutus or Cassius. Your designs should make the soldiers think about what they are fighting for when they get paid. Write a short explanation beside each design.

**durst not** dared not
**moved me** irritated me
**tempted him** provoked him

**honesty** uprightness, integrity

**respect not** take no notice of

**indirection** dishonesty

**covetous** greedy
**rascal counters** rubbishy coins

**rived** broken

| | | |
|---|---|---|
| CASSIUS | You wrong me every way, you wrong me, Brutus. | 55 |
| | I said an elder soldier, not a better. | |
| | Did I say 'better'? | |
| BRUTUS | If you did, I care not. | |
| CASSIUS | When Caesar lived, he durst not thus have moved me. | |
| BRUTUS | Peace, peace, you durst not so have tempted him. | |
| CASSIUS | I durst not? | 60 |
| BRUTUS | No. | |
| CASSIUS | What? Durst not tempt him? | |
| BRUTUS | For your life you durst not. | |
| CASSIUS | Do not presume too much upon my love, | |
| | I may do that I shall be sorry for. | |
| BRUTUS | You have done that you should be sorry for. | 65 |
| | There is no terror, Cassius, in your threats, | |
| | For I am armed so strong in honesty | |
| | That they pass by me as the idle wind, | |
| | Which I respect not. I did send to you | |
| | For certain sums of gold, which you denied me, | 70 |
| | For I can raise no money by vile means. | |
| | By heaven, I had rather coin my heart | |
| | And drop my blood for drachmaes than to wring | |
| | From the hard hands of peasants their vile trash | |
| | By any indirection. I did send | 75 |
| | To you for gold to pay my legions, | |
| | Which you denied me. Was that done like Cassius? | |
| | Should I have answered Caius Cassius so? | |
| | When Marcus Brutus grows so covetous | |
| | To lock such rascal counters from his friends, | 80 |
| | Be ready, gods, with all your thunderbolts, | |
| | Dash him to pieces! | |
| CASSIUS | I denied you not. | |
| BRUTUS | You did. | |
| CASSIUS | I did not. He was but a fool that brought | |
| | My answer back. Brutus hath rived my heart. | 85 |
| | A friend should bear his friend's infirmities, | |
| | But Brutus makes mine greater than they are. | |
| BRUTUS | I do not, till you practise them on me. | |

Stung by Brutus's criticism, Cassius asks Brutus to kill him. Brutus relents, admits blame himself and resolves to ignore Cassius's temper in future.

## Characters

### Cassius: a change of heart (in pairs)

Line 93 seems to mark a turning point in Cassius and Brutus's quarrel. Cassius openly expresses his weariness at having his faults picked over, and then offers his dagger to Brutus and urges him to 'Strike as thou didst at Caesar'.

a   Work through Cassius's speech (lines 93–107). Then write advice for the actor playing Cassius about how he should deliver his lines. In particular, focus on the dagger and how he offers his 'naked breast' to Brutus. Rehearse the lines and then take turns to perform the speech.

b   Write a paragraph about what this speech shows about Cassius's character and his relationship with Brutus.

## Write about it

### Brutus's private thoughts

After Cassius's outburst at lines 93–107, Cassius and Brutus suddenly become firm friends, and so they remain. The cultivation of friendship was an important duty in the ancient world. In the year of Caesar's death, Cicero wrote in his essay 'Of Friendship':

> Take away the bond of kindly feeling from the world, and no house or city can stand. Even the fields will no longer be cultivated. If that sounds exaggerated, consider the opposite state of affairs: note the disasters that come from dissension and enmity. When there is internal hatred and division, no home or country in the world is strong enough to avoid destruction.

Suppose Brutus were to confide his thoughts in a soliloquy at the end of this scene. Brutus is seen reading a book. Imagine he is reading the passage from Cicero above. He is full of sadness as Cicero has just been killed in the purge instigated by Antony, Octavius and Lepidus.

*   As you read through the rest of the scene, gather material for Brutus's additional soliloquy. In public, Brutus shows true Stoic self-control as he and the generals mull over news from Rome, but alone he can ponder aloud the whole enterprise he undertook with Cassius.

*   When you reach line 274, write Brutus's additional soliloquy.

---

**braved** defied
**Checked** rebuked, told off
**bondman** slave
**conned by rote** learned by heart
**To cast ... teeth** to throw at me

**Pluto's mine** infinite wealth (Pluto, Roman god of the Underworld, was said to possess all mineral wealth)
**If that thou beest** if you are

**dishonour ... humour** your bad behaviour will be tolerated

**much enforcèd** when struck violently

**blood ill-tempered** an unbalanced disposition
**vexeth** angers

**bear with me** be patient with me

**chides** nags

| | |
|---|---|
| CASSIUS | You love me not. |
| BRUTUS |                     I do not like your faults. |
| CASSIUS | A friendly eye could never see such faults. |

90

| | |
|---|---|
| BRUTUS | A flatterer's would not, though they do appear |
| | As huge as high Olympus. |
| CASSIUS | Come, Antony, and young Octavius, come, |
| | Revenge yourselves alone on Cassius, |
| | For Cassius is a-weary of the world: |

95

Hated by one he loves, braved by his brother,
Checked like a bondman, all his faults observed,
Set in a notebook, learned, and conned by rote,
To cast into my teeth. O, I could weep

100

My spirit from mine eyes! There is my dagger
And here my naked breast: within, a heart
Dearer than Pluto's mine, richer than gold.
If that thou beest a Roman take it forth,
I that denied thee gold will give my heart:

105

Strike as thou didst at Caesar. For I know
When thou didst hate him worst thou loved'st him better
Than ever thou loved'st Cassius.

| | |
|---|---|
| BRUTUS |                    Sheathe your dagger. |

Be angry when you will, it shall have scope;
Do what you will, dishonour shall be humour.
O Cassius, you are yokèd with a lamb

110

That carries anger as the flint bears fire,
Who, much enforcèd, shows a hasty spark
And straight is cold again.

| | |
|---|---|
| CASSIUS |                Hath Cassius lived |

To be but mirth and laughter to his Brutus
When grief and blood ill-tempered vexeth him?

115

| | |
|---|---|
| BRUTUS | When I spoke that, I was ill-tempered too. |
| CASSIUS | Do you confess so much? Give me your hand. |
| BRUTUS | And my heart too. |
| CASSIUS |            O Brutus! |
| BRUTUS |                 What's the matter? |
| CASSIUS | Have not you love enough to bear with me |
| | When that rash humour which my mother gave me |

120

| | |
|---|---|
| | Makes me forgetful? |
| BRUTUS |                Yes, Cassius, and from henceforth |

When you are over-earnest with your Brutus,
He'll think your mother chides, and leave you so.

A poet tries to intercede and reconcile Brutus and Cassius. With uncharacteristic fury, Brutus throws him out. Cassius is surprised. Brutus explains that his wife is dead.

## 1 Should the Poet be cut? (in threes)

The brief episode where the Poet interrupts Brutus and Cassius's conversation (lines 124–38) follows pretty closely the Greek historian Plutarch's account of events. Some argue that his intervention is used to highlight the increasing turbulence in Brutus's mind and actions. But Shakespeare could easily have left him out.

- Talk together about a) why the Poet was included and b) what the play might gain from cutting his part. Share your thoughts with other groups.

### Themes

#### The importance of language

Act 3 focused closely on the power of language and its capacity to dictate the course of history (although it ended with the death of a wordsmith: Cinna the poet). Shakespeare chooses to introduce another poet in this scene, who seeks to reconcile the sparring Cassius and Brutus. Cassius labels him as a 'cynic' and Brutus exclaims: 'What should the wars do with these jigging fools?'

- What do Cassius's and Brutus's attitudes to the poet and what he represents suggest about their characters? Write a short paragraph in response.

## 2 Portia's final moments

a **Show her death (in pairs)** The audience does not see Portia's death; Brutus reports it. One of you is Brutus, the other Portia. Brutus reads aloud lines 152–6; Portia silently enacts the events described, ending at a tableau that captures the moment of her death.

b **Portia's suicide note (in threes)** Talk together about what could have forced Portia to commit suicide and why she decided to do it this way. (Plutarch records how Portia put burning coals into her mouth and choked to death.) Each of you writes her suicide note. Then show your note to the others in your group and discuss similarities and differences.

c **Why does Portia die off stage? (in small groups)** Talk together about the reasons Shakespeare might have had for not showing Portia's death as part of the main action of the play. Be ready to contribute your strongest idea to a whole-class discussion.

**stay** prevent

**vildly** vilely, wretchedly
**cynic** follower of Cynic philosophy (see p. 172)
**sirrah** a mildly offensive term of address
**humour** eccentric behaviour
**when … his time** when he can choose the right time to show it
**jigging** rhyming

**your philosophy** (Brutus was a Stoic – see p. 173)
**give place** give way
**accidental evils** chance, bad luck

**scaped** escaped
**crossed** argued with
**insupportable** unbearable
**Impatient of** unable to endure

**tidings** news
**fell distract** became mad

*Enter a* POET, [LUCILIUS *and Titinius*]

| | |
|---|---|
| POET | Let me go in to see the generals. |
| | There is some grudge between 'em, 'tis not meet       125 |
| | They be alone. |
| LUCILIUS | You shall not come to them. |
| POET | Nothing but death shall stay me. |
| CASSIUS | How now, what's the matter? |
| POET | For shame, you generals, what do you mean?       130 |
| | Love and be friends, as two such men should be, |
| | For I have seen more years, I'm sure, than ye. |
| CASSIUS | Ha, ha, how vildly doth this cynic rhyme! |
| BRUTUS | Get you hence, sirrah; saucy fellow, hence! |
| CASSIUS | Bear with him, Brutus, 'tis his fashion.       135 |
| BRUTUS | I'll know his humour when he knows his time. |
| | What should the wars do with these jigging fools? |
| | Companion, hence! |
| CASSIUS |                Away, away, be gone! |

*Exit Poet*

| | |
|---|---|
| BRUTUS | Lucilius and Titinius, bid the commanders |
| | Prepare to lodge their companies tonight.       140 |
| CASSIUS | And come yourselves, and bring Messala with you |
| | Immediately to us. |

[*Exeunt Lucilius and Titinius*]

| | |
|---|---|
| BRUTUS | [*To Lucius within*]   Lucius, a bowl of wine! |
| CASSIUS | I did not think you could have been so angry. |
| BRUTUS | O Cassius, I am sick of many griefs. |
| CASSIUS | Of your philosophy you make no use       145 |
| | If you give place to accidental evils. |
| BRUTUS | No man bears sorrow better. Portia is dead. |
| CASSIUS | Ha? Portia? |
| BRUTUS | She is dead. |
| CASSIUS | How scaped I killing when I crossed you so?       150 |
| | O insupportable and touching loss! |
| | Upon what sickness? |
| BRUTUS |              Impatient of my absence, |
| | And grief that young Octavius with Mark Antony |
| | Have made themselves so strong – for with her death |
| | That tidings came. With this she fell distract       155 |
| | And, her attendants absent, swallowed fire. |

Reconciled, Brutus and Cassius drink wine. Titinius and Messala enter to report that the Triumvirate has executed Cicero and a hundred other senators, and now approach Philippi.

## 1 Friends reunited (in threes)

In the gathering darkness suggested by Lucius's tapers, Brutus and Cassius drain their bowl of wine. As he would at home, Lucius brings hospitality to Cassius even though they are in a tent many hundreds of miles from Rome and Portia is dead. Perhaps Shakespeare uses this moment to echo Act 2 Scene 2, where Brutus and Caesar drank together on the morning of Caesar's assassination.

- Read and mime the actions from Lucius's entrance to his exit (lines 158–62). Feel your way into the characters' minds as you act. At the end of your mime, pause to speak aloud the exact thoughts in your character's head.

## Themes

### Public versus private (in pairs)

In a play that contains many great public events, the reconciliation between Brutus and Cassius stands out as one of the more private and intimate moments.

- Discuss why you think Shakespeare focuses so intensely on this episode at this point in the play.

## Write about it

### Brutus's grief

Brutus tells that he is 'sick of many griefs' at the thought of Portia's death. But he gives away very little about his deeper feelings on hearing of her agonising suicide. In fact, he dismisses talk of her with an abrupt: 'Speak no more of her.'

- Imagine that later that evening, alone in his tent, he reads Portia's suicide note, which you were asked to produce in Activity 2 on page 126. Write Brutus's deeper and more intimate reflections on the loss of his wife. Look back at their dialogue in Act 2 Scene 1 for glimpses of the kind of relationship they shared.

o'erswell spills over

call in … necessities
consider what we must do

Bending their expedition
moving rapidly

Philippi where the Republicans
were finally defeated in 42 BC

selfsame tenor very similar news

proscription … outlawry
the 'proscriptio' (see p. 173) was a
list of Roman 'outlaws' who were
put to death and then whose goods
were confiscated

CASSIUS    And died so?

BRUTUS                    Even so.

CASSIUS                            O ye immortal gods!

*Enter* BOY [LUCIUS] *with wine and tapers*

BRUTUS    Speak no more of her. Give me a bowl of wine.
           In this I bury all unkindness, Cassius. *Drinks*

CASSIUS    My heart is thirsty for that noble pledge.                    160
           Fill, Lucius, till the wine o'erswell the cup,
           I cannot drink too much of Brutus' love. [*Drinks*]

                                                        [*Exit Lucius*]

*Enter* TITINIUS *and* MESSALA

BRUTUS    Come in, Titinius; welcome, good Messala.
           Now sit we close about this taper here
           And call in question our necessities.                        165

CASSIUS    Portia, art thou gone?

BRUTUS                            No more, I pray you.
           Messala, I have here receivèd letters
           That young Octavius and Mark Antony
           Come down upon us with a mighty power,
           Bending their expedition toward Philippi.                    170

MESSALA    Myself have letters of the selfsame tenor.

BRUTUS    With what addition?

MESSALA    That by proscription and bills of outlawry
           Octavius, Antony, and Lepidus
           Have put to death an hundred senators.                       175

BRUTUS    Therein our letters do not well agree:
           Mine speak of seventy senators that died
           By their proscriptions, Cicero being one.

CASSIUS    Cicero one?

MESSALA                    Cicero is dead,
           And by that order of proscription.                          180
           Had you your letters from your wife, my lord?

BRUTUS    No, Messala.

MESSALA    Nor nothing in your letters writ of her?

BRUTUS    Nothing, Messala.

MESSALA                    That, methinks, is strange.

Brutus philosophically receives news of Portia's death, then turns to military tactics. Take battle to the enemy, he says. Let battle come to us, says Cassius. Brutus insists his plan is best.

# 1 'Free Rome': social networking (in small groups)

Republicans at home and in exile stay in close touch. Those at home keep the Republican flame burning among the people; those abroad raise armies to recapture Rome.

- Imagine there is a communication network to keep all Republicans informed. Consider how you might utilise postings on social media sites, emails and text messages. Then put together a series of electronic texts that emphasise the horrors of Triumvirate rule, yet celebrate Republican achievement and give heart to those who carry on the struggle. Use excerpts from the play as part of the text you write, stage some photographs and invent interviews with leading Republicans.

# 2 Talking tactics (in pairs)

Although they are now reconciled as friends, Brutus and Cassius fall to a disagreement again – this time over the military tactics for the next day's battle.

**a** Take parts and read their discussion (lines 198–225). Then, continuing in role as the two men, improvise an extended discussion based on the core arguments you originally proposed.

**b** Brutus again wins the argument. In your pair, discuss how important you think this is to the way in which the scene is developing.

## Language in the play

### 'a tide in the affairs of men' (in pairs)

In the days of sail, trading ships often had to wait for the right wind and tide. Too long a wait and the cargo might lose its value, especially if it were perishable. Sail at the wrong time and the ship could be wrecked. Either way investors would lose money.

**a** Talk together about whether what Brutus says in lines 218–24 is true of life as you know it. Can you think of any real-life examples of individuals you might mention in support of the conclusions you reach?

**b** Write a short paragraph analysing the effectiveness of this very famous extended metaphor about seizing the initiative at the right moment.

**once** at some point

**Even so** just so
**I have … in art as you** I am as learned [in Stoicism] as you

**waste** exhaust
**offence** damage, harm

**of force** of necessity

**Do stand … forced affection** show only a grudging loyalty

**new added** newly reinforced

**tried the utmost of** made the greatest demands on

**Omitted** (i.e. if they fail to take the opportunity)
**bound in** limited, confined to

| | | |
|---|---|---|
| BRUTUS | Why ask you? Hear you aught of her in yours? | 185 |
| MESSALA | No, my lord. | |
| BRUTUS | Now as you are a Roman tell me true. | |
| MESSALA | Then like a Roman bear the truth I tell, | |
| | For certain she is dead, and by strange manner. | |
| BRUTUS | Why, farewell, Portia. We must die, Messala. | 190 |
| | With meditating that she must die once, | |
| | I have the patience to endure it now. | |
| MESSALA | Even so, great men great losses should endure. | |
| CASSIUS | I have as much of this in art as you, | |
| | But yet my nature could not bear it so. | 195 |
| BRUTUS | Well, to our work alive. What do you think | |
| | Of marching to Philippi presently? | |
| CASSIUS | I do not think it good. | |
| BRUTUS | Your reason? | |
| CASSIUS | This it is: | |
| | 'Tis better that the enemy seek us, | |
| | So shall he waste his means, weary his soldiers, | 200 |
| | Doing himself offence, whilst we, lying still, | |
| | Are full of rest, defence, and nimbleness. | |
| BRUTUS | Good reasons must of force give place to better: | |
| | The people 'twixt Philippi and this ground | |
| | Do stand but in a forced affection, | 205 |
| | For they have grudged us contribution. | |
| | The enemy, marching along by them, | |
| | By them shall make a fuller number up, | |
| | Come on refreshed, new added, and encouraged, | |
| | From which advantage shall we cut him off | 210 |
| | If at Philippi we do face him there, | |
| | These people at our back. | |
| CASSIUS | Hear me, good brother. | |
| BRUTUS | Under your pardon. You must note beside | |
| | That we have tried the utmost of our friends, | |
| | Our legions are brimful, our cause is ripe; | 215 |
| | The enemy increaseth every day, | |
| | We, at the height, are ready to decline. | |
| | There is a tide in the affairs of men | |
| | Which, taken at the flood, leads on to fortune; | |
| | Omitted, all the voyage of their life | 220 |
| | Is bound in shallows and in miseries. | |

Cassius agrees to march to face the enemy at Philippi. After a harmonious leave-taking, Brutus is left to sleep. He asks Lucius for music.

## Stagecraft

### The last night of the Roman Republic (in fives)

The story of what followed Julius Caesar's assassination would probably have been well known to Shakespeare's audience. Therefore they would be aware that this part of the play signals the calm before the storm – the night before the decisive battle that will destroy the Republican forces.

**a** In your group, read lines 226–74 (the entrance of Caesar's ghost). What clues are there in the text that after the frenzied arguments of earlier, the mood is now of peaceful relaxation, quietness and reflection?

**b** A few basic stage directions have been added to Shakespeare's original script. Now, as collaborative directors, add as many more as you can in order to show how your actors will use movement, gesture and voice to enhance the mood created by the language.

**c** A significant number of lines 30–42 in this scene were short and broken. Here, lines 229–40 are much more regular, though nearly all shared. Read both sets of lines with careful regard for the rhythm. Talk together about the possible reasons why Shakespeare created such contrasting effects.

**d** Brutus begins this episode with 'The deep of night is crept upon our talk' (line 226). Produce a lighting design for the episode which clearly reflects and enhances the mood you are striving to create. Add it to your Director's Journal.

## 1 Question Cassius (whole class)

Cassius begins the scene in an angry mood, even threatening that if he were accused in such terms by anyone other than Brutus, he would kill them (lines 13–14). Just before he exits, he calls Brutus his 'dear brother' and pledges eternal companionship (lines 233–5).

- Put Cassius in the hot-seat. Question him about how he now feels about Brutus and the state of their relationship.

**when it serves** when the opportunity arises

**ventures** investments, opportunities, things we have risked

**with your will go on** as you wish, we shall advance

**nature … necessity** our bodies need caring for

**niggard** put off temporarily

**hence** go from this place

**repose** rest

**instrument** musical instrument (probably a lute)

**drowsily** sleepily

**Poor knave** poor lad

**o'erwatched** weary from lack of sleep

On such a full sea are we now afloat,
And we must take the current when it serves
Or lose our ventures.

CASSIUS                      Then with your will go on,
We'll along ourselves and meet them at Philippi.      225

BRUTUS    The deep of night is crept upon our talk,
And nature must obey necessity,
Which we will niggard with a little rest.
There is no more to say?

CASSIUS                      No more. Good night.
Early tomorrow will we rise and hence.      230

BRUTUS    Lucius!

*Enter* LUCIUS

My gown.

                              [*Exit Lucius*]

             Farewell, good Messala.
Good night, Titinius. Noble, noble Cassius,
Good night and good repose.

CASSIUS                O my dear brother!
This was an ill beginning of the night.
Never come such division 'tween our souls!      235
Let it not, Brutus.

*Enter* LUCIUS *with the gown*

BRUTUS             Everything is well.
CASSIUS    Good night, my lord.
BRUTUS                 Good night, good brother.
TITINIUS AND MESSALA    Good night, Lord Brutus.
BRUTUS                   Farewell every one.

              *Exeunt* [*Cassius, Titinius, Messala*]

Give me the gown. Where is thy instrument?
LUCIUS    Here in the tent.
BRUTUS            What, thou speak'st drowsily.      240
Poor knave, I blame thee not, thou art o'erwatched.
Call Claudio and some other of my men,
I'll have them sleep on cushions in my tent.
LUCIUS    Varrus and Claudio!

## 1 Compose Lucius's song (in pairs)

No words or music survive for Lucius's song, and as musical directors you have to supply them.

• Think about the mood needed and the right words to express it. Compose your own music or set your words to a tune you know already. Then explain to another pair the reasons behind your choice.

## Characters

### Brutus: what's your reaction? (in pairs)

Brutus has dealt stoically with his wife Portia's death and is reconciled to Cassius. Again, he has overruled Cassius, urging action rather than caution. Now Shakespeare shows him treating his servant Lucius considerately and generously.

• Together, look back at this scene and consider how Brutus acts, what he says and what is said about him. Then each write a short paragraph outlining your response to the character of Brutus that Shakespeare presents. Remember to support all your points with quotations. After writing, compare your versions.

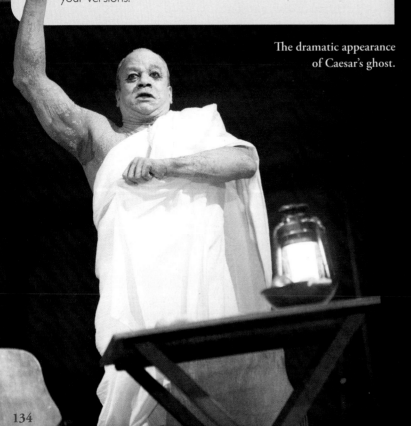

The dramatic appearance of Caesar's ghost.

**raise** rouse

**otherwise bethink me** change my mind

**sought for so** searched for

**strain** tune, song

**an't** if it

**I should not … might** I should not ask you to do more than you are capable of

**young bloods** hot-blooded youngsters

**murd'rous** death-like

**leaden mace** heavy staff (used by a bailiff arresting someone)

**ill** badly, poorly

*Enter* VARRUS *and* CLAUDIO

| | | |
|---|---|---|
| VARRUS | Calls my lord? | 245 |
| BRUTUS | I pray you, sirs, lie in my tent and sleep, | |
| | It may be I shall raise you by and by | |
| | On business to my brother Cassius. | |
| VARRUS | So please you, we will stand and watch your pleasure. | |
| BRUTUS | I will not have it so. Lie down, good sirs, | 250 |
| | It may be I shall otherwise bethink me. | |

*[Varrus and Claudio lie down]*

| | | |
|---|---|---|
| | Look, Lucius, here's the book I sought for so, | |
| | I put it in the pocket of my gown. | |
| LUCIUS | I was sure your lordship did not give it me. | |
| BRUTUS | Bear with me, good boy, I am much forgetful. | 255 |
| | Canst thou hold up thy heavy eyes awhile | |
| | And touch thy instrument a strain or two? | |
| LUCIUS | Ay, my lord, an't please you. | |
| BRUTUS | It does, my boy. | |
| | I trouble thee too much, but thou art willing. | |
| LUCIUS | It is my duty, sir. | 260 |
| BRUTUS | I should not urge thy duty past thy might, | |
| | I know young bloods look for a time of rest. | |
| LUCIUS | I have slept, my lord, already. | |
| BRUTUS | It was well done and thou shalt sleep again, | |
| | I will not hold thee long. If I do live | 265 |
| | I will be good to thee. | |

*Music, and a song*

| | | |
|---|---|---|
| | This is a sleepy tune. O murd'rous slumber, | |
| | Layest thou thy leaden mace upon my boy, | |
| | That plays thee music? Gentle knave, good night, | |
| | I will not do thee so much wrong to wake thee. | 270 |
| | If thou dost nod thou break'st thy instrument. | |
| | I'll take it from thee and, good boy, good night. | |
| | Let me see, let me see, is not the leaf turned down | |
| | Where I left reading? Here it is, I think. | |

*Enter the* GHOST OF CAESAR

| | | |
|---|---|---|
| | How ill this taper burns! Ha, who comes here? | 275 |

Promising a second appearance, the ghost disappears. Brutus wakes the servants and orders immediate preparations for marching to Philippi to do battle with Antony and Octavius.

# 1 Caesar's ghost

Ghosts were highly significant for Elizabethans. They believed that ghosts could be good or bad, silent or talkative, truthful or deceptive. Evil spirits could disguise themselves to mislead mortals. If you knew how to talk to a ghost, you could gain valuable (or misleading) information about the past, present or future.

**a** **What should Caesar's ghost look like? (in small groups)**
Every director must decide how to portray the 'monstrous apparition': Bloodstains? Larger than life? A floating head? Voiceover rather than physical presence? Talk together about how you could present Caesar's ghost to make the greatest impression on the audience. Then write a 'design brief' for your Director's Journal giving justification for the choices you have made.

**b** **The first appearance of Caesar's ghost (in pairs)** Read or stage lines 273–88 as dramatically as you can. The ghost has only sixteen words. Make each of them count!

**c** **'Art thou some god, some angel, or some devil?'**
Write six more lines to add to the end of Brutus's speech (lines 275–81), beginning 'If you are a god …'

**d** **Why does only Brutus see the ghost? (in threes)**
After the ghost's exit (at line 286) Brutus is desperate to check with his companions whether they, too, have seen Caesar's spirit. But Shakespeare deliberately has the ghost appear just to Brutus (Lucius, Varro and Claudio are asleep). Try to come up with two or three possible reasons Shakespeare might have had for staging the episode in this way.

# 2 Fluctuating moods (in pairs)

The final scene of Act 4 is both long and varied in dramatic mood, with some episodes of heightened dramatic intensity and others more reflective.

- Split the scene into episodes. Then draw a 'mood graph', with a y-axis numbered −10 to +10 to reflect the dramatic mood in each episode. Label the x-axis with the different episodes. Allocate a number to each epidode showing its dramatic intensity (+10 for extreme dramatic intensity; −10 for extremely reflective).
- Display your graphs for other pairs to look at. How similar are they?

**upon me** towards me

**stare** stand on end

**false** out of tune

**set on his powers** get his forces moving

**betimes** early in the morning

|  | I think it is the weakness of mine eyes |  |
|---|---|---|
|  | That shapes this monstrous apparition. |  |
|  | It comes upon me. Art thou any thing? |  |
|  | Art thou some god, some angel, or some devil, |  |
|  | That mak'st my blood cold and my hair to stare? | 280 |
|  | Speak to me what thou art. |  |
| GHOST | Thy evil spirit, Brutus. |  |
| BRUTUS | Why com'st thou? |  |
| GHOST | To tell thee thou shalt see me at Philippi. |  |
| BRUTUS | Well, then I shall see thee again? |  |
| GHOST | Ay, at Philippi. | 285 |
| BRUTUS | Why, I will see thee at Philippi then. |  |

*[Exit Ghost]*

|  | Now I have taken heart thou vanishest. |  |
|---|---|---|
|  | Ill spirit, I would hold more talk with thee. |  |
|  | Boy, Lucius! Varrus! Claudio! Sirs, awake! |  |
|  | Claudio! | 290 |
| LUCIUS | The strings, my lord, are false. |  |
| BRUTUS | He thinks he still is at his instrument. |  |
|  | Lucius, awake! |  |
| LUCIUS | My lord? |  |
| BRUTUS | Didst thou dream, Lucius, that thou so cried'st out? | 295 |
| LUCIUS | My lord, I do not know that I did cry. |  |
| BRUTUS | Yes, that thou didst. Didst thou see anything? |  |
| LUCIUS | Nothing, my lord. |  |
| BRUTUS | Sleep again, Lucius. Sirrah Claudio! |  |
|  | *[To Varrus]* Fellow, thou, awake! | 300 |
| VARRUS | My lord? |  |
| CLAUDIO | My lord? |  |
| BRUTUS | Why did you so cry out, sirs, in your sleep? |  |
| BOTH | Did we, my lord? |  |
| BRUTUS | Ay. Saw you anything? |  |
| VARRUS | No, my lord, I saw nothing. |  |
| CLAUDIO | Nor I, my lord. | 305 |
| BRUTUS | Go and commend me to my brother Cassius. |  |
|  | Bid him set on his powers betimes before, |  |
|  | And we will follow. |  |
| BOTH | It shall be done, my lord. |  |

*Exeunt*

# Looking back at Act 4
## Activities for groups or individuals

## 1 From Rome to Asia

The action of the play switches at the beginning of Act 4 Scene 2 from Rome to Asia.

- Work out a set design that could quite easily accommodate the change in location required. Base your ideas on the opportunities afforded by a modern theatre. Add notes to explain how you would manage any scene-shifting so that the attention of the audience is not lost.

## 2 Is updating possible?

Some productions of *Julius Caesar* are given a setting in more modern times, for example Fascist Italy in the 1930s.

- Imagine that you have been invited to direct a production set in the twenty-first century. Take one of the scenes in Act 4, and talk in pairs about a possible modern setting and about appropriate costumes for the characters.

## 3 Comparing alliances

Act 4 shows two sets of political partnerships in operation: Antony, Octavius and Lepidus (Scene 1); Brutus and Cassius (Scenes 2 and 3).

- Look back through the act and make notes on the comparative strengths and weaknesses of the two alliances. After collecting your evidence, write a paragraph on which partnership seems the more cohesive and why.

## 4 Giving Octavius a presence

Octavius does not appear in the play until Act 4, yet by that time he is already established as a key member of the Triumvirate.

- How would you organise the opening of Act 4 to give Octavius a genuine stage presence and authority?

## 5 Keeping up the tempo

Many critics feel that the last two acts of the play are an anticlimax after the superlative assassination and funeral scenes in Act 3.

- Quickly remind yourself of the events of Act 4, and then write notes for your cast about how to sustain the dramatic energy through this act.

## 6 A sense of foreboding

The death of Caesar marked the end of stability in Rome. The Republicans' hopes of 'Peace' are badly threatened in Act 4 and Shakespeare shows that all is not well in Brutus's world: he quarrels with Cassius, Portia commits suicide, and he is visited ominously by Caesar's ghost.

a  Take these points in turn. Write a paragraph about how each is used to increase a sense of foreboding.

b  Look back to earlier acts to consider how Shakespeare has used other ominous episodes to increase dramatic tension.

## 7 Claudio

Claudio is one of Shakespeare's near-silent characters (he has only six words in the last scene).

- Your task is to give him a voice. Study his brief appearance in the play (he enters at line 244) and then write a few entries for his diary. Express his views on life with the Republican army in Asia.

## 8 Brutus and Cassius

Study the photograph opposite in which Cassius (left) and Brutus argue passionately.

a  How effectively does this photograph capture the moment when two friends fall out?

b  In this production, Brutus and Cassius wore modern suits in the first three acts. They now dress in combat fatigues. What do you think the director had in mind?

Octavius and Antony argue about why the enemy has come down to them, and both vie for leadership in the coming battle. Brutus and Cassius enter with their army.

## 1 Leaders disagree – again (in pairs)

The first time we saw Antony and Octavius together they argued. Here, the two men disagree over the advance of the Republican army and over which of them should lead the Triumvirate forces.

**a** Read lines 1–20 (missing out the Messenger's speech), bringing what you know of their characters into your performance.

**b** Antony and Octavius's confrontation mirrors that between Brutus and Cassius in the previous scene. Look back at Act 4 Scene 3. Then, in your Director's Journal, make a list of the similarities between:

- the issues at the centre of the arguments
- the ways in which the four men quarrel.

## Stagecraft

**a** **Battle decisions (in large groups)** This scene calls for the two opposing sides to be on stage with their armies at the same time. How does a director achieve this?

- In your groups, discuss different ideas about how to stage this demanding scene. Remember they have to be practical!
- If enough space is available, act out your best idea for the entrance of both armies. You may want to appoint a director. If more actors are needed, borrow from another group.

**b** **Who's on the right? (in small groups)** Much has been written about how Shakespeare used his source material (see p. 166). Often the changes he made demonstrate where he wants to place the emphasis in his play. According to Plutarch, the battlefield of Philippi looked like this:

The superior general always fought on the right of the line of battle: that's why lines 16–20 are so important. Shakespeare retains who fought whom, but leaves right and left open to directors of the play to decide.

- In your groups, discuss why Shakespeare might have chosen not to specify who fought where.

**proves** turns out to be

**battles** armies

**warn us** challenge us

**Answering … of them** answering a call to battle before we have issued it

**I am in their bosoms** I know what they are thinking

**could be … other places** would rather be somewhere else

**With fearful bravery** with a show of splendour that conceals the fear they are feeling

**face** pretence (of bravery)

**fasten** fix the idea

**bloody sign** red flag (the Roman battle signal)

**lead your battle softly on** advance your army slowly

**cross me** oppose me

**exigent** crisis

**I do not cross you** I am not opposing you perversely

**parley** talks under truce

# Act 5 Scene 1
## The battlefield at Philippi in Greece

*Enter* OCTAVIUS, ANTONY, *and their army*

OCTAVIUS  Now, Antony, our hopes are answerèd.
You said the enemy would not come down
But keep the hills and upper regions.
It proves not so: their battles are at hand,
They mean to warn us at Philippi here,                    5
Answering before we do demand of them.

ANTONY  Tut, I am in their bosoms, and I know
Wherefore they do it. They could be content
To visit other places and come down
With fearful bravery, thinking by this face             10
To fasten in our thoughts that they have courage.
But 'tis not so.

*Enter a* MESSENGER

MESSENGER          Prepare you, generals,
The enemy comes on in gallant show,
Their bloody sign of battle is hung out,
And something to be done immediately.                   15

ANTONY  Octavius, lead your battle softly on
Upon the left hand of the even field.

OCTAVIUS  Upon the right hand I, keep thou the left.

ANTONY  Why do you cross me in this exigent?

OCTAVIUS  I do not cross you, but I will do so.            20

*March*

*Drum. Enter* BRUTUS, CASSIUS, *and their army;* [LUCILIUS,
*Titinius,* MESSALA, *and others*]

BRUTUS  They stand and would have parley.

CASSIUS  Stand fast, Titinius, we must out and talk.

# Language in the play

## Trading insults (in fours)

Before battle commences the four generals meet to parley, but quickly start taunting each other. Brutus's opening salvo 'Words before blows' underlines a major issue: the importance of language to the action of the play. Remember how much plotting and planning there was before Caesar was actually killed in Act 3.

**a** Take parts and read lines 27–66. Begin line 27 at a whisper. With each subsequent speech, increase the volume slightly until you are virtually shouting the lines.

**b** Re-read lines 30–2. Work out exactly what Antony means. How do you think Brutus might react to such a description of events?

**c** In lines 39–44, Antony strikingly creates four powerful, insulting similes to hurl at his enemies. Two of you are Antony. Deliver the lines simultaneously (or with a slight time delay or echo effect) as you circle the seated Brutus and Cassius. How menacing can you make them? Afterwards talk about how the experience felt.

**d** Look back to the assassination of Caesar in Act 3. Now improvise a discussion on the accuracy of Antony's description of the event (which he did not witness) between Antony and three of the conspirators. See if you can include an accusation against Antony of hyperbole (exaggeration).

**e** Choose one of Antony's similes and illustrate it.

# Write about it

## Brutus's thoughts

At line 45, things get worse for Brutus when Cassius turns upon him.

**a** Look back to Act 2 Scene 1 and read lines 154–65 to find out what decision by Brutus Cassius is referring to in lines 46–7.

**b** Imagine that that the action freezes after line 47. Write Brutus's thoughts at that point.

# 1 Is battle inevitable? (in pairs)

Can battle be avoided? Talk together about whether honourable negotiation might be possible and desirable after line 58.

**answer on their charge** wait until they attack

**Make forth** go forward

**posture** nature

**Hybla** Sicilian town famous for its honey

**showed your teeth** grinned insincerely or showed hostility

**might have ruled** could have had his way

**cause** business at hand

**proof** testing

**goes up** is sheathed

**Have added slaughter to** has also been killed by

| | |
|---|---|
| OCTAVIUS | Mark Antony, shall we give sign of battle? |
| ANTONY | No, Caesar, we will answer on their charge. |
| | Make forth, the generals would have some words. |
| OCTAVIUS | Stir not until the signal. |
| BRUTUS | Words before blows; is it so, countrymen? |
| OCTAVIUS | Not that we love words better, as you do. |
| BRUTUS | Good words are better than bad strokes, Octavius. |
| ANTONY | In your bad strokes, Brutus, you give good words. |
| | Witness the hole you made in Caesar's heart, |
| | Crying, 'Long live, hail, Caesar!' |
| CASSIUS | Antony, |
| | The posture of your blows are yet unknown; |
| | But for your words, they rob the Hybla bees |
| | And leave them honeyless. |
| ANTONY | Not stingless too? |
| BRUTUS | O yes, and soundless too, |
| | For you have stolen their buzzing, Antony, |
| | And very wisely threat before you sting. |
| ANTONY | Villains! You did not so when your vile daggers |
| | Hacked one another in the sides of Caesar. |
| | You showed your teeth like apes and fawned like hounds, |
| | And bowed like bondmen, kissing Caesar's feet, |
| | Whilst damnèd Casca, like a cur, behind |
| | Struck Caesar on the neck. O you flatterers! |
| CASSIUS | Flatterers? Now, Brutus, thank yourself. |
| | This tongue had not offended so today |
| | If Cassius might have ruled. |
| OCTAVIUS | Come, come, the cause. If arguing make us sweat, |
| | The proof of it will turn to redder drops. |
| | Look, |
| | I draw a sword against conspirators; |
| | When think you that the sword goes up again? |
| | Never, till Caesar's three and thirty wounds |
| | Be well avenged, or till another Caesar |
| | Have added slaughter to the sword of traitors. |
| BRUTUS | Caesar, thou canst not die by traitors' hands |
| | Unless thou bring'st them with thee. |
| OCTAVIUS | So I hope. |
| | I was not born to die on Brutus' sword. |

Line numbers: 25, 30, 35, 40, 45, 50, 55

Cassius insults the triumvirs. Octavius defies him and the triumvirs leave with their troops. Cassius, whose birthday it is, confides to Messala his newfound respect for omens.

# 1  Is Cassius right?

You are a keen young war correspondent who has just overheard Cassius's summing up of the opposition, in lines 61–2. First decide whether your newspaper is objective or partisan (supporting one side). Then write your first dispatch from the front assessing the accuracy of Cassius's description. Which description matches which member of the triumvirate?

## Characters

### Cassius – 'all is on the hazard' (in small groups)

Cassius seems to have become particularly superstitious. Unlike the super-confident Octavius ('If you dare fight today'), he speaks of fateful storms and chance throws of the dice ('on the hazard'). Furthermore, it's Cassius's birthday and he is conscious of powerful natural omens such as the carrion birds ('ravens, crows, and kites') that shadow his army.

- Read together lines 70–91, changing speakers at each full stop.
- One of you now becomes Cassius. The rest put him in the hot-seat. What has brought about the change in his philosophy and beliefs? How will it affect his approach to the crucial battle at Philippi? Quiz him about the assassination of Caesar and where and why it all went wrong.

## Themes

### Fate and omens

Just as the battle is about to start, Cassius confesses to Messala that he has had a change of philosophical viewpoint. He had been a follower of Epicurus, who did not believe in the power of omens. In Act 1 Scene 3, he says that the tempestuous night that is terrifying others is 'a very pleasing night to honest men' and 'most wonderful'. Now he says he does put some store by omens ('partly credit things that do presage') and describes two recent ones which involve birds.

- Read lines 80–8. On a large piece of paper draw an image or images inspired by Cassius's description of the omens. Then around them, write down quotations, references and ideas that relate to the theme of fate and omens in the play so far. Remember the Soothsayer? What about Julius Caesar's ghost?

---

**strain** family

**peevish** silly or childish
**masker** amateur actor and dancer
**reveller** lover of parties

**stomachs** courage, inclination

**bark** ship, vessel
**on the hazard** to be played for

**(As Pompey was)** at the Battle of Pharsalia where Pompey was forced to fight Caesar against his better judgement
**Epicurus** Greek philosopher (see p. 172) who believed that as the gods were indifferent to the affairs of humans, omens and portents did not mean anything
**partly credit** partially believe in
**presage** foretell the future
**former ensign** foremost banner or standard

**fatal** forboding death

| | | |
|---|---|---|
| BRUTUS | O, if thou wert the noblest of thy strain, | |
| | Young man, thou couldst not die more honourable. | 60 |
| CASSIUS | A peevish schoolboy, worthless of such honour, | |
| | Joined with a masker and a reveller! | |
| ANTONY | Old Cassius still! | |
| OCTAVIUS | Come, Antony, away! | |
| | Defiance, traitors, hurl we in your teeth. | |
| | If you dare fight today, come to the field; | 65 |
| | If not, when you have stomachs. | |

*Exeunt Octavius, Antony, and army*

| | | |
|---|---|---|
| CASSIUS | Why now blow wind, swell billow, and swim bark! | |
| | The storm is up, and all is on the hazard. | |
| BRUTUS | Ho, Lucilius, hark, a word with you. | |

*Lucilius and Messala stand forth*

| | | |
|---|---|---|
| LUCILIUS | My lord. | |

[*Brutus speaks apart to Lucilius*]

| | | |
|---|---|---|
| CASSIUS | Messala! | |
| MESSALA | What says my general? | |
| CASSIUS | Messala, | 70 |
| | This is my birthday, as this very day | |
| | Was Cassius born. Give me thy hand, Messala. | |
| | Be thou my witness that against my will | |
| | (As Pompey was) am I compelled to set | |
| | Upon one battle all our liberties. | 75 |
| | You know that I held Epicurus strong | |
| | And his opinion. Now I change my mind | |
| | And partly credit things that do presage. | |
| | Coming from Sardis, on our former ensign | |
| | Two mighty eagles fell, and there they perched, | 80 |
| | Gorging and feeding from our soldiers' hands, | |
| | Who to Philippi here consorted us. | |
| | This morning are they fled away and gone, | |
| | And in their steads do ravens, crows, and kites | |
| | Fly o'er our heads and downward look on us | 85 |
| | As we were sickly prey. Their shadows seem | |
| | A canopy most fatal under which | |
| | Our army lies, ready to give up the ghost. | |
| MESSALA | Believe not so. | |

Cassius is in high spirits despite the omens. He persuades Brutus to prefer suicide to captivity. They part in friendship and readiness for whatever the future holds.

## 1 Can you guess who is speaking? (in fours)

**a** Talk together about the differences between Cassius's and Brutus's language that we find in the play: lines 103–15 of Act 1 Scene 3 are typical of Cassius; lines 12–21 of Act 2 Scene 1 are typical of Brutus. Have a look at these lines to remind yourselves of their individual styles.

**b** Two of you close your eyes. The other two read aloud lines 92–126 of Act 5 Scene 1, omitting any mention of the names Brutus and Cassius. After the reading, guess who read Cassius and who Brutus, and give your reasons. Is it easy to tell who is who at this point? Explore the answers to this question in your group.

## Themes

**a** **What it is to be a Roman (in pairs)** Although he is a Roman, Brutus seems to be feeling his way towards the Christian doctrine condemning suicide in lines 101–8. His words seem prophetic, but after a pause for thought at line 108 he decides to take the noble Roman's way out and kill himself if he is defeated.

- Talk together about Brutus's pause for thought and speculate on what must have gone through his mind in that moment before he said 'No, Cassius, no'.

**b** **Friendship** Unlike many of Shakespeare's tragedies, the character after whom the play is named is not the most fully drawn. We see much more of Brutus and Cassius than we do of Caesar, hear of the changes in their view of the world and witness the fluctuations in their friendship.

- Look back at the key scenes in which Brutus and Cassius are together and draw a 'friendship graph' that charts the highs and lows of their relationship. Put the name of the scenes along one axis and use the other axis to indicate the state of their friendship.
- Bearing in mind how important male friendship was to the Romans, discuss as a class what the drama of their relationship adds to the play.
- Follow this up with a discussion of what other examples of male friendship there are in the play so far. You may want to revisit this after reading Act 5 Scene 5, when Brutus is with his 'poor remains of friends'.

**but** only

**constantly** resolutely

**The gods ... friendly** may the gods today remain on our side

**still incertain** always uncertain

**philosophy** (i.e. Stoicism, which advocated suicide)

**Cato** Portia's father, who took his own life (see also p. 56)

**fall** happen

**prevent / The time of life** end one's life before the proper time

**stay the providence** wait for the decision

**led in triumph** (as a humiliated captive)

| CASSIUS | I but believe it partly, |  |
|---|---|---|
|  | For I am fresh of spirit and resolved | 90 |
|  | To meet all perils very constantly. |  |
| BRUTUS | Even so, Lucilius. [*Advancing*] |  |
| CASSIUS | Now, most noble Brutus, |  |
|  | The gods today stand friendly that we may, |  |
|  | Lovers in peace, lead on our days to age! | 95 |
|  | But since the affairs of men rests still incertain, |  |
|  | Let's reason with the worst that may befall. |  |
|  | If we do lose this battle, then is this |  |
|  | The very last time we shall speak together. |  |
|  | What are you then determinèd to do? | 100 |
| BRUTUS | Even by the rule of that philosophy |  |
|  | By which I did blame Cato for the death |  |
|  | Which he did give himself – I know not how, |  |
|  | But I do find it cowardly and vile, |  |
|  | For fear of what might fall, so to prevent | 105 |
|  | The time of life – arming myself with patience |  |
|  | To stay the providence of some high powers |  |
|  | That govern us below. |  |
| CASSIUS | Then if we lose this battle, |  |
|  | You are contented to be led in triumph |  |
|  | Through the streets of Rome? | 110 |
| BRUTUS | No, Cassius, no. Think not, thou noble Roman, |  |
|  | That ever Brutus will go bound to Rome: |  |
|  | He bears too great a mind. But this same day |  |
|  | Must end that work the Ides of March begun. |  |
|  | And whether we shall meet again I know not, | 115 |
|  | Therefore our everlasting farewell take: |  |
|  | For ever and for ever, farewell, Cassius! |  |
|  | If we do meet again, why, we shall smile; |  |
|  | If not, why then this parting was well made. |  |
| CASSIUS | For ever and for ever, farewell, Brutus! | 120 |
|  | If we do meet again, we'll smile indeed; |  |
|  | If not, 'tis true this parting was well made. |  |
| BRUTUS | Why then, lead on. O, that a man might know |  |
|  | The end of this day's business ere it come! |  |
|  | But it sufficeth that the day will end, | 125 |
|  | And then the end is known. Come ho, away! |  |

*Exeunt*

Battle. As Octavius weakens, Brutus orders all his troops to attack. On another part of the battlefield, Cassius reports that his soldiers have fled. Flee, says Pindarus, Antony is in our camp.

## 1 'Over now to our reporter at Philippi'
**(in small groups)**

War reporters on television tell us about:

- what is happening and the commander's overall strategy
- the state of morale, from general to footsoldier.

Devise a short national news report about the events at Philippi described opposite. Use reporters' commentary, newsreel, maps and interviews.

## Stagecraft

### Theatre of war (in large groups)

This activity could be planned in the classroom and then acted out in a larger space. The stage direction 'Alarum' means that the events in this scene are preceded by a loud battle noise of drums, trumpets, voices and clashing weapons off stage.

- Start at Act 5 Scene 1, line 120, and use all the resources you have available to make the sound effects for scene changes up to Scene 3, line 4. Each scene has a different mood, and your effects must make this clear. The right volume and quality of noise take careful planning.
- While some work out sound effects, others work on the staging. How are you going to show the difference between the battlefield and the high place overlooking it? A plan of the stage area in your Director's Journal may help.
- The number of actors on stage is another crucial consideration; either restrict yourself to the four named characters, or bring on a host of soldiers. Work out blocking (where the characters move on stage) either on your stage space or on your diagram in your Journal. Have the whole field of battle in mind when you plot entrances and exits. Ensure that you show the armies' contrasting moods: thoughtful, joyful, fearful, dejected, fast, slow – or whatever you feel is appropriate.
- What would your actors wear? Perhaps you can also think of some token piece of clothing that will indicate which side they are on in your production.
- When you have seen the work of different groups, come together in one large group and discuss what was successful and what was difficult about this activity.

*Alarum* sounds of battle (see 'Stagecraft' activity)

**bills** written orders

**on the other side** (i.e. Cassius's wing of the battle formation)

**set on** attack

**cold ... in Octavio's wing** low spirits in Octavius's troops

**sudden push ... overthrow** a sudden attack will beat them

**the villains fly** (i.e. his own troops are running away)

**ensign** standard-bearer

**did take it** took the standard

**fell to spoil** began plundering and looting

**tents** encampment

# Act 5 Scene 2
## The battlefield at Philippi

*Alarum. Enter* BRUTUS *and Messala*

BRUTUS Ride, ride, Messala, ride, and give these bills
Unto the legions on the other side.
*Loud alarum*
Let them set on at once, for I perceive
But cold demeanour in Octavio's wing,
And sudden push gives them the overthrow.  5
Ride, ride, Messala, let them all come down.

             *Exeunt*

# Act 5 Scene 3
## A high place overlooking the battlefield at Philippi

*Alarums. Enter* CASSIUS *and* TITINIUS

CASSIUS O, look, Titinius, look, the villains fly!
Myself have to mine own turned enemy.
This ensign here of mine was turning back;
I slew the coward and did take it from him.

TITINIUS O Cassius, Brutus gave the word too early,  5
Who, having some advantage on Octavius,
Took it too eagerly. His soldiers fell to spoil
Whilst we by Antony are all enclosed.

*Enter* PINDARUS

PINDARUS Fly further off, my lord, fly further off!
Mark Antony is in your tents, my lord,  10
Fly therefore, noble Cassius, fly far off.

CASSIUS This hill is far enough. Look, look, Titinius,
Are those my tents where I perceive the fire?

Titinius leaves, on Cassius's orders. Pindarus reports that Titinius has been captured. Cassius decides on suicide and orders Pindarus to kill him. Pindarus obeys his command.

## Characters

### Snapshots of Cassius (in pairs)

Cassius's life has come full circle. It is his birthday:

*This day I breathèd first, time is come round*
*And where I did begin there shall I end*

Plutarch describes Cassius as a 'choleric' (angry, hot-tempered) man, with a personal hatred of Caesar, who 'even from his cradle, could not abide any manner of tyrants'. But little else is known of the historical Cassius.

**a** Discuss and list Cassius's main characteristics, both professional and personal. What do you think of his decisions at key points in the play? It may help to look back at previous notes you have made. Include any relevant brief quotations in your list.

**b** Compare your list with the brief description above of Cassius in Shakespeare's source material. Speculate on why Shakespeare developed the character in the way that he did. Make a note of your observations to share with the class.

**c** Cassius orders his loyal servant Pindarus to kill him (ironically with the sword that had previously killed Caesar). One of you reads Cassius's death speech (lines 33–46). The other is Pindarus. Work together on staging an effective end to Cassius's life. Finish the presentation with a tableau that 'freezes' at the instant of death.

**d** Cassius is a complex and passionate character. Discuss in your pair your feelings at his death.

## Write about it

### Pindarus – grief and joy

Pindarus is consumed with conflicting feelings: of grief as he kills his master and of ecstasy at Cassius releasing him from slavery so he can begin a new life 'Where never Roman shall take note of him' (line 50).

- Pindarus does not appear again in the play. Write his diary entry once he has arrived 'far from this country'. What is his 'non-Roman' view of recent events?

**even with a thought** as quick as a thought

**thick** weak, dim
**thou not'st** you observe, see

**is run his compass** has come full circle

**make to** approach
**on the spur** riding hard
**light** dismount
**ta'en** taken, captured

**Parthia** (modern-day Iran/Iraq)
**I swore thee** I made you promise
**saving of** when I spared
**attempt** perform

**search** probe, penetrate
**Stand not** do not delay

| | |
|---|---|
| TITINIUS | They are, my lord. |
| CASSIUS | Titinius, if thou lovest me, |
| | Mount thou my horse and hide thy spurs in him 15 |
| | Till he have brought thee up to yonder troops |
| | And here again that I may rest assured |
| | Whether yond troops are friend or enemy. |
| TITINIUS | I will be here again even with a thought. *Exit* |
| CASSIUS | Go, Pindarus, get higher on that hill, 20 |
| | My sight was ever thick: regard Titinius |
| | And tell me what thou not'st about the field. |

[*Pindarus goes up*]

This day I breathèd first, time is come round
And where I did begin there shall I end:
My life is run his compass. Sirrah, what news? 25

| | |
|---|---|
| PINDARUS | (*Above*) O my lord! |
| CASSIUS | What news? |
| PINDARUS | Titinius is enclosèd round about |
| | With horsemen that make to him on the spur, |
| | Yet he spurs on. Now they are almost on him. 30 |
| | Now Titinius – Now some light; O, he lights too. |
| | He's ta'en. |

(*Shout*)

And hark, they shout for joy.

| | |
|---|---|
| CASSIUS | Come down, behold no more. |
| | O, coward that I am to live so long |
| | To see my best friend ta'en before my face. 35 |

*Pindarus* [*descends*]

Come hither, sirrah.
In Parthia did I take thee prisoner,
And then I swore thee, saving of thy life,
That whatsoever I did bid thee do
Thou shouldst attempt it. Come now, keep thine oath. 40
Now be a freeman, and with this good sword,
That ran through Caesar's bowels, search this bosom.
Stand not to answer; here, take thou the hilts
And when my face is covered, as 'tis now,
Guide thou the sword.

[*Pindarus stabs him*]

Caesar, thou art revenged 45
Even with the sword that killed thee. [*Dies*]

151

Pindarus flees. Messala and Titinius enter with news of Brutus's success over Octavius. They hope to cheer Cassius but find him dead.

## Stagecraft

### Pause for thought?

Several directors slow the pace of their productions after Pindarus exits, in order to allow the audience time to focus on Cassius's body.

* Write a short note in your Director's Journal to explain whether or not you would do this in your production.

## 1 The end of the Republic (in groups of four or five)

After five hundred years the Republic is about to end. Like millions of persecuted, defeated or outlawed people in history – Jews in Nazi Germany, for example – Republicans anywhere in the Roman world realise that life as they knew it is over. Pindarus flees, Messala will fight on, Titinius will kill himself.

* Lines 60–4 are Titinius's lament for the Republic. Take a line each and keep repeating it, building your lament like a piece of music. Speaking the verses in any order, start softly and chime your line into the ensemble of voices sparingly, then increase in volume and frequency as grief deepens. Savour the sadness of the words, which reach the listener as a collage of broken phrases.

## Characters

### Cassius again (in small groups)

a Lines 60–4 are also a lament for Cassius, showing that he inspired feelings of admiration and respect amongst his followers. Discuss how these lines fit with your impressions of Cassius in response to the activity on page 150.

b Is Messala right to claim that 'Mistrust of good success' (looking on the dark side of things) was responsible for Cassius's downfall?

c How do you now feel about Cassius's death, given that it was the result of a fatal error? The battle is not yet lost.

d As a final piece of work on Cassius, discuss in your group, and then write on your own, his obituary from the point of view of a friend and co-conspirator. You may want to include consideration of Brutus's lines 100–1 on page 155.

---

**Durst I** had I dared to

**change** exchange, tit for tat

**Mistrust of** doubts about

**error** (Messala personifies error here, describing its nature and how it was born)

**melancholy's child** Melancholics (like Cassius) were believed to have a tendency to imagine evils which are non-existent

**apt thoughts** impressionable minds

**mother** (i.e. the person who has the mistaken thoughts, in this case Cassius)

**engendered** conceived

**Hie** hasten

| | |
|---|---|
| PINDARUS | So I am free, yet would not so have been |
| | Durst I have done my will. O Cassius, |
| | Far from this country Pindarus shall run, |
| | Where never Roman shall take note of him.        [*Exit*]        50 |

*Enter* TITINIUS *and* MESSALA

| | |
|---|---|
| MESSALA | It is but change, Titinius, for Octavius |
| | Is overthrown by noble Brutus' power, |
| | As Cassius' legions are by Antony. |
| TITINIUS | These tidings will well comfort Cassius. |
| MESSALA | Where did you leave him? |
| TITINIUS |       All disconsolate,        55 |
| | With Pindarus his bondman, on this hill. |
| MESSALA | Is not that he that lies upon the ground? |
| TITINIUS | He lies not like the living. O my heart! |
| MESSALA | Is not that he? |
| TITINIUS |      No, this was he, Messala, |
| | But Cassius is no more. O setting sun,        60 |
| | As in thy red rays thou dost sink to night, |
| | So in his red blood Cassius' day is set. |
| | The sun of Rome is set. Our day is gone, |
| | Clouds, dews, and dangers come. Our deeds are done. |
| | Mistrust of my success hath done this deed.        65 |
| MESSALA | Mistrust of good success hath done this deed. |
| | O hateful error, melancholy's child, |
| | Why dost thou show to the apt thoughts of men |
| | The things that are not? O error, soon conceived, |
| | Thou never com'st unto a happy birth        70 |
| | But kill'st the mother that engendered thee. |
| TITINIUS | What, Pindarus? Where art thou, Pindarus? |
| MESSALA | Seek him, Titinius, whilst I go to meet |
| | The noble Brutus, thrusting this report |
| | Into his ears. I may say 'thrusting' it,        75 |
| | For piercing steel and darts envenomèd |
| | Shall be as welcome to the ears of Brutus |
| | As tidings of this sight. |
| TITINIUS |       Hie you, Messala, |
| | And I will seek for Pindarus the while. |

[*Exit Messala*]

Titinius places a victory wreath on Cassius's head, then loyally kills himself. Brutus and others enter and mourn the two dead men. Brutus orders his fellow Romans to fight on.

## Themes

### Appearance and reality

Pindarus got it wrong first. Titinius was not captured by the enemy (which was what Pindarus 'saw', lines 28–30), but greeted by welcoming comrades. The victory garland sent by Brutus now becomes Cassius's funeral wreath. Titinius mourns that Cassius 'misconstrued everything'.

- Head up two columns with 'Brutus' and 'Cassius' and fill them in with details about how each character has misinterpreted or misjudged what they have 'seen' during the course of the whole play.

## 1 The story of Cassius's sword (in small groups)

Weapons can be objects of reverence and exquisite craftsmanship. In stories they often have magical powers. Shakespeare's characters often swear on, or by, their swords. Cassius introduces us to his in Act 1 Scene 3, line 89: 'I know where I will wear this dagger then: / Cassius from bondage will deliver Cassius.' He stabs Caesar with it (Act 3 Scene 1, line 76) and invites Brutus to kill him with it (Act 4 Scene 3, lines 100–5). By the time we reach this scene, it has a life of its own. In line 45 Cassius asks Pindarus to 'Guide thou the sword'; in line 90 it is told to 'find Titinius' heart'; in lines 94–6 Brutus imagines the dead Caesar wields it 'and turns our swords / In our own proper entrails'.

- Each group takes one episode in the sword's story and works on a presentation. This could take the form of a tableau, a rewriting of the scene in which the sword has a voice or something more symbolic.
- Show your presentations in chronological order.

## Write about it

### Is Brutus right?

- Read Brutus's lines 94–6, and then write two or three paragraphs analysing whether or not his assessment of events since Caesar's death is accurate. Remember to back up your points with evidence from the text and quotations.

**misconstrued** misinterpreted (see 'Themes' activity)

**hold thee** wait a moment

**regarded** honoured

**By your leave, gods!** (he asks permission to end his life before the time allotted to him by the gods is ended)

**a Roman's part** how a Roman should die (i.e. by suicide)

**own proper** very own

**Look whe'er** see how

**Thasos** island near Philippi

**discomfort us** dishearten our troops

**Labeo and Flavio** two of Brutus's friends

**battles** forces

Why didst thou send me forth, brave Cassius? 80
Did I not meet thy friends? And did not they
Put on my brows this wreath of victory
And bid me give it thee? Didst thou not hear their shouts?
Alas, thou hast misconstrued everything.
But hold thee, take this garland on thy brow; 85
Thy Brutus bid me give it thee, and I
Will do his bidding. Brutus, come apace,
And see how I regarded Caius Cassius.
By your leave, gods! – This is a Roman's part.
Come, Cassius' sword, and find Titinius' heart. *Dies* 90

*Alarum. Enter* BRUTUS, MESSALA, YOUNG CATO, *Strato, Volumnius,*
*and Lucilius,* [*Labeo, and Flavius*]

| | |
|---|---|
| BRUTUS | Where, where, Messala, doth his body lie? |
| MESSALA | Lo yonder, and Titinius mourning it. |
| BRUTUS | Titinius' face is upward. |
| CATO | He is slain. |
| BRUTUS | O Julius Caesar, thou art mighty yet, |

Thy spirit walks abroad and turns our swords 95
In our own proper entrails.
*Low alarums*

| | |
|---|---|
| CATO | Brave Titinius! |

Look whe'er he have not crowned dead Cassius.

| | |
|---|---|
| BRUTUS | Are yet two Romans living such as these? |

The last of all the Romans, fare thee well!
It is impossible that ever Rome 100
Should breed thy fellow. Friends, I owe mo tears
To this dead man than you shall see me pay.
I shall find time, Cassius, I shall find time.
Come therefore and to Thasos send his body;
His funerals shall not be in our camp 105
Lest it discomfort us. Lucilius, come,
And come, young Cato, let us to the field.
Labeo and Flavio, set our battles on.
'Tis three o'clock, and, Romans, yet ere night
We shall try fortune in a second fight. 110
*Exeunt*

Battle. Brutus encourages his troops, then leaves. Left behind, Cato is killed in combat and Lucilius (posing as Brutus) captured. Lucilius drops his pretence when Antony enters.

## Stagecraft

### Time to fight (in eights)

This is the only actual fight called for by a stage direction, so it must be performed well. Display fighting was a popular entertainment in Elizabethan times. Real fighting had its place, too, and not just in Elizabeth's foreign wars. Young men used to swagger in the streets of London, shouting and banging their swords on their 'bucklers' (little shields) as a general challenge to fight. The authorities thought they were a public menace. It is reported that some women found them attractive.

- Plan how you would stage a slow-motion version of the fight, from 'Enter SOLDIERS' to 'Young Cato is slain'. Your fight should be convincing, but not dangerous. The golden rule of stage-fighting is safety first!
- Perform your version to the rest of the class.

## 1 Brutus's men (in pairs)

a Work out what is happening in the scene and what it tells us about Brutus and his men (especially Cato and Lucilius). In particular, consider why Lucilius pretends to be Brutus.

b Improvise a scenario in which one of you explains to the other, who is a younger reader of the play, what is happening in this scene.

▼ Why do you think the director decided to depart from the script and have Antony threaten Young Cato in this way?

**Yet** keep going!

**What bastard doth not?** who is of such low parentage that he does not (want to keep fighting)?

**I am the son of Marcus Cato** (here he identifies himself as Portia's brother)

**Only I yield to die** (i.e. I will die before I surrender)

**There is … straight** there is good reason for you to kill me quickly (i.e. because I am Brutus)

**like himself** true to his own noble nature

# Act 5 Scene 4
## The battlefield at Philippi

*Alarum. Enter* BRUTUS, *Messala,* [YOUNG] CATO, LUCILIUS,
*and Flavius,* [*Labeo*]

| | |
|---|---|
| BRUTUS | Yet, countrymen, O, yet hold up your heads! |
| | [*Exit with Messala, Flavius, and Labeo*] |
| CATO | What bastard doth not? Who will go with me? |
| | I will proclaim my name about the field. |
| | I am the son of Marcus Cato, ho! |
| | A foe to tyrants, and my country's friend. |
| | I am the son of Marcus Cato, ho! |

*Enter* SOLDIERS *and fight*

| | |
|---|---|
| LUCILIUS | And I am Brutus, Marcus Brutus, I, |
| | Brutus, my country's friend. Know me for Brutus! |
| | [*Young Cato is slain*] |
| | O young and noble Cato, art thou down? |
| | Why, now thou diest as bravely as Titinius |
| | And mayst be honoured, being Cato's son. |
| 1 SOLDIER | Yield, or thou diest. |
| LUCILIUS | Only I yield to die. |
| | There is so much that thou wilt kill me straight. |
| | Kill Brutus and be honoured in his death. |
| 1 SOLDIER | We must not. A noble prisoner! |

*Enter* ANTONY

| | |
|---|---|
| 2 SOLDIER | Room ho! Tell Antony, Brutus is ta'en. |
| 1 SOLDIER | I'll tell the news. Here comes the general. |
| | Brutus is ta'en, Brutus is ta'en, my lord! |
| ANTONY | Where is he? |
| LUCILIUS | Safe, Antony, Brutus is safe enough. |
| | I dare assure thee that no enemy |
| | Shall ever take alive the noble Brutus. |
| | The gods defend him from so great a shame! |
| | When you do find him, or alive or dead, |
| | He will be found like Brutus, like himself. |

Line numbers: 5, 10, 15, 20, 25

Antony gives safe custody to Lucilius and sends for word of Brutus. Brutus and followers enter and rest. Separately and secretly he asks them to kill him.

# Characters

## What are Antony's motives? (in small groups)

Far from being angry at Lucilius's attempt to impersonate Brutus, Antony treats him with the greatest respect and kindness (lines 26–9).

- Discuss the different motives Antony might have for doing this.

## 1 Contrasts of war (in large groups)

Scene 4 is all about violence, glory and action. Scene 5 opens peacefully and quietly. Some dialogue is a whisper – so quiet that the audience can't hear it. Strato falls asleep. But as the voice of battle steadily grows in volume, Brutus's plea for help in his suicide becomes urgent.

- Bring out these contrasts by making a recording of the script from the start of Act 5 Scene 4 to Act 5 Scene 5, line 57. Rehearse and coordinate sound effects and dialogue very carefully.

# Themes

## Fate and omens (in pairs)

The Elizabethans were not sure what to make of ghosts. They certainly suggested unsettled times, but were they good or evil? See page 136 for more discussion of ghosts.

a Speculate on why Shakespeare has Brutus say that Caesar's ghost has appeared to him again but does not show the event on stage.

b What does it show about the state of Brutus's mind that he says 'I know my hour has come' after describing the appearance of the ghost?

c Write and stage the scene in which Caesar's ghost appears to Brutus 'here in Philippi fields'. It may help to look back to the ghost's appearance in Act 4 Scene 3, line 274. Note how the ghost speaks in simple but ominous statements. After the ghost leaves in Act 4, Brutus says 'I would hold more talk with thee'. What will he take the opportunity to say to the ghost in your scene? Finally, when writing your scene, consider what frame of mind you want Brutus to be in after the encounter. Bear in mind your answer to the question about Brutus above.

**whe'er** whether

**poor remains** pitiful survivors

**showed the torchlight** gave the signal when he reached Cassius's camp

**or ta'en or slain** either captured or killed

**deed in fashion** popular thing to do at the moment (suicide)

**Now is ... vessel full of grief** the noble [Brutus] is like a jug brimful with sad tears

**several** separate

ANTONY  This is not Brutus, friend, but, I assure you,
A prize no less in worth. Keep this man safe,
Give him all kindness. I had rather have
Such men my friends than enemies. Go on,
And see whe'er Brutus be alive or dead,                    30
And bring us word unto Octavius' tent
How everything is chanced.

                                              *Exeunt*

# Act 5 Scene 5
## A rocky place near the battlefield at Philippi

*Enter* BRUTUS, DARDANIUS, CLITUS, STRATO, *and* VOLUMNIUS

BRUTUS      Come, poor remains of friends, rest on this rock.
CLITUS      Statilius showed the torchlight but, my lord,
He came not back. He is or ta'en or slain.
BRUTUS      Sit thee down, Clitus. Slaying is the word,
It is a deed in fashion. Hark thee, Clitus. [*Whispering*]       5
CLITUS      What, I, my lord? No, not for all the world.
BRUTUS      Peace then, no words.
CLITUS                          I'll rather kill myself.
BRUTUS      Hark thee, Dardanius. [*Whispers*]
DARDANIUS                      Shall I do such a deed?
CLITUS      O Dardanius!
DARDANIUS   O Clitus!                                        10
CLITUS      What ill request did Brutus make to thee?
DARDANIUS   To kill him, Clitus. Look, he meditates.
CLITUS      Now is that noble vessel full of grief,
That it runs over even at his eyes.
BRUTUS      Come hither, good Volumnius, list a word.        15
VOLUMNIUS   What says my lord?
BRUTUS                      Why, this, Volumnius:
The ghost of Caesar hath appeared to me
Two several times by night, at Sardis once
And this last night here in Philippi fields.
I know my hour is come.
VOLUMNIUS                      Not so, my lord.              20

Volumnius refuses to aid Brutus's suicide. Brutus bids farewell to his friends. He urges them to fly. But he detains Strato, who helps Brutus to take his own life.

## 1 'Brutus' tongue' (in fives)

In taking his own life Brutus is his own biographer. He writes himself a noble death: 'Brutus' tongue / Hath almost ended his life's history'. Volumnius, an old school friend, disagrees with Brutus twice, but as usual we hear only Brutus's side of the argument.

- To let Clitus, Dardanius and Volumnius give their point of view, delay Antony's approach and have them refuse to leave at line 43. Improvise what happens as they probe the wisdom and sincerity of Brutus's motives in committing suicide both now and in the future. Brutus and Strato defend his actions and intentions.

- After your improvisation, see if you can read Brutus's part with more conviction and realism than before.

> ## Stagecraft
>
> ### Brutus alone (in pairs)
>
> Shakespeare deliberately increases Brutus's isolation as his death approaches. The increasing intensity of the 'alarums' (sounds of battle) suggests the Triumvirate's unstoppable advance. Brutus's last few friends flee until only Strato is left as his companion.
>
> **a** Rehearse and present Brutus's lines 50–1 in slow motion, ending with a freeze-frame, then talk with other pairs about the effects you have created.
>
> **b** Several critics write of the 'humiliation' of Brutus (and Cassius) at the end of the play. Discuss whether you agree with this view or whether you consider it a glorious end, as Brutus does: 'I shall have glory by this losing day'. After your discussion, consider how you would infuse your production of this scene with glory or humiliation and note your ideas in your Director's Journal.

> ## Language in the play
>
> ### How does Brutus persuade? (in small groups)
>
> When Cassius was recruiting the conspirators to his cause, there was need of much persuasive language and rhetoric. In this scene, Brutus seeks to persuade one of his 'poor remains of friends' to assist him in his suicide.
>
> - Discuss and list the techniques he uses to do this.

**beat us to the pit** driven us before them (like hunted animals into a pit)

**more worthy** nobler

**vile conquest** shameful victory

**at once** without further ado

**this hour** the hour of his death

**good respect** good reputation

**smatch** trace, smack

**Caesar, now be still** Caesar's ghost can now rest peacefully, as Caesar's death has been avenged

| | |
|---|---|
| BRUTUS | Nay, I am sure it is, Volumnius. |
| | Thou seest the world, Volumnius, how it goes: |
| | Our enemies have beat us to the pit. |

*Low alarums*

It is more worthy to leap in ourselves
Than tarry till they push us. Good Volumnius, 25
Thou know'st that we two went to school together;
Even for that our love of old, I prithee
Hold thou my sword-hilts whilst I run on it.

VOLUMNIUS That's not an office for a friend, my lord.

*Alarum still*

CLITUS Fly, fly, my lord, there is no tarrying here. 30

BRUTUS Farewell to you, and you, and you, Volumnius.
Strato, thou hast been all this while asleep:
Farewell to thee too, Strato. Countrymen,
My heart doth joy that yet in all my life
I found no man but he was true to me. 35
I shall have glory by this losing day
More than Octavius and Mark Antony
By this vile conquest shall attain unto.
So fare you well at once, for Brutus' tongue
Hath almost ended his life's history. 40
Night hangs upon mine eyes, my bones would rest,
That have but laboured to attain this hour.

*Alarum. Cry within, 'Fly, fly, fly!'*

CLITUS Fly, my lord, fly!

BRUTUS             Hence! I will follow.

          *[Exeunt Clitus, Dardanius, and Volumnius]*

I prithee, Strato, stay thou by thy lord.
Thou art a fellow of a good respect, 45
Thy life hath had some smatch of honour in it.
Hold then my sword and turn away thy face,
While I do run upon it. Wilt thou, Strato?

STRATO Give me your hand first. Fare you well, my lord.

BRUTUS Farewell, good Strato.

         *[Runs on his sword]*

              Caesar, now be still, 50
I killed not thee with half so good a will.     *Dies*

To the sound of the retreating conspirators' trumpets, the triumvirs enter and accept Brutus's followers into their service. Antony honours Brutus as the only selfless conspirator.

## 1 Clemency – wisdom or folly? (in fours)

Octavius shows clemency (mercy) to all of Brutus's followers when he spares their lives. Julius Caesar also showed clemency to the followers of Pompey after he had defeated them. Among those same followers were Brutus and Cassius, who later assassinated the merciful Caesar. Is Octavius making the same mistake as Caesar?

- One of you takes the part of Octavius. The others play advisers who are not happy with Octavius's decision. Debate who is right.

## Characters

### Brutus or Antony the hero? (in groups of five or six)

Antony's tribute to Brutus (lines 68–75) is fulsome in its praise of 'the noblest Roman of them all'. He singles out Brutus amongst the conspirators as not being driven by 'envy of great Caesar' but by a concern for the 'common good to all'.

- One person reads through Antony's final lines in the play. Discuss their dramatic impact and what they add to your opinions of Brutus's character and Antony's. Which man is the greater hero? Feed back your opinions in a class discussion. At the end, take a vote.

## Stagecraft

### An ending – but what is to come? (in large groups)

When Octavius speaks the last words of the play, he unceremoniously (but tellingly) asserts his leadership and authority. Many productions choose to suggest an irony in the ending. Caesar disposed of Pompey to become sole ruler of Rome, but will there now be a new power struggle between Antony and Octavius?

- **a** Look carefully at the language of the final two speeches. Discuss what advice about tone, pace, emotion and gesture you would give to the actors delivering these speeches. Experiment with different actors delivering the speeches in different ways.

- **b** Now present the play's closing moment as a tableau that suggests future hostility between the two victorious generals.

162

*Alarum. Retreat. Enter* ANTONY, OCTAVIUS, MESSALA,
LUCILIUS, *and the army*

| | | |
|---|---|---|
| OCTAVIUS | What man is that? | |
| MESSALA | My master's man. Strato, where is thy master? | |
| STRATO | Free from the bondage you are in, Messala. | |
| | The conquerors can but make a fire of him: | 55 |
| | For Brutus only overcame himself, | |
| | And no man else hath honour by his death. | |
| LUCILIUS | So Brutus should be found. I thank thee, Brutus, | |
| | That thou hast proved Lucilius' saying true. | |
| OCTAVIUS | All that served Brutus I will entertain them. | 60 |
| | Fellow, wilt thou bestow thy time with me? | |
| STRATO | Ay, if Messala will prefer me to you. | |
| OCTAVIUS | Do so, good Messala. | |
| MESSALA | How died my master, Strato? | |
| STRATO | I held the sword, and he did run on it. | 65 |
| MESSALA | Octavius, then take him to follow thee, | |
| | That did the latest service to my master. | |
| ANTONY | This was the noblest Roman of them all: | |
| | All the conspirators, save only he, | |
| | Did that they did in envy of great Caesar. | 70 |
| | He only, in a general honest thought | |
| | And common good to all, made one of them. | |
| | His life was gentle, and the elements | |
| | So mixed in him that Nature might stand up | |
| | And say to all the world, 'This was a man!' | 75 |
| OCTAVIUS | According to his virtue let us use him, | |
| | With all respect and rites of burial. | |
| | Within my tent his bones tonight shall lie, | |
| | Most like a soldier, ordered honourably. | |
| | So call the field to rest, and let's away | 80 |
| | To part the glories of this happy day. | |

*Exeunt*

# Looking back at the play
## Activities for groups or individuals

## 1 Fifteen-minute version

Divide the class into five groups, each group taking one act of the play. You are going to produce a three-minute version of your allocated act, using only the words from the script itself. When you are ready, put each of the five acts together in turn; you have created a fifteen-minute version of the whole play. As a variation, mime or perform each act in a different style (documentary investigation, soap opera, melodrama, and so on).

## 2 Press statement

In modern warfare, after a great victory the triumphant generals often meet the press, have their photographs taken and issue a press statement.

- Two people take the roles of Antony and Octavius, while the others prepare to be members of the press or a television crew. Question the two leaders and get as much out of them as you can. Afterwards, write the press statement issued by the victors. (They might decide to release separate statements.)

## 3 Octavius or Antony?

Octavius Caesar speaks the final lines of the play. As a key member of the Triumvirate he has risen slickly to power. Antony, however, is older, more experienced and arguably more likeable. Lepidus has not been seen for a while. Such a team may be unstable.

- a Gather some of the plebeians together and improvise a lively discussion about which man they would prefer as leader and why. Refer to the military careers of Antony, Octavius and Lepidus, as well as to their handling of events after the death of Caesar.

- b Now you have the feel of what the populace think, write a speech as either Octavius or Antony, putting their case for being sole ruler of the Roman world. Use whichever rhetorical techniques will strengthen your case. Deliver your speech to the waiting crowd.

## 4 Cast the play

Imagine that you are a film director about to put together a new and ambitious version of Julius Caesar. Go through the list of characters on page 5, and choose the eight that you think are most important in the play. Decide which well-known film actors you would cast in each part – money no object! In each case, say what it is about that particular actor that makes you think they are right for the part.

## 5 Julius Caesar

Julius Caesar, the character after whom the play is named, dies in Act 3. We see far more of several other characters, most notably Brutus and Cassius.

- Discuss or write answers to the questions: Why do you think Shakespeare called the play Julius Caesar? If you were to rename it, what would you call it? Why?

## 6 Women in the play

The case has been made that this is one of Shakespeare's most male plays. Female characters only appear in Acts 1 and 2, although there may be female crowd members. Answer one of the following:

- 'The female characters add nothing to the play'. Discuss.
- 'The power of Rome could not be fully understood without the female characters in Julius Caesar.' To what extent do you agree?

## 7 Why read Julius Caesar now?

One of the claims that is frequently made about Shakespeare is that he has something to say to everyone, whatever their age and culture.

- Explore in writing the point of studying this play in the twenty-first century and what it says to you personally. Looking back at the 'Themes' boxes may help you.

▼ ▶ What suggestions are being made about the future here as Octavius looks at Antony contemplating the dead Brutus?

# Perspectives and themes

## What is the play about?

*Julius Caesar* was probably written in 1599 and first performed in the same year on the stage of the Globe Theatre on London's Bankside. Although essentially a tragedy, it is also a history play dealing with politics and war. However, unlike most of Shakespeare's other history plays, it is not drawn from English history or from Tudor England's recent past.

Shakespeare's main source for his story of *Julius Caesar* is a text that he probably studied at school: Plutarch's *Lives of the Noble Grecians and Romans*, translated into English by Thomas North in 1579. Shakespeare may have been drawn to Plutarch's *Lives* because it contained interesting, biographically detailed, rich and complex appreciations of famous people at the centre of historical events, rather than simply retelling those events. Plutarch also made studies of power and the personal dilemmas faced by political leaders. All this provided fertile source material for Shakespeare to shape and fashion in his own distinctive way. The changes that he made to Plutarch's historical account include:

- having Calpurnia present at the Lupercal festival and using Casca to report Caesar's three-time refusal of the crown (Act 1 Scene 2)
- adding Brutus's long soliloquy in Act 2 Scene 1
- having Caesar reject Artemidorus's warning about the conspiracy (Act 2 Scene 3 and Act 3 Scene 1)
- showing the assassins ritually bathing their arms in Caesar's blood (Act 3 Scene 1)
- adjusting the sequence of events so Antony's funeral oration follows directly after Brutus's speech of explanation to the Roman people; having Antony read out the details of Caesar's will (Act 3 Scene 2).

◆ Choose one of the changes listed above. Write a paragraph discussing what the play gains from the alteration that Shakespeare made.

To help you deepen your understanding of the narrative or **plot** of Shakespeare's *Julius Caesar,* try one or more of the following activities.

### The bare bones of the script

◆ Have a go at retelling the story of the play in just one sentence, or rewrite the play as a mini-saga (exactly fifty words).

◆ Imagine you are a newspaper sub-editor. Decide what type of paper you work for ('serious' or 'popular'). Your job is to write brief, memorable headlines for each of the five acts in the play. Of course, they may include puns or clever wordplay to gain attention and interest, but they must also be accurate!

### Longer versions

◆ In a group of five, each take responsibility for retelling the story of an individual act, and then put the narrative together. Display your version on the classroom wall and compare it with those of other groups. What have they included that you have missed out? Argue your case.

◆ Try writing a sentence about Act 1 Scene 1, and then pass your paper to another student who should pick up the narrative. Keep working around the group, adding a sentence about each scene until you reach the end of the play.

◆ Review the photo gallery at the start of this edition, which gives a version of the play in pictures and captions. What pictures have been missed out? Suggest three other images you would include, giving reasons for your choices.

◆ Stage a TV production meeting in which you must decide how to cut the narrative of the play to two hours ready for filming. Decide which episodes and incidents to keep and then storyboard the main elements of your newly adapted version.

## Sculpture park

◆ The class divides into two groups. As one group looks away, the other half of the class – working as pairs – freezes into 'sculptures' that represent some of the key moments of the play. When the first group of students turns round, they see various statues depicting moments from the play set out before their eyes. Their task is to identify as many of the sculptures as possible.

### Whose story is it?

Caesar, who gives his name to the title of the play, dies at the start of Act 3. Many critics argue that the central character is Brutus, rather than Caesar, as we witness many events from his perspective. Thus the play would be completely different if it were Cassius's story, Portia's story, Octavius's story or Antony's story.

◆ Have a go at retelling the story of *Julius Caesar* from the perspective of one of the four characters mentioned above. Choose your own text format for this (for example, letter, diary, monologue, short story, narrative poem).

## Politics

The feeling that great events are happening – events that will shape all subsequent history – is unmistakable in this play. This may be ancient history, but it is told with racy vitality.

This is probably achieved by the play's mixture of old and new. Shakespeare's Rome owes much to Tudor London – its people even dress in doublets – but it is spiced with specifically pre-Christian superstition and cruelty, such as the sacrifice of animals and the mob slaughter of the poet Cinna. The pagan world had not yet learned of the teaching of Jesus Christ, though intelligent and educated men like Cicero had brought it 'civilisation' and 'culture'.

By setting his play in ancient Rome, Shakespeare could present a debate about authority without fear of offending Queen Elizabeth I and her government or arousing religious controversy. The fact that the conspirators' attempt to save the Roman Republic actually failed was no doubt conveniently reassuring

to the Tudor authorities. However, Caesar's assassination would have been an uncomfortable reminder to Elizabethans of the many attempts on the life of the queen (her Jewish physician was executed for allegedly trying to poison her). Similarly, some Elizabethans believed that the queen's power, like Caesar's, was growing too great. Others were as concerned as the ancient Romans about the threat of political upheaval and civil war when their ageing and childless queen finally died.

## Tragedy

*Julius Caesar* is often viewed as a tragedy. Some argue that in writing the play Shakespeare was responding to a growing public demand for such types of drama, especially those that featured elements of bloody and violent revenge or retribution in their narrative structure. In the First Folio (the first published collection of Shakespeare's plays in 1623), *Julius Caesar* is placed with the other major tragedies.

In some ways, *Julius Caesar* conforms to Aristotle's model of classical Greek tragedy:

- A great man is destroyed through an error of judgement (**hamartia**).
- Caesar suffers from pride and arrogance (**hubris**).
- There are several important deaths in the play.
- The final scenes are meant to inspire pity and a release of the audience's emotion (**catharsis**).

However, it is also possible to recognise that Shakespeare has added his own distinctive and individual features to this well-known model. For example, Caesar is the 'hero' after whom the play is named, yet he dies at the start of Act 3 rather than the end of the play. And Brutus is given typically 'tragic' soliloquies in which he reflects agonisingly on the prospect of murdering Caesar.

◆ Research Aristotle's views about tragedy in the library or on the Internet. Expand your research by exploring other, more recent, definitions. Then write a short essay in which you consider how closely you feel *Julius Caesar* conforms to the different possible models of tragedy.

# Themes in *Julius Caesar*

Another way of looking at the play is to discuss its themes. Themes are ideas, issues or topics that recur throughout the play. They suggest that Shakespeare was preoccupied by particular ideas as he wrote, and sought to explore them through a drama that would entertain his audiences – and make them think. Such major themes include: death and its physical representation; sickness and disease; public versus private; love and friendship; blood and blood ties; and appearance versus reality.

## Death and its physical representation

The idea of death and its physical representation runs through the play:

- Flavius and Murellus are killed for removing the decorations from Caesar's statues (Act 1 Scene 2).
- Cassius frequently mentions the possibility of suicide. Brutus resolves to kill Caesar: 'It must be by his death' (Act 2 Scene 1).
- After the frenzied stabbing of Caesar, his bloodied body is vividly present on stage and used to rouse the crowd to an avenging fury against the 'traitors' who killed him (Act 3 Scene 2).
- The innocent poet Cinna is pointlessly killed by the Roman mob (Act 3 Scene 3).
- Antony coolly approves the execution of his nephew as the Triumvirate seek to establish control of Rome (Act 4 Scene 1).
- Portia kills herself; Caesar's ghost appears to Brutus (Act 4 Scene 3).
- Pindarus helps Cassius to commit suicide; Titinius, displaying loyalty to Cassius, takes his own life (Act 5 Scene 3).
- Strato helps Brutus to kill himself (Act 5 Scene 5).

◆ Use the examples above, and any of your own, as the basis for an essay plan on how death in *Julius Caesar* creates moments of great dramatic impact.

## Sickness and disease

Disease and infection were rife in Elizabethan England. Unpleasant sexual diseases and, particularly, the bubonic plague were a constant threat, and epidemics were frequent. *Julius Caesar* contains many references to sickness and ill-health. When Murellus urges the common people to 'Pray to the gods to intermit [prevent] the plague' his words carry a strong contemporary resonance.

Caesar's human frailty is highlighted by focusing on his deafness and his epilepsy. Like Elizabeth I, Caesar is unable to beget an heir (Calpurnia is attending the Lupercal ceremony in an attempt to 'cure' her infertility). Cassius has poor eyesight.

Shakespeare frequently connects the sickness of the body with that of the mind. In Act 2 Scene 1, Portia asks 'Is Brutus sick?' when she witnesses his troubled sleeplessness in 'the vile contagion of the night' and concludes that her husband has 'some sick offence within [his] mind'; Ligarius's sickness is cured when he joins the conspiracy against Caesar; and to Brutus the assassination is 'A piece of work that will make sick men whole'.

◆ Research the prevalence of sickness and disease in Elizabethan England and prepare a short presentation to the class on how vulnerable and frightened Shakespeare's audiences may have been.

## Public versus private

Many aspects of the play explore the dramatic tension between public and private events. At its heart are the big 'set-piece' public scenes involving Caesar's assassination and the speeches by Brutus and Antony to the Roman crowd after Caesar's death. The play begins with the common people applauding Caesar's victory over Pompey (Act 1 Scene 2), then shows the Lupercal festival where Antony is reported as offering a crown to Caesar three times; Caesar's epileptic seizure is reported to have happened publicly 'in the market-place'.

After the murder, the play focuses increasingly on the nationwide repercussions of Caesar's assassination as mob violence drives Brutus and Cassius from Rome and precipitates civil war. The play's final scenes show faction fighting against faction and destruction and disorder on a grand scale. Shakespeare even includes a self-indulgent reference by Cassius to the way in which future actors will re-enact 'our lofty scene'.

Yet the play is also keen to explore issues at an individual 'private' level. There is Cassius's expression of his personal hatred of Caesar (Act 1 Scene 3); Brutus's agonised soliloquy in his orchard (Act 2 Scene 1); the domestic scenes showing Portia with Brutus and Calpurnia with Caesar (Act 2 Scenes 1 and 2); the presentation of Caesar's human frailties against his grand public self-confidence (Act 2 Scene 2); Antony's private outpourings of grief ('O, pardon me, thou bleeding piece of earth') and revenge ('Now let it work. Mischief, thou art afoot') which immediately follow his apparently equally sincere public speeches to the conspirators and the Roman crowd (Act 3 Scenes 1 and 2); and Brutus and Cassius's private reconciliation (Act 4 Scene 3).

◆ Write an analysis of one scene in the play in which you think Shakespeare skilfully explores the tension between 'public' and 'private'.

### Love and friendship

The nature of the male friendships presented in the play reflects Elizabethan values. The main male characters express deep and loyal affection for each other. Antony's friendship and admiration for Caesar are first suggested in Act 1 and given full dramatic play in Act 3 after Caesar's murder: 'Thou art the ruins of the noblest man / That ever livèd in the tide of times'. Brutus and Cassius share a similarly powerful friendship, even though they are not like-minded characters. In Act 4 Scene 3, after their bitter quarrel, Shakespeare stresses the importance of their

reconciliation as Cassius declares 'I cannot drink too much of Brutus' love.' Brutus also inspires love and affection in Portia, his servant Lucius and his friends. This makes Brutus's betrayal of Caesar all the more treacherous. Caesar's dying words in Act 3 Scene 1 ('*Et tu, Brute*? [Even you, Brutus?] – Then fall, Caesar!') express his disbelief at what is happening. Brutus's betrayal is almost as fatal to Caesar as the conspirators' savage stab wounds.

In striking contrast, the young and inexperienced Octavius is portrayed in Acts 4 and 5 as controlled, detached and calculating. Shakespeare developed this coldly formidable, efficient character in much greater detail in his later play *Antony and Cleopatra*.

◆ Working in small groups, make a list of the main characters. For each character, write a short paragraph about their attitudes to love and friendship. Link all your comments to quotations from the play.

## Blood: loyalty, sacrifice and betrayal

Both images and actual representations of blood abound in the play. In the opening scene the common people champion Caesar 'over Pompey's blood'. Antony speaks of how Pompey's statue ran with blood as Caesar fell dead at its base. Brutus agonises about behaving like a 'butcher' during the assassination and is cautious about killing Antony lest their 'course will seem too bloody'.

After the murder the conspirators smear their arms with Caesar's blood. Portia wounds herself to prove her devotion to Brutus. Calpurnia dreams of clouds that 'drizzled blood' and of her husband's statue that 'Did run pure blood'. As Antony shakes the hand of each conspirator his own is smeared with Caesar's blood. During his funeral oration Antony makes moving use of Caesar's bloodied robe and conjures up powerful images of Caesar's blood: 'Caesar's wounds, poor, poor, dumb mouths'.

As the references to blood diminish after Act 3, we are reminded that it is Caesar's spirit rather than his body that will now dominate events. Only when Brutus dies can he declare: 'Caesar, now be still.'

◆ **Find all the references to blood in the play. Display your findings as a striking presentation.**

## Appearance versus reality

One of Shakespeare's major preoccupations in his plays seems to have been an exploration of the difference between what things are like on the surface (appearance) and what they are really like (reality). This is a theme that is well matched to a play such as *Julius Caesar*, in which the conspirators often need to conceal their murderous intentions and sinister plotting beneath a veneer of apparent honesty, trust and friendship. In Act 2 Scene 1 Brutus, in particular, expresses his shame as he urges that the 'monstrous visage' of their conspiracy be hid 'in smiles and affability'. As the conspirators approach the assassination (Act 2 Scene 2) Caesar's assured public confidence is set against Trebonius's and Brutus's threatening asides.

◆ **Look back at the 'Themes' boxes on pages 44, 66 and 154. Use the material from those boxes to help you produce a short presentation for your class on how Shakespeare uses the theme to create a range of dramatic effects in the play.**

# The Roman world

This alphabetical section provides details about some of the Roman people, places and customs that Shakespeare incorporated into his play.

**Aeneas** (see p. 16) was a Trojan hero, the son of Anchises and the goddess Venus. According to legend, Aeneas's journey from Troy (retold in Virgil's epic poem the *Aeneid*) led to the founding of the city that was to become Rome.

**Armies** At the time of the late Republic, some Roman armies were privately owned. Troops swore an oath of allegiance to their commander and the commanders looked to their soldiers for political support.

◆ Study the image on this page and other photographs in this edition of Romans in military dress. Then conduct your own research on the equipment and fighting techniques of the Roman soldier. Suggest ways of using your information to devise suitable costumes for a modern stage production. Draw and label them to add to your Director's Journal.

**Augurers** (see p. 50) Any decision of importance was referred to the augurers, who had various ways of determining the will of the gods and deciding whether it was lucky or unlucky to proceed on that day. Sometimes a live animal was cut open and its insides studied. In Act 2 Scene 1, line 200, Cassius refers to Caesar's belief in the power of augurers, omens and dreams, which he fears will prevent him from going to the Capitol and thereby ruin the conspirators' plans.

◆ Look back at Act 2 Scene 2, lines 1–107, where Caesar debates whether to go to the Capitol. Describe how Shakespeare has used dreams, omens and auguries to add to the scene's dramatic tension.

◆ Remind yourself of the 'Themes' box on page 144 and use the material generated as a starting point for a mini-essay on the importance of fate and omens in the play.

**Cicero (106–43 BC)** (see p. 20) was the leading orator of his day. His writings were studied intensely in Elizabethan schools. His style was held up as the ideal model for students. His essays, letters and imaginary conversations between historical figures popularised the ideas of Greek philosophers, presenting them in a pleasurable and accessible style.

◆ Conduct your own research into the historical character Cicero. Then look back at Cicero's part in the play (Act 1 Scenes 2 and 3). Suggest ways in which an actor might portray something of the historical Cicero in the way he performs his role.

**The city of Rome** was built around two locations. The forum (market-place) was the central area where commerce and the administration of justice were focused. The Capitol, on one of its seven hills, was the political and religious centre of ancient Rome.

The site of the ancient Roman forum.

The Roman Capitol seen from the Palatine Hill in the 19th century.

◆ Research what ancient Rome looked like. Choose one 'public' scene from the play and design the set and costumes for that scene. Suggest ways of bringing out the atmosphere of ancient Rome.

**Colossus** (see p. 18) was a giant statue of the Greek god Apollo that bestrode the harbour entrance to the Greek island of Rhodes. Over 30 metres high (the tallest statue of its time), it was known as one of the seven wonders of the ancient world.

**Cynics** (see p. 126) believed primarily in two key principles: that the individual was responsible for their own morality and that a person's mental determination ('will') was all-important. They rejected the social values of the time, preached the avoidance of pleasure and denied social relationships. Cynicism was the forerunner of Stoicism (see p. 173).

**Epicurus** (see p. 144) was a Greek philosopher who founded Epicureanism. He believed that seeking simple and modest pleasures was the route to tranquillity and freedom from fear.

**Honour** (see also **Suicide**) in ancient times and in Shakespeare's day was not the vague concept it is today. Aristotle, a famous ancient Greek philosopher, explained how the magnanimous man (the perfect ruler) made public honour his 'chief concern'.

◆ Discuss how Shakespeare explores the theme of honour in the play. Refer to the 'Themes' box on page 24 and look closely at what Brutus and Cassius say about it (e.g. in Act 1 Scene 2 and Act 3 Scene 2) and how they approach their deaths. What does 'honour' mean to them? Prepare a short talk for younger students of Shakespeare on the importance of honour to classical Romans.

**The Lupercal** (see p. 10) was originally a farming festival held on 15 February to ward wolves off the newborn lambs and kids in the flocks. Later it was adopted by the city of Rome to ward off evil spirits. Just as the billy goats brought fertility to the flocks, barren women thought the flick of a goatskin flail would enable them to have children.

◆ Caesar's first appearance in the play is to attend the Lupercal (Act 1 Scene 2). Sketch a set design for that scene which reflects some of the ideas above.

**Octavius Caesar (63 BC–AD 14)**, grand-nephew to Julius Caesar, achieved high office at an early age. Caesar treated him as his heir. After Caesar's assassination (as seen in the play), Octavius established the Second Triumvirate with Antony and Lepidus, but later (as seen in *Antony and Cleopatra*) Lepidus was disposed of, and then Octavius and Antony quarrelled and battled with each other. Octavius won and became sole ruler of the Roman Empire, with the title of Emperor Caesar Augustus.

**Pompey (106–48 BC)** (see p. 8) was, like Caesar, a very popular general; both were members of the First Triumvirate (with Crassus). He married Caesar's daughter Julia. Pompey remained in Rome, while Caesar campaigned in Europe, becoming increasingly powerful. When Caesar returned and became dictator, Pompey fled and was finally murdered. Shakespeare's *Julius Caesar* opens after Caesar has wiped out a final pocket of resistance headed by Pompey's sons.

**Proscription** (see pp. 112 and 128) was the imposition of the death penalty; three hundred out of nine hundred senators were executed along with two hundred equites (aristocrats). The newly formed Triumvirate (Antony, Octavius and Lepidus) used it ruthlessly to organise a purge of their political opponents. They were even willing to sacrifice members of their own families.

**Sacrifice** of animals was an important ritual in Roman religious observance. Caesar shows his superstitious nature in Act 2 Scene 2 when he urges the priests to 'do present [immediate] sacrifice' on the morning of his assassination – a ceremony that threatens ill-fortune as the priests 'could not find a heart within the beast'.

**Stoics** (see p. 126) held to the philosophy of Stoicism. This taught that self-control, inner strength and freedom from unsettling emotions were ideal principles that made people indifferent to pleasure and pain and led to clear thinking, balanced judgement and absolute truth. If life became unendurable, it was appropriate to kill yourself.

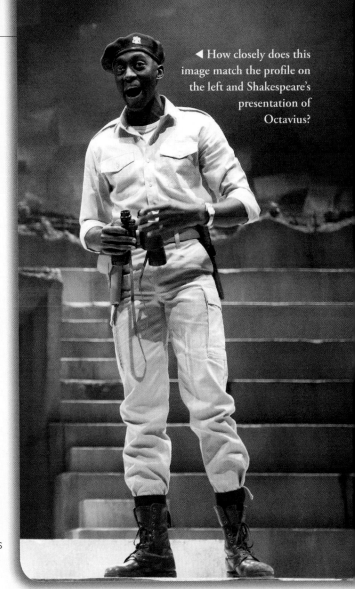

◄ How closely does this image match the profile on the left and Shakespeare's presentation of Octavius?

**Suicide** was seen as a noble action in the ancient world. The Roman code of honour dictated that suicide was preferable to ignominious death or disgrace. Brutus vows he will never 'go bound to Rome'; Cassius commits suicide remarking: 'O, coward that I am to live so long'.

◆ Many of the major characters believe their lives are not sacrosanct (see the 'Themes' box on p. 24). But can suicide ever be a 'noble' act? What do you think Shakespeare's play suggests? Talk about this in a small group and be ready to offer your main conclusions in a class discussion.

# Characters

Recent literary critical thinking has questioned the validity of considering characters in plays as 'real people'. In fact, this idea has generally been dispensed with in favour of seeing them as dramatic constructs that function only within the social and political contexts of the play. The 'identities' of these characters are also considered to be much less fixed than they were in the past, as characters may be interpreted differently in each production. They only exist for the length of the play.

It is, therefore, useful to summarise what you discover about the characters through their speech, actions and what others say about them during the course of the play. These are the three main ways in which characters are established.

Remember you are always entitled to your own views on the characters and their roles – just make sure you can back those views up with reference to the play itself.

## Julius Caesar

*Julius Caesar* has been called Shakespeare's 'great political thriller'. Many historians agree that Caesar was a man of immense talent and great military skill, yet at the same time a mass of contradictions and complexities. Shakespeare makes great use of the paradoxical mixture of qualities chronicled by historians to portray the man whom several conspirators were desperate to wipe from the face of the Roman world.

Shakespeare's Caesar dominates the play from the start: the crowd rejoices at his triumph and the Tribunes Flavius and Murellus resentfully describe him as the man who intends to 'soar above the view of men'. It is significant that the play begins with Caesar's popularity being demonstrated by the crowd's reaction to him, as the people were a powerful force in the Republic. At the Lupercal ceremony in Act 1 Scene 2, Antony also affirms Caesar's towering authority (line 10): 'When Caesar says, "Do this", it is performed.' Any dissenting voices are ruthlessly silenced (line 275).

Yet Caesar, though powerful, betrays signs of physical weakness and emotional vulnerability. He is deaf in his left ear (a detail that Shakespeare seems to have invented), suffers from epilepsy and in Act 1 Scene 2, Caesar says that Calpurnia suffers from the 'sterile curse', but this reflects upon him too – having no heir was a weakness in a leader. Public spectacle, the 'holy chase' in celebration of the Feast of Lupercal, is mixed with personal vulnerability and susceptibility to superstition. Similarly, at the very moment when Caesar was publicly being offered a crown we are told how 'He fell down in the market-place, and foamed at mouth, and was / speechless' (Act 1 Scene 2, lines 246–7). Cassius also recounts how once he had to rescue Caesar during a swimming contest and how, during a bout of fever, he had cried out 'As a sick girl'.

However, Cassius also acknowledges Caesar to 'bestride the narrow world / like a Colossus'. Arrogant enough to constantly talk of himself in the third person (as 'Caesar' rather than 'I'), nineteen times in total in fact, Caesar is at one moment a shrewd and astute judge of character, warning Antony to be on his guard against Cassius with his 'lean and hungry look', then moments later boasting of his own immunity from fear: 'I rather tell thee what is to be feared / Than what I fear: for always I am Caesar' (Act 1 Scene 2, lines 211–12).

Perhaps foolhardy, perhaps fearless, Caesar finally ignores his wife's pleas for him not to go to the Capitol, and in the lead-up to his assassination many of his more unattractive traits are given prominence. Adamantly refusing to repeal the order to banish Metellus's brother, Caesar spurns Metellus 'like a cur [dog]', declaring himself 'constant as the northern star'. This inflexible pride seals his fate.

But Caesar's spirit lives on. Antony's moving funeral oration, the blood-drenched corpse, the appearance of his ghost and the fact that both Cassius and Brutus die with Caesar's name on their lips – all help keep Caesar clearly in the audience's mind to the end of the play.

◆ In order to help your thinking about Caesar, discuss or write about the following questions:

**a** In your own production of *Julius Caesar* would you stress Caesar's weakness or his power? Justify your answer.

**b** What would the effect be of having a female Caesar in a production with male conspirators?

**c** Is it fierce courage or dangerous pride that makes Caesar say, 'Danger knows full well / That Caesar is more dangerous than he' (Act 2 Scene 2, lines 44–5)? Justify your answer.

**d** In a review of a recent production, the actor's performance of Caesar was described as 'thuggish'. Is there evidence in the play to suggest that this is a valid interpretation?

**e** Do you find Caesar a likeable leader? Why or why not?

**f** 'In dramatising the character of Caesar, Shakespeare avoids soliciting sympathy for him or arousing alienation towards him.' Discuss.

◆ 'Could the way in which Julius Caesar is portrayed as somewhat petulant and past his prime, almost the old maid, have offered a whispered suggestion of Queen Elizabeth at the end of her life, fearful of conspiracy and assassination?' Try acting out a few scenes, with Caesar being 'petulant and past his prime'. Follow this up with an analysis of how successful you think this interpretation is.

▼ Which of these two photos better captures your impressions of Caesar? Give reasons for your answer.

# Brutus

Brutus was a highly educated man from a distinguished family; an ancestor of his overthrew the tyrannous Tarquin royal family and established the Roman Republic. He fought with Pompey against Caesar, but was pardoned and became Caesar's trusted and close friend. He now sees Caesar's increasing power and the rumoured impending coronation as a danger to his Republican idealism and Rome itself.

Perhaps the key to Shakespeare's presentation of Brutus is the sense of conflict that haunts him. By his own admission he is 'Brutus, with himself at war'. In his soliloquy (Act 2 Scene 1, lines 10–34) he reasons very carefully why Caesar must die, concerned to justify all his actions to the highest ethical standard. He believes passionately in the power of rational and logical argument, yet his judgement is sometimes flawed. He fails to see how Cassius manipulates him, suggests conspirators dip their hands in Caesar's blood, spares Antony's life, and then lets Antony speak at Caesar's funeral. He heads the conspirators with unquestioned authority, overruling the others on the need to swear an oath, Cicero's suitability as a fellow conspirator and the best way to do battle.

Brutus's integrity and reputation are admired by his colleagues and he brings respectability to the conspiracy. Cassius judges: 'Well, Brutus, thou art noble'. Casca remarks that he 'sits high in all the people's hearts'. To Ligarius he is the 'Soul of Rome'. Brutus himself boasts: 'Set honour in one eye and death i'th'other / And I will look on both indifferently.'

Although these traits lend him a pompous and self-righteous air (perhaps most clearly seen in his quarrel with Cassius in Act 4 Scene 3), his idealism often makes him tragically vulnerable. He has a soft and caring side, which surfaces in the domestic scenes where he shows tenderness and concern for his wife, Portia and his servant, Lucius. It is noticeable that Cassius has no comparable scenes, and consequently Brutus can be said to show greater emotional range than Cassius.

At the end of the play, even though he is presented as increasingly isolated, he is still seen with the 'remains of friends', who loyally refuse to help him die. Antony's epitaph celebrates powerfully 'the noblest Roman of them all', motivated only by 'common good' rather than 'envy of great Caesar'.

Below are some comments from critics about Brutus.

*I used to think Brutus was the idealist in a world of realpolitik: [the actor] excellently shows him to be a self-righteous blunderer.*

Michael Billington, 2012

*Brutus's vision is obscured by Utopian assumptions (his belief that people can be persuaded by rational argument and that they are as consistent and trustworthy as he believes himself to be).*

Anthony Davies, 2002

*[Brutus] is a man who thinks much, but none too well; a man whose assumptions about the world he lives in are almost all mistaken; a man who, acting on these assumptions, achieves the exact opposite of what he intended. He is a political disaster – and yet he is not without a certain nobility.*

John Nettles, 2000

*It cannot be seriously doubted that Brutus is the focus – dramatically, psychologically, politically, and morally.*

Marvin Spevack, 2004

*Shakespeare treats him [Brutus] with delicate sympathy.*

Frank Kermode, 1974

◆ **Choose one of the above quotations and, having discussed your ideas about it in a group, write up your answer making clear whether or not you agree with the view expressed. Make sure you back up your points with evidence and quotations from the text.**

◆ **Look back at all the work you did on Brutus throughout your study of the play. Make the case for him being the most interesting and sympathetic character in the whole play. You could do this in the form of a speech and then take questions.**

◆ Without going back to your notes, write down all the times you can remember that Brutus and Cassius disagree and what they disagree about. What is the significance of these arguments?

◆ Imagine a production of the play without Brutus. What difference would his absence make?

▼ Which of Brutus's qualities does this actor show in his expression and gesture?

## Cassius

Cassius fought with Pompey against Caesar and was pardoned, but he did not receive Caesar's favour. It is he who drives the initial stages of the conspiracy. Like Brutus, he is troubled by the thoughts of what Caesar has become: 'Upon what meat doth this our Caesar feed / That he is grown so great?'

Cassius is prompted by personal resentment and antagonism. These feelings surface powerfully in the way he tries to 'seduce' Brutus to the cause of toppling Caesar. In Act 1 Scene 2, in particular, his words seethe with energy and passion as he compares 'we petty men' to the demi-god Caesar. Although Shakespeare does not elaborate on his motives, Cassius expresses his contempt for 'So vile a thing as Caesar' because he 'doth bear me hard' (has a grudge against me). Later in the play (Act 4

Scene 3) Shakespeare suggests that Cassius's temper was inherited from his mother.

Caesar's assessment of Cassius (Act 1 Scene 2) is astute and accurate. Cassius looks predatory and he 'thinks too much'. A shrewd judge of character, he rarely smiles and abjures entertainment. But he is particularly dangerous because such men will forever be restless: 'Whiles they behold a greater than themselves'.

In contrast to Brutus, Cassius has political acumen and cleverness. He knows that the conspiracy will only be successful if all threats are removed (Brutus is obsessed by the need to be 'sacrificers' rather than 'butchers'). However, Cassius knows that he needs Brutus's support in order to lend dignity and nobility to their enterprise and to quash any accusations of self-interest on the part of the conspirators.

A key aspect of Cassius's presentation is the change that his character undergoes. He becomes much more sympathetic after the assassination. Like Brutus, he attracts loyal followers and shows the deep value of friendship (his reconciliation with Brutus in Act 4 Scene 3 is very moving). Frenzied outbursts give way to calmness. Brutus pays a mournful tribute to him: 'The last of all the Romans'. But perhaps Titinius's ironic comment ('thou hast misconstrued everything'), capping Cassius's impetuous suicide, is the more appropriate assessment.

◆ A theatre critic wrote of Cassius in the 2012 RSC production: 'Wary and sly, scared and manipulative, Mr Nri is an excellent Cassius.' Would you want the Cassius in your production to show these characteristics?

◆ 'Cassius is branded as a figure of disorder on both the personal and political levels.' Is this an accurate way of considering Cassius, in your view?

◆ Consider Cassius the leader:

a Why is Cassius so successful in binding the conspirators together?

b If you had been in Rome at the time and had harboured feelings against Caesar, do you think you would have joined Cassius? Give reasons for your answer. Compare your answer with others'.

◆ In the course of the play, Cassius refers to himself fourteen times in the third person. Explore the significance of this, bearing in mind that Brutus (thirteen times) and Caesar (nineteen times) also refer to themselves in this way.

◆ You are the director of a new production of the play. What advice would you offer the actor playing Cassius about how to make the change in his character after the assassination plausible? With a partner, perform a role play – what ideas does Cassius have?

Cassius and Brutus could be said to be dramatic 'foils' for each other. This means that the contrasting qualities and actions of one help to highlight the qualities and actions of the other.

◆ Using the list of disagreements you compiled for the activity on page 177 to help you, draw up a table to show how their qualities and actions contrast.

◆ 'The conspiracy would not have gone ahead if Brutus had refused to join it.' Do you agree? Improvise a discussion between two conspirators who hold different views.

◆ Brutus and Cassius are the two most important conspirators. They need to be considered separately, but it is also useful to compare their roles and traits, as you have been offered the opportunity to do on some of the left-hand pages. How would the play be different if there were no dramatic contrast between these two characters?

## Antony

Antony was a soldier with a reputation for womanising and riotous living. Shakespeare stresses his virility and social pursuits – he is a Lupercalian runner 'given / To sports, to wildness, and much company'. This reputation endures into Act 5, where Cassius labels him 'a masker and a reveller'. He campaigned with Caesar, reaching high government office through Caesar's favour. Prior to Caesar's assassination Antony speaks only five lines; in his first appearance he is presented as Caesar's close friend, a man who respects his absolute authority: 'When Caesar says, "Do this", it is performed.' Like Brutus, his judgement is seen to be flawed, and he mistakenly rates Cassius as harmless.

After Caesar's death Antony really comes into his own. As a deeply grieving friend, master tactician and political opportunist, he holds the stage during the pivotal 'funeral' scene in a mesmerising way.

First he must engage with the murderers. Whilst holding loyally to his love for Caesar, he skilfully negotiates with the assassins, shaking their bloodied hands in an ironic gesture of friendship and respect. But his main objective is to set up his funeral oration to Caesar, and his soliloquy (from Act 3 Scene 1, line 254) shows how false his earlier words have been, the true depth of his grief and the anticipated fury of his revenge.

His funeral speech (from Act 3 Scene 2, line 65), widely regarded as the climactic moment of the play, shows off all Antony's rhetorical skills. Careful not to antagonise the crowd, he first denies he has come to praise Caesar. Dealing with claims about Caesar's ambition, he shows ironic respect for Brutus and sets up memorable choruses and refrains ('honourable man').

The pause to allow the common people to digest his message is a masterstroke. By the time he has re-established Caesar's greatness, planted ideas of mutiny in the minds of the crowd and made reference to the violation of Caesar's cloak, it remains only for him to mention the munificence of Caesar's will and he has unleashed the force of mob violence.

He appears in only four further scenes and is, arguably, eclipsed by Octavius's cool assurance and control by the end of the play. However, Antony's ruthlessness is underlined by his willing sacrifice of his nephew. He also shows contempt for Lepidus and the integrity of Caesar's will (by siphoning off money to pay for the war against Brutus and Cassius).

At the end of the play, Shakespeare perhaps attempts to recalibrate his presentation of Antony, firstly by having him pardon Lucilius and secondly by the generosity of his tribute to Brutus in the closing moments.

◆ Discuss these differing views of Antony:

*Antony is the most charismatic character in the play. It is not surprising that he is often played by well-known and attractive actors.*

*Antony's main role in the play is as a superb speech-maker.*

*Antony [is] a calculating opportunist.*

◆ Refer back to the photos of Antony in this book (pp. x, 20, 82, 88, 96, 98, 165, 170). Which one most closely fits your idea of him? Why?

◆ Write a list of the incidents when Antony shows the vicious or cruel side of his character. Pick out a quotation for each incident that sums up his attitude to it. Now list his acts of kindness or generosity and pick out a quotation for each of them. What conclusions can you draw about him from reading through your lists?

◆ What are Antony's political views? Are they as well defined as those of Cassius and Brutus?

◆ In what ways is Antony a foil to Octavius? What evidence does the play offer that they will work well together and with Lepidus, the other member of the Triumvirate, in the future?

▼ Does this photo of Antony add anything to your understanding of the dramatic function of the character?

# Portia and Calpurnia

These are the only female characters in what is known as Shakespeare's 'most male' play. They have several features in common: they mirror Elizabethan attitudes to women; they inhabit a world in which men hold complete power and authority and in which women's lives are subservient. In more recent productions their roles have been highlighted in different ways (see page 194) and feminist criticism has questioned the issue of the importance of gender in the play.

**Portia** appears in only two scenes. In Act 2 Scene 1 part of her role is to reveal the impact of Brutus's mental turmoil on his domestic life. Portia has sensitively and discreetly witnessed the changes in Brutus, but is keen for him to share his burden with her. She makes clear what a loving wife expects 'By all your vows of love' and, in turn, provokes a tender response from Brutus: 'You are my true and honourable wife'. As testament to her love and devotion she has wounded herself in the thigh, a gesture that wrings pity and admiration from her husband. He begs that he might be 'worthy of this noble wife', noble not only because of her actions but also because she is descended from a noble family: Marcus Porcius Cato is her (and Young Cato's) father and Brutus's uncle. Marcus Porcius Cato was a famous soldier, orator and statesman of high moral standing who committed suicide rather than be captured. Thus, Cato's life has several parallels with Brutus's and Portia refers to herself as a 'woman well reputed' because she is his daughter.

In the scene at the Capitol (Act 2 Scene 4), Portia displays the gender stereotyping so prevalent in Shakespeare's time, confessing that she finds it hard to keep quiet. It is likely that Brutus has shared the conspirators' plan with her and Portia's natural agitation and nervous anxiety ratchet up the dramatic energy of this episode. Her suicide (by swallowing hot coals) is only reported in Act 4. This painful death is further evidence of her nobility and bravery.

'**Calpurnia**' is the first word that Caesar speaks in the play. Perhaps Shakespeare is drawing attention to Caesar's intimate side as well as reminding the audience that the couple are childless. Later (Act 2 Scene 2) she signals the terrifying portents of the storm and relates a striking dream about her husband's death. In entreating him not to go to the Senate house she provides him with an excuse: 'Call it my fear / That keeps you in the house, and not your own.' Momentarily, Caesar listens, only for Decius to sway the decision by mocking Caesar's adherence to his wife's 'dreams'.

◆ In a recent production, Portia was obviously pregnant, in contrast to Calpurnia's childlessness. What do you think of this idea?

◆ If you were given the choice of playing either Portia or Calpurnia in a production of *Julius Caesar*, which role would you choose and why?

◆ Set up a debate within a group of four. Two of you argue that the women in the play are too sketchily drawn to be significant. The other two argue against this view.

◆ Traditionally, the scenes that included the women were considered to be rather limited. More recently critics have highlighted the mixture of both public and private concerns in these domestic scenes. What ideas that have a public significance (for example, political ideas) do you find in these scenes with Calpurnia and Portia?

◆ As a director you decide that Portia's death should not happen off stage – it should be given more prominence, as Brutus's death is. Write the speech she might make before committing suicide.

▼ As in Shakespeare's time, this 1999 production was all male. What challenges would be presented for a male actor playing Portia in the present day?

▼ A tender moment between Calpurnia and Caesar. How far can this be justified from the script?

## The people

The people have a significant dramatic function. Indeed, some critics would consider the importance of the Roman people in the play as rivalling that of Caesar, Brutus and Antony. This is for political as well as dramatic reasons. The Republic is under threat at the start of the play in the eyes of those who are concerned about Caesar's ambition. The Tribunes and the conspirators talk resentfully about Caesar elevating himself above the people on whose support he depends.

Civic unrest is shown at the start of *Julius Caesar* when the crowd gathers to 'make holiday to see Caesar and to rejoice in his triumph', as the Cobbler says. The right and desire of the crowd to do this is challenged by two Tribunes and this leads to lively exchanges and threats. Several individuals (Plebeians 1, 2, 3 and 4) emerge each time the crowd is present, expressing different views. Such scenes would have been familiar to contemporary audiences, as riots frequently broke out when it was holiday time.

Antony's skilful manipulation of the crowd in Act 3 at the funeral of Caesar is demonstrated by the crowd's reactions to his words. Having begun by supporting Brutus, even to the extent of Plebeian 3 shouting 'Let him be Caesar', the crowd begins to assess Antony's words, at first acknowledging that 'there is much reason in his sayings'. From there, Antony works on their natural greed with the promise of Caesar's will, significantly comes down from the pulpit to their level and then works the crowd up to a frenzy of grief, drawing attention to Caesar's body. Without the crowd's reactions, the rhetoric would be empty. It needs to be seen to work. Antony then works on them to feel aggressive towards the conspirators who are responsible for this. He finally reveals what Caesar has promised them in his will and then watches as the crowd departs, intent on the 'mischief' he has encouraged them to. This is directly followed by the shocking scene of the terrorising of Cinna, showing the horrors of mob violence.

In more recent productions, members of the cast have been planted among the audience, taking the plebeian speaking parts. The audience then becomes the crowd and hence part of the drama. Arguably this helps to extend the people's involvement in politics to every member of the audience.

◆ How would you stage the crowd scenes in your production of the play?

◆ Can you think of any other plays or films in which the crowd plays a significant role? What comparisons could you usefully make with this play?

In this play and others, the crowd is often talked of disparagingly. Flavius calls them 'idle creatures'. Murellus calls them:

*You blocks, you stones, you worse than senseless things!*
*O you hard hearts, you cruel men of Rome*

In Shakespeare's play *King Henry IV Part 2* the people are reviled for being

*the blunt monster with uncounted heads,*
*The still-discordant wav'ring multitude*

◆ Do the people deserve such criticism in *Julius Caesar*? You could tackle this question in a group, with two speech-makers, one saying the people do deserve such criticism, the other saying they don't. The speech-makers should use rhetorical techniques in their speeches (see pp. 185–6). The other members of the group play the crowd, heckling and supporting.

◆ 'Without the crowd, this play would be a dry political drama'. Do you agree?

# The language of *Julius Caesar*

## Imagery

Some critics have claimed that *Julius Caesar* does not contain much **imagery**: vivid words and phrases that help create atmosphere as they conjure up emotionally charged pictures or associations in the mind. Yet when Flavius describes the removal of decorations from Caesar's statues, claiming that 'These growing feathers plucked from Caesar's wing / Will make him fly an ordinary pitch' (Act 1 Scene 1, lines 71–2), he is using a striking animal image to compare the limiting of Caesar's power to the way a falconer restricts the 'pitch' of a falcon (the height to which it rises before swooping) by plucking its feathers. When Flavius adds that Caesar wants to keep his subjects in 'servile [slave-like] fearfulness', the impression of Caesar as a tyrannical predator is complete.

Shakespeare uses metaphor, simile and personification. All are comparisons that in effect substitute one thing (the image) for another (the thing described).

A **simile** compares one thing to another using 'like' or 'as'. For example, Cassius contemptuously dismisses Caesar dealing with his fever 'As a sick girl'. Caesar 'doth bestride the narrow world / Like a Colossus'. Brutus, contemplating how to execute Caesar rather than slaughter him, implores his fellows to 'carve him as a dish fit for the gods, / Not hew him as a carcass fit for hounds.' Caesar makes his death inevitable by asserting: 'I am constant as the northern star'.

A **metaphor** is also a comparison, suggesting that dissimilar things are the same. Brutus slights Antony, saying he is so dependent on his friend that he is 'but a limb of Caesar'. Urging the conspirators to be 'sacrificers, but not butchers', Brutus shows a high-minded, ethical approach to the killing of Caesar. Portia, aware of an increasingly distant relationship with Brutus, asks: 'Dwell I but in the suburbs / Of your good pleasure?' To Antony the conspirators' 'purpled hands do reek and smoke'.

**Personification** turns things into persons, giving them human feelings or attributes. Cassius bemoans the state of Rome 'groaning underneath this age's yoke'. Brutus describes 'conspiracy' as like a person ashamed 'to show thy dang'rous brow by night' and celebrates the assassination of Caesar by declaring: 'Ambition's debt is paid.' For Antony, Caesar's bleeding wounds 'like dumb mouths do ope their ruby lips'.

◆ Find the sources of the four similes, four metaphors and four personifications cited above. In each case identify the specific comparison being made and write a sentence commenting on the impact of the image.

◆ Now test yourself with the following images. First, identify whether it is metaphor, simile or personification. Then locate the image in the text and analyse it as outlined above.

   **a** 'But hollow men, like horses hot at hand, / Make gallant show and promise of their mettle'

   **b** 'Tiber trembled underneath her banks / To hear the replication of your sounds'

   **c** 'When you are waspish'

   **d** 'and put a tongue / In every wound of Caesar, that should move / The stones of Rome to rise and mutiny'

   **e** 'For I am armed so strong in honesty / That they pass by me as the idle wind'

   **f** 'There is a tide in the affairs of men / Which, taken at the flood, leads on to fortune'

   **g** 'sweet Caesar's wounds, poor, poor, dumb mouths'

   **h** 'The deep of night is crept upon our talk'

   **i** 'let me not stir you up / To such a sudden flood of mutiny'

   **j** 'He shall but bear them as the ass bears gold'

◆ Identify five additional striking and powerful images in the play. Draw them in a bold way that highlights the comparisons at the heart of each one. Collate them into a whole-class display.

### 'Animal' imagery

Images enrich particular moments and can also illuminate key themes. Consider the effect of the following animal images in the play.

- Caesar dismisses the conspirators' pleas to repeal Metellus's brother's banishment by affirming that he will not respond to 'base spaniel fawning' (behaviour like that of an eager-to-please dog).
- As Antony contemplates the civil strife that will follow Caesar's murder, he imagines Caesar's ghost will 'Cry havoc and let slip the dogs of war', linking the frenzied mob violence that he has unleashed to the savagery of unruly hounds.
- Caesar is a 'brave hart [deer]' felled by 'hunters' and 'crimsoned in thy Lethe' (Lethe was the river of oblivion in the underworld), or 'like a deer strucken by many princes'.

Other animal images provide insight into character, and intensify meaning and emotional force. When Brutus muses on 'the bright day that brings forth the adder', his train of thought connects hidden danger with the idea of a snake ... and Caesar. Once Caesar is crowned, 'we put a sting in him / That at his will he may do danger with'. Thus Brutus resolves to 'think him as a serpent's egg ... And kill him in the shell.'

◆ **Write a short paragraph exploring each of the above images. Focus on the specific qualities that the animal comparison brings to that image.**

## Creating atmosphere

Shakespeare often uses language to create atmosphere. Remember that his plays were originally staged in broad daylight so words had to establish setting and atmosphere (see p. 190). A good example of his technique is Act 2 Scene 1, where the language has to suggest a night-time setting in Brutus's orchard for the conspirators' meeting. This darkness gradually gives way to the breaking of dawn (line 106).

◆ **Choose a favourite scene. Talk with a partner about its atmosphere (aggressive, fearful, joking, and so on). Compile a 'language list' of phrases or lines from your chosen scene that create the atmosphere.**

◆ **Use your list to make up a short play with your own plot and characters. Create as powerful an atmosphere as you can in your play by using Shakespeare's words.**

## Creating character

Most of Shakespeare's characters have a distinctive way of speaking, but their style can change from situation to situation. For example, Casca's language in Act 1 changes from a relaxed, cynical style in Scene 2 (when he is with his patrician friends) to one of fear and apprehension in the storm of Scene 3.

◆ **Choose a character, follow them through the play and compile a list of their typical language in different situations.**

## Rhetoric

Public speaking (or oratory) was hugely significant in ancient Rome. The art of persuasive speaking and writing, known as **rhetoric**, was a skill that all public figures aspired to master. Scholars developed sophisticated and memorable language techniques that were often used to establish and maintain political power. The art of rhetoric was still considered crucial in Elizabethan times and Shakespeare undoubtedly studied it at school.

In all centuries since Shakespeare's time, the art of rhetoric has played a very important part in public and political events across the world. Perhaps one of the most famous public speeches was delivered by Martin Luther King on 28 August 1963. Luther was a major leader of the American civil rights movement and his seventeen-minute speech to over 200,000 civil rights supporters on the steps of the Lincoln Memorial after a march through Washington has become world famous.

Largely as a result of the powerful repetition of the phrase, it has become known as his 'I have a dream' speech. In it, King plays significantly on:

- the pattern and repetition of language (for example, 'Now is the time'; 'Let freedom ring')
- the use of balanced phrases and antithesis (for example, 'It came as a joyous daybreak to end the long night of captivity')
- paralinguistic features (that is, the non-lexical components of the speech, such as the musicality of the rhythm, the preacher's 'call-and-response' technique, the varying of pitch, pace and volume)
- the use of the 'rule of three' (words or ideas repeated three times: 'Free at last!')
- emotive language ('crippled by the manacles of segregation')
- language that makes use of strong sounds (using onomatopoeia and alliteration).

◆ **The speech is widely available as a transcript and it can be viewed on the Internet. Working in pairs, analyse a small portion of the speech. See if you can identify other examples of some (or all) of the techniques listed above. Talk together about the kind of impact the speech makes on an audience.**

◆ **Try your hand at writing your own 'persuasive' speech, modelled on the same core strategies. The choice of subject is entirely yours!**

*Julius Caesar* also contains many examples of rhetoric: speeches that similarly seek to persuade by using striking and memorable vocabulary and language strategies. Language is used to create atmosphere, persuade people, move them to action, seek to change them. It appeals to their reason, emotions and imagination and builds their confidence in the speaker. In the play, rhetoric is used to great effect in several contexts:

- Murellus and Flavius's reprimand of the common people (Act 1 Scene 1)
- Cassius's speeches to Brutus in Act 1 Scene 2

- Brutus in soliloquy where he tries to persuade himself that Caesar's death is justified; Portia's emotional speeches to her husband, imploring him to confide in her (Act 2 Scene 1)
- The Soothsayer's cryptic and ominous warnings to Caesar (Act 2 Scene 4)
- Brutus's speech to the common people, 'Romans, countrymen, and lovers'; Antony's funeral oration, 'Friends, Romans, countrymen' (Act 3 Scene 2)
- Caesar's arrogant assertions of fearlessness (Act 2 Scene 2, Act 3 Scene 1).

Rhetoric is discussed in detail in the 'Language' boxes on pages 8, 16, 18, 92 and 120. It uses a range of methods to make language more memorable, in terms of both language selection and its delivery. As well as making extensive use of lists and repetition (see p. 187), it is very precisely structured and ordered. Key phrases and ideas are reinforced through striking imagery, as in 'Our day is gone, / Clouds, dews, and dangers come' (Act 5 Scene 3, lines 63–4). Listeners are directly engaged through rhetorical questions that direct the audience towards the speaker's desired conclusion without the speaker overtly stating it – for example, 'Did this in Caesar seem ambitious?' (Act 3 Scene 2, line 82).

◆ **Choose one rhetorical speech from the play (either from the list above, or one of your own). First, identify and annotate its specific 'persuasive' features. Then write a short critical evaluation of how it creates its effects.**

◆ **Perform or record your own interpretation of the speech in a way that highlights those specific rhetorical effects. Play your version alongside those of other students so that you create a sequence of persuasive speeches that you can compare.**

## Antithesis

**Antithesis** is the opposition of words or phrases to each other, as in 'Set honour in one eye and death i'th'other' (Act 1 Scene 2, line 86); 'honour' and 'death' stand against each other. The setting of word against word is one of Shakespeare's favourite language devices. He uses it extensively in his plays because antithesis powerfully expresses conflict through the use of opposites, and conflict is the essence of drama. Antony remarks of Caesar after his death 'O mighty Caesar! Dost thou lie so low?' Brutus's argument that Antony should not be killed by the conspirators (Act 2 Scene 1, lines 162–83) contains at least a dozen antitheses – 'head' versus 'limbs', 'sacrificers' versus 'butchers' and so on. These antitheses highlight the debate that Brutus is conducting as he tries to present Caesar's assassination as noble rather than brutal and vicious.

◆ Collect more examples of antithesis. Use them in an essay exploring how antithesis creates a sense of conflict in *Julius Caesar*.

▼ How effectively does this image explore antithesis?

## Repetition

The **repetition** that is apparent in the play's language is yet another rhetorical device, used by Shakespeare to create atmosphere, character and dramatic impact. The names 'Caesar' and 'Brutus' each occur over a hundred times in the play. The next most popular words are 'good', 'men' and 'man'. The pattern of repetition reflects some of the play's main concerns: personal identity, the justification and morality of actions, and the appropriate behaviour of men in a patriarchal society like Rome.

Shakespeare also repeats language techniques to create particular effects. In the first scene, for example, Murellus fires off a multitude of rhetorical questions as he reproaches the plebeians.

◆ Remind yourself of the 'Language' box on page 8, and then track the repeated use of rhetorical questions through the play. Write a short essay comparing their impact in different situations.

On a grander scale, Shakespeare uses repetition in the public speeches.

◆ In small groups, discuss how Antony's repeated use of 'honourable' in his funeral oration (Act 3 Scene 2) turns the crowd against the conspirators.

◆ Explore the use of repetition in Brutus's funeral oration (also Act 3 Scene 2). Look closely at the ways in which he restates and echoes key words and ideas (for example, 'Believe me for mine honour, and have respect to / mine honour that you may believe.') and his use of the 'rule of three' (see p. 186) and rhetorical questions.

## Lists

Another of Shakespeare's favourite language methods is to accumulate words or phrases rather like a list. He intensifies and varies description, atmosphere and argument as he 'piles up' item on item, incident on incident. Brutus uses lists in his funeral oration addressed to the people of Rome (Act 3 Scene 2, lines 13–39): 'There is tears for his love, joy for his fortune, honour for his valour, / and death for his ambition.'

Antony likewise lists 'all thy conquests, glories, triumphs, spoils' (Act 3 Scene 1, line 149), and towards the end of his funeral oration (Act 3 Scene 2, lines 211–13) ironically suggests that as a speaker he has 'neither wit, nor words, nor worth, / Action, nor utterance, nor the power of speech / To stir men's blood.'

◆ Lists also help to accentuate the details of the storm (Act 1 Scene 3, lines 59–78) and Calpurnia's description of the omens seen by the guards (Act 2 Scene 2, lines 13–24). In pairs, discuss the effects created by these lists.

## Verse and prose

How did Shakespeare decide whether to write in verse or prose? One answer is that he followed theatrical convention. Prose was traditionally used by comic and low-status characters. High-status characters spoke verse. Comic scenes were written in prose (as were letters), but audiences expected verse in the serious scenes: the poetic style was thought to be particularly suitable for moments of high dramatic or emotional intensity, and for tragic themes.

The Commoners (low-status characters) speak in prose in the first scene although Flavius and Murellus (high status) use verse. However, during Caesar's funeral individual members of the crowd speak in verse, perhaps to underline the emotional intensity of the scene. Another remarkable departure from this prose or verse convention is Brutus's funeral oration (Act 3 Scene 2), which is in prose, although Brutus's language here clearly demonstrates that Shakespeare can use prose just as effectively as verse to express the deepest feelings and the most profound thoughts.

With few other exceptions, the verse of *Julius Caesar* is **blank verse**: unrhymed verse written in **iambic pentameter**. Shakespeare would probably have learned the technical definition of iambic pentameter at school. In Greek, the word *pente* means 'five'. An **iamb** is a 'foot' (or group) of two syllables, the first unstressed and the second stressed, as in the pronunciation of 'alas': a LAS.

Iambic pentameter is therefore metrical verse in which each line has five stressed syllables (/) alternating with five unstressed syllables (×), as in this line by Cassius:

×  /   ×   / ×   /   ×   /  ×  /
*I know where I will wear this dagger then*

◆ Read the line aloud in unison with a partner, pronouncing each syllable very clearly. As you read, beat out the five-stress rhythm (e.g. clap hands, tap the desk).

◆ Now turn to the closing eight lines of Act 1 Scene 3. Repeat what you have just done. Can you find the rhythm? Is it clearly discernible and regular in each line or do you sense some subtle variations?

◆ Choose another verse speech and learn it ready to deliver in a way that emphasises the metre (five beats). Then speak it as you feel it should be delivered on stage.

By the time Shakespeare wrote *Julius Caesar*, he was becoming more flexible and experimental in his use of the iambic pentameter. **End-stopped** lines (lines with a pause at the end) are less frequent and there is a greater use of **enjambement** (where one line flows into the next).

◆ Find examples of both end-stopping and enjambement in Brutus's speech (Act 2 Scene 1, lines 162–83). Describe the different effects Shakespeare creates using these metrical techniques.

## Soliloquy

As in all Shakespeare's tragic plays, he uses the dramatic device of the soliloquy powerfully in *Julius Caesar* – although there are fewer such speeches than in his other tragedies. In order to appreciate the impact of some of the language, try one of the following activities based on Brutus's soliloquy in Act 2 Scene 1 or Antony's in Act 3 Scene 1.

In a small group take one line at a time and agree what you consider to be the key word. Write down that key word – just one per line. This will give you a 'bare bones' script of a handful of words.

◆ Keeping the words in their original order, present this new script in any ways that seem appropriate. Think about using choral speech, echoes, repetitions, sound effects or movement. Share your performance with the rest of the class for comment.

◆ Read through your chosen soliloquy, with each person handing over the reading at each full stop, colon, semi-colon or question mark.

◆ Now consider ways of performing this speech as i it's a conversation (which it is, in a way, as it's like a piece of internal dialogue or a character debating with himself or herself). Experiment with other ways of dividing up the speech and ways of speaki to create different effects.

◆ Then think about how you might layer in moveme where you might stand (back-to-back, facing each other, one kneeling the other standing etc.). Share your final response with others in the class.

◀ Match this image to a line of Antony's soliloquy.

# *Julius Caesar* in performance

## In Shakespeare's time

*Julius Caesar* was probably first performed in 1599 and seems to have been a popular play from the start. It was almost certainly one of the earliest productions by Shakespeare's own company at the newly built Globe Theatre. There were no elaborate sets on the Globe stage, so Shakespeare had to rely on language to set the scene.

◆ Identify a scene in which Shakespeare has relied heavily on the power of language to evoke a particular atmosphere. Pick out several phrases that you find especially descriptive and share them with a partner, explaining what senses the words appeal to. Design your own set for this scene and write a commentary on your design, making clear which words from the script have prompted your ideas.

At the Globe, plays were performed only in the summer months and in broad daylight in the open air. At about 2 p.m. the audience would gather with food and drink, eager to be entertained. They were not required to be silent or to stay in the theatre – they could come and go as they wanted. This meant that the actors had to cope with significant background noise.

The audience also often found it difficult to hear what was taking place on the stage. The Globe could hold approximately three thousand people: the 'groundlings' stood in the pit around the stage, while those who paid more were seated on three levels around the pit. Most of the audience could hear well when the actor was at the front of the stage, but it would be dull if all the action happened there. Elsewhere, upstage, furthest away from the audience, and downstage, closer to the audience, only certain sections of the audience could hear. In order to ensure that everyone heard the vital parts of the plot, the same idea was sometimes developed in three different ways in a speech. Shakespeare did this by using different imagery and the accumulation of detail. When such a repetition is present, it may have been a prompt to the actor to move around the stage.

◆ Research further how plays were staged at the Globe in Shakespeare's time. Visit the website for the recreated Shakespeare's Globe in London, or better still go and see a play there!

◆ Having done your research, consider whether there are any features of the stage and layout of the Globe that could be exploited to make a production of *Julius Caesar* particularly dramatic. Make a list, so you are ready to participate in a group discussion.

◆ Look ahead to the short review of the Globe's 400th anniversary production of *Julius Caesar* in 1999 on page 193. Historical authenticity was a significant feature and the cast was all male, as it would have been in Shakespeare's time. Using the Internet, research this production in detail, in order to understand the stagecraft and theatrical constraints of Shakespeare's time more fully.

# Performances after Shakespeare's time

Today, Shakespeare's words are treated with greater reverence than they were during the centuries after his death. The short survey of performances that follows outlines how freely the script was altered. It also touches on which aspects of the play were stressed, modified or removed.

During the seventeenth and eighteenth centuries, Shakespeare's script was often modified to suggest more strongly that Brutus was the central character and thereby heighten his tragic status. He was, for example, given a more impressive death scene in one production, where he was allowed to kill himself without the aid of Strato. A lengthy and patriotic death speech was also given to Brutus, adding to the sense of him as the fallen Roman hero. There was also a trend to scale down the importance of the 'supernatural' elements.

In the nineteenth century, some productions focused on the recreation of the splendid setting of Rome with lavish scenery and costume. The architecture was carefully designed and the 'public' elements, such as the grand processions and crowd scenes, were handsomely staged.

The text continued to be adjusted to showcase Brutus as a noble and patriotic hero and Antony as a high-minded avenger. This meant that some of the play had to be cut (e.g. Antony's ruthless political activity in Act 4 Scene 1) because it jarred with the overall tone of the production.

William Charles Macready, staging the play in the early 1800s, gave the crowd scenes greater dramatic prominence, which set the trend for late nineteenth-century versions, in which the market-place scene (and Antony) were seen as central to the play.

John Philip Kemble's 1812 production in Covent Garden in London was influential for the rest of the century. He cut the script significantly and altered many of the minor characters, replacing the new ones in the later acts with some from the earlier ones. For example, Artemidorus and the Soothsayer were made into the same character. Brutus was a grand, patriotic philosopher and he was definitely the main character.

◆ Antony's eulogy to Brutus ended Kemble's version of the play. Why do you think Kemble decided to cut Octavius's speech?

Kemble also wanted to create a significant spectacle. His production was notable for its lavish costumes and the vast number of actors that made up Caesar's retinue. Brutus, the classical hero, was played by Kemble in a grand style.

Herbert Beerbohm Tree's production in 1898 emphasised the active involvement of the crowd and highlighted the way in which Antony manipulated them, so that he now became the leading figure in the play. Tree – who thought that Antony provided the 'glamour of the play' – took that role himself. There was also an attempt to instil greater complexity and richness into the presentation of Caesar. Tree's commitment to visual spectacle produced a series of 'Roman daily life' scenes, which he inserted before Shakespeare's opening scene in order to establish a Roman context.

◆ In Tree's production, Calpurnia enters to mourn her husband at the end of the assassination scene. How would this alter the drama at this point in the play?

*Julius Caesar* became a popular play in the United States during the nineteenth century, possibly because the political ideas it explored were close to American political experience at that time. Edwin Booth's 1871 production of the play in New York was especially influential. Interestingly, Booth and his brothers had put on a production in 1864 as a fundraiser. Booth's brother, John Wilkes Booth, played Antony in this production. Only a few months later, he assassinated the American president, Abraham Lincoln.

◆ If you are interested in researching particular productions, see what you can find out about Booth's 1871 production in New York. The characterisation of Brutus was particularly significant. Present your findings to the class.

▲ This painting gave Booth the inspiration for his staging of the assassination scene. How well does it capture the drama of the moment?

## Recent productions

The twentieth century saw a return to much simpler stagings of the play. There was still some extravagance, but the dependence on theatrical illusion disappeared and productions concentrated on the clear delivery of the language. Just as Shakespeare probably intended, scenes flowed swiftly into each other and the action was not held up by clumsy stagecraft. Although scenes were often still cut, additional scenes were not added. Orson Welles's landmark 1937 production was subtitled *Death of a Dictator* and was heavily focused on the play's political elements. Welles also took the radical decision to dress the actors in Fascist uniforms and everyday clothes. Importantly, Welles was the first to play Brutus as a self-questioning, ineffectual liberal. For the first time ever in the United States, the scene involving Cinna the poet was kept.

In the last decades of the twentieth century, many productions tried to link the play with contemporary events. Caesar was played as a Latin American dictator,

resembled Egypt's assassinated President Sadat and was identified with the freedom fighter Che Guevara. Rome was used to symbolise Germany in the 1930s and East European dictatorships. In the last of these interpretations, a promenade staging, Caesar was followed continually by a secret policeman and TV camera and the actors moved amongst the audience, who found themselves playing the part of the Roman citizens.

◆ Can you think of a contemporary political regime that could be used as a setting for *Julius Caesar*? Debate the advantages and disadvantages of locating a production of the play so specifically.

◆ In the end, this is a play about Rome. Do you agree?

◆ Coleridge, the Romantic poet, praised the impartiality of Shakespeare's politics in this play. Do you think that Shakespeare balances the claims of Caesar and the conspirators, or does he suggest that one side is right and the other wrong?

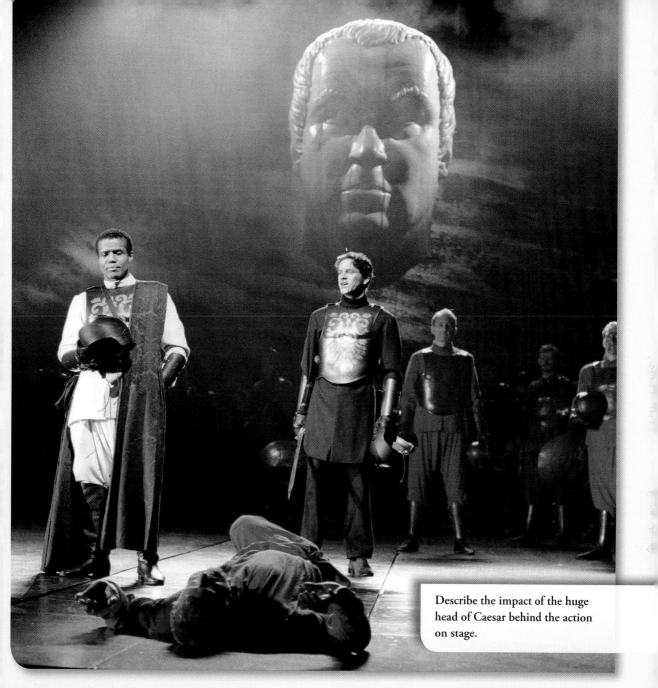

Describe the impact of the huge head of Caesar behind the action on stage.

## Short reviews of more recent productions

- The 1995 RSC production was cut to two hours' running time. A 2.5-metre (8-foot) marble head of Caesar dominated the beginning and ending, and there was a huge amount of visual imagery – buckets of blood, red togas and a blood-red crack through Caesar's image in the storm scene. It was a production that emphasised the symbolism of the play.

- In 1999, a 400th anniversary production of the play was staged at the newly finished Shakespeare's Globe in London. Historical reconstruction was its most notable feature with the women's parts being played by men, lavish Elizabethan costumes and a jig being danced at the end (this detail had been recorded by a member of the audience in 1599). The Soothsayer and the plebeians were among the audience.

- In 2001, the RSC again stressed the play's political dimensions, this time by creating a set that resembled the Nazi Nuremberg rallies (see p. vii, bottom). The Fascist references were echoed by the wearing of ceremonial togas combined with jackboots and black shirts.

- The RSC took their 2004 production on tour, using improvised and unconventional venues (see pp. x and 139). The rawness and toughness of the set, reminiscent of industrial Eastern Europe, attracted a young audience. The Roman mob was dressed in fashionable casual clothes, while the soundtrack and lighting were sinisterly threatening.

- The 2005 Barbican production deployed a hundred extras, which gave the mob tremendous energy and power (see pp. x top, 4, 10 and 182–3). Very much a modern-dress version, it opened like a movie premiere based around cool, slick marble and glass. For the battle scenes the fighters wore American-style battle dress and the set was like a vast, devastated warehouse.

- The 2006 RSC production (see pp. v top, vii top, 14 and 39 top) used a minimalist set, just a gravel area surrounded by a pitch-black void. The storm scene was very dramatic, using real water and crackling electricity. The senators wore predominantly red outfits under crisp white togas.

- The 2012 RSC production set the play in an unidentified African state sometime in the last fifty years and had an all-black British cast. There was no interval. The vast statue of a dictator, its back turned to the audience, dominated the back of the stage. Caesar wore a white suit and carried a fly whisk; the others wore a mixture of modern dress and desert khakis. The Soothsayer's skin was painted white and the production was punctuated by a beating drum.

- The Donmar Warehouse staged an all-female production of the play in 2012. The key staging idea was that the inmates of a women's prison were putting on a production of Julius Caesar. The play opened with the whole cast doing military-style aerobics. Caesar, a prison warder whom they wanted to be rid of, was their instructor. Their weapons were water pistols and the music was punk. This production also had no interval.

◆ Choose one or more ideas from the above production reviews that you find interesting and describe in detail what special qualities you think they added to those productions.

◆ Some critics feel that setting Julius Caesar in a different historical or political period from ancient Rome causes problems for a modern audience. What do you think?

◆ What is gained by the play having no interval? Would you structure your performance like this?

◆ Watch a performance of Julius Caesar and write your own review of it.

◆ Comment on the set design of the Dutch production in the photograph below. What ideas from the play lie behind it?

All stars in the heavens give off light, but only one stays in the same place.

Min. until Julius Caesar's death

Are all-male or all-female productions of the play a gimmick or do they make a serious point?

# Screen versions

There are around fifteen screen versions of adaptations of the play. The 1938 BBC *Julius Caesar* was the first full-length Shakespeare play ever broadcast on television; sadly, it does not survive. Some of the most notable screen versions are described below.

**The 1953 MGM version** Produced by John Houseman and directed by Joseph L. Mankiewicz, this version was made in Hollywood. Although colour was available, they decided to use black and white for artistic reasons. The set of another movie was reused to create a grand imperial backdrop and there were hundreds of actors involved, making the crowd scenes impressive. There were many contemporary resonances, including the black and white of World War II newsreels. A subtext referenced the rise and fall of the 1930s Fascist leaders Hitler and Mussolini. The film was released at the height of the McCarthy era in the United States, and many parallels can be drawn. For example, we can link Cinna the poet's fate to incidents where some communities turned against individuals for being Communist sympathisers, based on little or no evidence.

◆ The casting of Marlon Brando as Antony in the film was controversial. Use the Internet to find out why.

**The 1979 BBC version** This low-budget television version was filmed in a studio with a small cast. There was no Roman grandeur and the emphasis was placed on verse speaking and the quality of the acting. It was only fractionally cut, unlike all other screen versions.

**The RSC's 2012 stage production** (see p. 194) Set in Africa, this version was adapted and filmed on location and in Stratford. Not only was Africa's turbulent political history referenced, but there were resonances of recent events during the Arab Spring, when dictators were removed by the actions of the people.

***Caesar Must Die*** The Taviani brothers' movie came out in 2012. As in Phyllida Lloyd's 2012 production at the Donmar Warehouse, a prison performance of *Julius Caesar* is the framing device. This time the prisoners are tough Mafia men in the all-male, high-security wing of Rome's Rebibbia prison, auditioning for parts in the production. The roles of Portia and Calpurnia do not exist. Although the movie begins and ends with the prisoners performing the play in colour, the audition scenes in the middle are shot in black and white, which the directors consider to be a less realistic format.

◆ Discuss what is gained and lost by setting a production of *Julius Caesar* in a prison.

◆ There is certainly scope for a new big-budget movie version of *Julius Caesar*. In a group, develop the pitch you will make to a group of media moguls. You will need to convince them that Shakespeare can pull in big audiences even now. Can you sell this as a political thriller? An outline of your ideas for the setting will be needed and a list of current big-name actors you would like to employ. Another group play the media moguls who will question you closely about your ideas. Will they give you the go-ahead?

◆ If you were given the choice of directing either a stage or a screen version of *Julius Caesar*, which would you choose and why?

▼ A still from the 2012 film *Caesar Must Die*.

## Stage your own production of *Julius Caesar*

Talk together about the period and place in which you will set your production. Clearly any historical setting other than a Roman one could have wider political resonances. Then choose one or more of the following activities.

◆ Design the basic set. If your production is going to be school-based, you will need to work with a particular space in mind (either indoors or outdoors). Decide where you want the audience to be seated. Consider whether you want a thrust stage or to present your play 'in the round' or as a promenade performance. Sketch your set or make a three-dimensional model of it. Work out how you will depict the domestic scenes (inside Brutus's and Caesar's homes), the Capitol scenes and the battles.

◆ Design the costumes. Study some of the ways Caesar and the conspirators have been presented. Think about how you will dress Portia and Calpurnia to reflect their roles and relationships with their husbands. How will you dress the common people?

◆ Design the props. Three important ones are Cassius's sword (see p. 154), Pompey's statue and Caesar's battle cloak.

◆ Design a sound-effects programme to accompany any one scene.

◆ Design a publicity poster. Use illustrations and language that will make people take notice.

◆ Design the programme. It could include a summary of the plot, a cast list, interviews with the actors, a history of recent productions and photographs from rehearsals.

◆ Cast the play. Suggest people at your school or college, or from the world of television, theatre or the media.

◆ Choose any scene from the play and produce your version of a director's prompt book for it. Your prompt book should include detailed notes about the ways in which you want the actors to perform the script, notes on the setting and props, on entrances and exits – anything to help you to bring that scene to life.

▼ For your production, would you choose costumes that locate the play in a particular period or not? Begin your discussion by considering the costumes in these photos.

197

# Writing about Shakespeare

## The play as text

Shakespeare's plays have always been studied as literary works – as words on a page that need clarification, appreciation and discussion. When you write about the plays, you will be asked to compose short pieces and also longer, more reflective pieces like controlled assessments, examination scripts and coursework – often in the form of essays on themes and/or imagery, character studies, analyses of the structure of the play and on stagecraft. Imagery, stagecraft and character are dealt with elsewhere in this edition. Here, we concentrate on themes and structure. You might find it helpful to look at the 'Write about it' boxes on the left-hand pages throughout the play.

## Themes

It is often tempting to say that the theme of a play is a single idea, like 'death' in *Hamlet*, or 'the supernatural' in *Macbeth*, or 'love' in *Romeo and Juliet*. The problem with such a simple approach is that you will miss the complexity of the plays. In *Romeo and Juliet*, for example, the play is about the relationship between love, family loyalty and constraint; it is also about the relationship of youth to age and experience; and the relationship between Romeo and Juliet is also played out against a background of enmity between two families. Between each of these ideas or concepts there are tensions. The tensions are the main focus of attention for Shakespeare and the audience; this is also how the best drama operates – by the presentation of and resolution of tension.

Look back at the 'Themes' boxes throughout the play to see if any of the activities there have given rise to information that you could use as a starting point for further writing about the themes of the specific play you are studying.

## Structure

Most Shakespeare plays are in five acts, divided into scenes. These acts were not in the original scripts, but have been included in later editions to make the action more manageable, clearer and more like 'classical' structures. One way to get a sense of the structure of the whole play is to take a printed version (not this one!) and cut it up into scenes and acts, then display each scene and act, in sequence, on a wall, like this:

As you set out the whole play, you will be able to see the 'shape' of each act, the relative length of the scenes, and how the acts relate to each other (such as whether one act is shorter, and why that might be). You can annotate the text with comments, observations and questions. You can use a highlighter pen to mark the recurrence of certain words, images or metaphors to see at a glance where and how frequently they appear. You can also follow a particular character's progress through the play.

Such an overview of the play gives you critical perspective: you will be able to see how the parts fit together, to stand back from the play and assess its shape, and to focus on particular parts within the context of the whole. Your writing will reflect a greater awareness of the overall context as a result.

## The play as script

There are different, but related, categories when we think of the play as a script for performance. These include *stagecraft* (discussed elsewhere in this edition and throughout the left-hand pages), *lighting*, *focus* (who are we looking at? Where is the attention of the audience?), *music and sound*, *props and costumes*, *casting*, *make-up*, *pace and rhythm*, and other *spatial relationships* (e.g. how actors move around the stage in relation to each other). If you are writing about stagecraft or performance, use the notes you have made as a result of the 'Stagecraft' activities throughout this edition of the play, as well as any information you can find about the plays in performance.

## What are the key points of dispute?

Shakespeare is brilliant at capturing a number of key points of dispute in each of his plays. These are the dramatic moments where he concentrates the focus of the audience on difficult (sometimes universal) problems that the characters are facing or embodying.

First, identify these key points in the play you are studying. You can do this as a class by brainstorming what you consider to be the key points in small groups, then debating the long-list as a whole class, and then coming up with a short-list of what the class thinks are the most significant. (This is a good opportunity for speaking and listening work.) They are likely to be places in the play where the action or reflection is at its most intense, and which capture the complexity of themes, character, structure and performance.

Second, drill down at one of the points of contention and tension. In other words, investigate the complexity of the problem that Shakespeare has presented. What is at stake? Why is it important? Is it a problem that can be resolved, or is it an insoluble one?

## Key skills in writing about Shakespeare

Here are some suggestions to help you organise your notes and develop advanced writing skills when working on Shakespeare:

- Compose the title of your writing carefully to maximise your opportunities to be creative and critical about the play. Explore the key words in your title carefully. Decide which aspect of the play – or which combination of aspects – you are focusing on.
- Create a mind map of your ideas, making connections between them.
- If appropriate, arrange your ideas into a hierarchy that shows how some themes or features of the play are 'higher' than others and can incorporate other ideas.
- Sequence your ideas so that you have a plan for writing an essay, review, story – whichever genre you are using. You might like to think about whether to put your strongest points first, in the middle, or later.
- Collect key quotations (it might help to compile this list with a partner), which you can use as evidence to support your argument.
- Compose your first draft, embedding quotations in your text as you go along.
- Revise your draft in the light of your own critical reflections and/or those of others.

The following pages focus on writing about *Julius Caesar* in particular.

# Writing about *Julius Caesar*

The purpose of this section is to help you to write about *Julius Caesar* in an informed, coherent and convincing fashion. Before you begin to commit to writing down your ideas, remember to keep two key considerations in mind:

1   *Julius Caesar* is a play, so you should always appreciate its form and genre. In Caesar's first scene (Act 1 Scene 2), for example, there is a huge amount of 'stagecraft' built in to the writing (entrances, exits, 'stage business', action and so on). It's all about what the audience sees, hears and experiences.

◆   **Look at the script of the first 31 lines of Act 1 Scene 2 in this edition. Try writing about how the language might be brought to life on stage. Speculate about different ways of playing this short episode.**

2   *Julius Caesar* is not about 'real' people and 'real' situations, so don't treat it as such. When Shakespeare pays close attention to the presentation of Brutus's home life in the play in Act 2, it's as much about making a dramatic point (the privacy and stability of his home being invaded by the conspiracy) as trying to make it all credible and naturalistic. The play is a dramatic construct and often characters, for example, are vehicles for ideas about themes and structure. Remember Artemidorus? Lucius? The Soothsayer? Shakespeare presents them very sketchily as figures (and they've been played on stage in a variety of ways) but they have crucial roles in the drama.

## How many different kinds of writing might you tackle?

You could write about:

•   an extract (a key speech, such as Antony's 'If you have tears, prepare to shed them now' [Act 3 Scene 2], or a longer passage of dialogue, such as the reconciliation between Brutus and Cassius in Act 4 Scene 3)

•   a key scene (such as the death of Brutus in Act 5 Scene 5)

•   a character (Cassius), or group of characters (the 'Triumvirate')

•   a core theme (the concept of honour)

•   an element of the text re-creatively (that is, rewriting it in another genre or from another perspective or in the persona of one of the characters).

◆   **Individually, consider each of these 'types' of writing in turn. See if you can come up with three additional focuses or frameworks for questions besides the ones that are mentioned in brackets above. Then pass your ideas to a partner for consideration. Together, settle on two questions for each category that you think would generate interesting written responses. Keep these in mind as you work through the next section.**

## Writing about an extract or a key scene

**Consider the dramatic effectiveness of the opening 120 lines of Act 3 Scene 1.**

1   Locate the extract in the play, and contextualise it. What has just happened? (The conspirators' plot has been settled.) What is about to come? (Caesar is assassinated; the conspirators attempt to justify their actions and bathe themselves in his blood.)

2   Concentrate on exploring the mood or atmosphere of the extract. (Caesar ignores any attempts to warn him and reaffirms that he is 'constant' in his principles. The dramatic intensity escalates as the conspirators stab Caesar. Shakespeare focuses on Caesar's bewilderment at Brutus's betrayal.)

3   How might the lines be spoken – tone, emphasis, pace, pauses, etc. What are key words and images ('constant', '*Et tu, Brute?*', 'death', 'blood')?

4   Think about Shakespeare's stagecraft – how he assembles and groups characters (the big public gathering and the warnings from the Soothsayer and Artemidorus at the start of the scene), the gradual narrowing of focus onto Caesar, the use of entrances/exits and the blocking on stage (how the conspirators close in on Caesar).

**5** Link the details of the extract to key themes or issues rooted in the text as a whole (the presentation of Caesar, the motivation of the conspirators, the exploration of death and honour).

**6** Show how the extract links to the dramatic construction of the play (a turning point, and a prelude to the rise of Antony and the discrediting of the conspiracy).

◆ Working in a group of six, take one numbered section each of the above essay framework. Plan your answer by researching your specific area of focus. Then divide up a large sheet of sugar paper into six sections. Take turns to fill in the notes you have compiled. Use this large sheet as a resource to help you produce an essay plan of no more than one side that you could include in a revision booklet to be given to students for examination preparation.

## Writing about character

### Planning an essay on the character of Antony

**1** Summarise what Antony does in each act, his interactions with other characters, his decisive actions.

**2** Explore how Antony relates to other characters and note down the different ways he treats them. How do they speak to him and about him?

**3** Focus on the type of language that Antony uses – the imagery he employs, the tone he strikes, his typical way of speaking. Identify quotations that will back up your points. Link Antony's role to key themes and aspects of the drama.

**4** Finally, think about the ways in which Shakespeare shows the development and change within his character over the course of the play.

## Writing creatively

Many assessments offer you the opportunity to write about *Julius Caesar* creatively as well as critically. There are a number of such activities which you have been encouraged to try act by act. The great thing is that you can be as imaginative and original within the framework

of such responses as you choose to be: *Julius Caesar* is a complex, rich and intriguing text that offers many opportunities for creative approaches.

## Summing up

Keep in mind the focus on *Julius Caesar* as a dramatic text. What features of the play as a theatrical performance enhance the impact of key issues? Remember that there is no single, right interpretation – both from you as a critic, but also from a director. How might an audience respond – in Shakespeare's time, and now? How do you respond? What are your own personal responses to the question and how can you justify them?

## Possible questions

◆ Below you'll find questions on character, theme, extracts and re-creative tasks. Have a go at one of each, or invent your own!

**1** Neither Portia nor Calpurnia has an important role in *Julius Caesar*. What is your view, and why?

**2** 'Although the play is called *Julius Caesar*, it's really Brutus who is the main character.' Discuss.

**3** Discuss the presentation and development of the theme of honour and ambition in the play.

**4** Explore the dramatic construction of Act 4 Scene 2.

**5** Explore the contrasts between appearance and reality.

**6** In role as one of the characters, write about a key incident in the play from your point of view.

**7** Brutus's character is full of irreconcilable differences. Explore the presentation of Brutus in the light of this comment.

**8** Argue the case for retaining Acts 4 and 5 in a production of the play.

**9** Write an additional speech for a character or script a section of dialogue between a character who appears in the play and one who doesn't.

# William Shakespeare 1564–1616

| | |
|---|---|
| **1564** | Born Stratford-upon-Avon, eldest son of John and Mary Shakespeare. |
| **1582** | Marries Anne Hathaway of Shottery, near Stratford. |
| **1583** | Daughter Susanna born. |
| **1585** | Twins, son and daughter Hamnet and Judith, born. |
| **1592** | First mention of Shakespeare in London. Robert Greene, another playwright, described Shakespeare as 'an upstart crow beautified with our feathers'. Greene seems to have been jealous of Shakespeare. He mocked Shakespeare's name, calling him 'the only Shake-scene in a country' (presumably because Shakespeare was writing successful plays). |
| **1595** | Becomes a shareholder in The Lord Chamberlain's Men, an acting company that became extremely popular. |
| **1596** | Son, Hamnet, dies aged eleven. |
| | Father, John, granted arms (acknowledged as a gentleman). |
| **1597** | Buys New Place, the grandest house in Stratford. |
| **1598** | Acts in Ben Jonson's *Every Man in His Humour*. |
| **1599** | Globe Theatre opens on Bankside. Performances in the open air. |
| **1601** | Father, John, dies. |
| **1603** | James I grants Shakespeare's company a royal patent: The Lord Chamberlain's Men become The King's Men and play about twelve performances each year at court. |
| **1607** | Daughter Susanna marries Dr John Hall. |
| **1608** | Mother, Mary, dies. |
| **1609** | The King's Men begin performing indoors at Blackfriars Theatre. |
| **1610** | Probably returns from London to live in Stratford. |
| **1616** | Daughter Judith marries Thomas Quiney. |
| | Dies. Buried in Holy Trinity Church, Stratford-upon-Avon. |

## The plays and poems

(no one knows exactly when he wrote each play)

| | |
|---|---|
| **1589–95** | *The Two Gentlemen of Verona, The Taming of the Shrew, First, Second* and *Third Parts* of *King Henry VI, Titus Andronicus, King Richard III, The Comedy of Errors, Love's Labour's Lost, A Midsummer Night's Dream, Romeo and Juliet, King Richard II* (and the long poems *Venus and Adonis* and *The Rape of Lucrece*). |
| **1596–99** | *King John, The Merchant of Venice, First* and *Second Parts* of *King Henry IV, The Merry Wives of Windsor, Much Ado About Nothing, King Henry V,* **Julius Caesar** (and probably the Sonnets). |
| **1600–05** | *As You Like It, Hamlet, Twelfth Night, Troilus and Cressida, Measure for Measure, Othello, All's Well That Ends Well, Timon of Athens, King Lear.* |
| **1606–11** | *Macbeth, Antony and Cleopatra, Pericles, Coriolanus, The Winter's Tale, Cymbeline, The Tempest.* |
| **1613** | *King Henry VIII, The Two Noble Kinsmen* (both probably with John Fletcher). |
| **1623** | Shakespeare's plays published as a collection (now called the First Folio). |

# Acknowledgements

Cambridge University Press would like to acknowledge the contributions made to this work by Rex Gibson, Mike Clamp and Tim Seward.

Extract from Michael Billington's review of *Julius Caesar* at The Royal Shakespeare Theatre, Stratford-upon-Avon on p. 176 copyright © Guardian News & Media Ltd 2012.

## Picture Credits

p. iii: Barbican Theatre, London 2005, © Donald Cooper/Photostage; p. v top: RSC/Royal Shakespeare Theatre 2006, © Donald Cooper/Photostage; p. v bottom: RSC/The Courtyard Theatre, Stratford-upon-Avon 2009, © Geraint Lewis; p. vi: RSC/Royal Shakespeare Theatre 1991, © Donald Cooper/Photostage; p. vii top: RSC/Royal Shakespeare Theatre 2006, © Donald Cooper/Photostage; p. vii bottom: RSC/Royal Shakespeare Theatre 2001, © Donald Cooper/Photostage; p. viii top: RSC/Royal Shakespeare Theatre 2012, © Donald Cooper/Photostage; p. viii bottom: RSC/Royal Shakespeare Theatre 2001, © Donald Cooper/Photostage; p. ix: RSC Tour/Lyric Hammersmith, London 2005 © Donald Cooper/Photostage; p. x top: Barbican Theatre, London 2005, © Donald Cooper/Photostage; p. x bottom: RSC/Lyric Hammersmith, London 2005, © Donald Cooper/Photostage; p. xi top: Barbican Theatre, London 2005, © Donald Cooper/Photostage; p. xi bottom: Barbican Theatre, London 2005, © Donald Cooper/Photostage; p. xii: Barbican Theatre, London 2005, © Donald Cooper/Photostage; p. 3: Shutterstock/ecco; p. 4: Barbican Theatre, London 2005, © Donald Cooper/Photostage; p. 6: RSC/Royal Shakespeare Theatre 1983, © Donald Cooper/Photostage; p. 10: Barbican Theatre, London 2005, © Donald Cooper/Photostage; p. 14: RSC/Royal Shakespeare Theatre 2006, © Donald Cooper/Photostage; p. 20: RSC/Royal Shakespeare Theatre 2012, Nigel Norrington/ArenaPAL/TopFoto; p. 26: Shutterstock/nortivision; p. 34: Barbican Theatre, London 2005, © Donald Cooper/Photostage; p. 39 top: RSC/Royal Shakespeare Theatre 2006, © Donald Cooper/Photostage; p. 39 bottom: RSC/Royal Shakespeare Theatre 1991, © Donald Cooper/Photostage; p. 42: Barbican Theatre, London 2005, © Donald Cooper/Photostage; p. 46: RSC/Royal Shakespeare Theatre 2012, © Geraint Lewis; p. 56: RSC/The Courtyard Theatre, Stratford-upon-Avon 2009, © Donald Cooper/Photostage; p. 62: Barbican Theatre, London 2005, © Donald Cooper/Photostage; p. 73 top: RSC/Royal Shakespeare Theatre 2012, Nigel Norrington/ArenaPAL/TopFoto; p. 73 bottom: RSC/The Courtyard Theatre, Stratford-upon-Avon 2009, Nigel Norrington/ArenaPAL/TopFoto; p. 74: The Granger Collection/TopFoto; p. 76: RSC/Moscow Chekhov Art Theater 2012, RIA Novosti/ArenaPAL; p. 80: Barbican Theatre, London 2005, © Donald Cooper/Photostage; p. 82: Barbican Theatre, London 2005, © Donald Cooper/Photostage; p. 88: RSC/Barbican Theatre, London 1996, © Donald Cooper/Photostage; p. 96 top: RSC/Royal Shakespeare Theatre 2012, © Donald Cooper/Photostage; p. 96 bottom: RSC/Royal Shakespeare Theatre 2001, © Donald Cooper/Photostage; p. 98: RSC/Royal Shakespeare Theatre 1991, © Donald Cooper/Photostage; p. 108: Barbican Theatre, London 2005, © Donald Cooper/Photostage; p. 111 top left: RSC/Barbican Theatre, London 1996, © Donald Cooper/Photostage; p. 111 top right: RSC/The Other Place, Stratford-upon-Avon 1993, © Donald Cooper/Photostage; p. 111 bottom left: Barbican Theatre, London 2005, © Donald Cooper/Photostage; p. 111 bottom right: National Youth Theatre/Bloomsbury Theatre, London 1993, © Donald Cooper/Photostage; p. 114: © TopFoto; p. 116: Belasco Theatre, Broadway, New York 2005, © Joan Marcus/ArenaPAL/TopFoto; p. 122: The Granger Collection/TopFoto; p. 134: RSC/Royal Shakespeare Theatre 2012, © Geraint Lewis; p. 139: RSC Tour, Ebbw Vale, 2004, © Donald Cooper/Photostage; p. 154: Shutterstock/greglith; p. 156: RSC/Royal Shakespeare Theatre 2012, © Donald Cooper/Photostage; p. 165 top: Barbican Theatre, London 2005, © Donald Cooper/Photostage; p. 165 bottom: RSC/Royal Shakespeare Theatre 2012, © Geraint Lewis; p. 169: Shakespeare's Globe, London 1999, © Donald Cooper/Photostage; p. 170: RSC/The Courtyard Theatre, Stratford-upon-Avon 2009, Nigel Norrington/ArenaPAL/TopFoto; p. 171: Shutterstock/Meunierd; p. 172 top: Shutterstock/Jeff Banke; p. 172 bottom: The Granger Collection/TopFoto; p. 173: RSC/Royal Shakespeare Theatre 2012,

Produced for Cambridge University Press by White-Thomson Publishing
+44 (0)843 208 7460
www.wtpub.co.uk

Project editor: Clare Collinson
Designer: Clare Nicholas
Concept design: Jackie Hill